Pane e Lavoro:
The Italian American
Working Class

Inquiries regarding the proceedings of *Pane e Lavoro:*
The Italian American Working Class should be
addressed to the Multicultural History Society of
Ontario, 43 Queen's Park Crescent East, Toronto,
Ontario M5S 2C3 or to the American Italian Historical
Association, 209 Flagg Place, Staten Island, New York
10304.

ISBN 0-919045-00-6

The Multicultural History Society of Ontario is a non-
profit organization, founded in 1976, which supports
research and publication on topics in ethnic and
immigration studies. The Society's administrative office
is at 43 Queen's Park Crescent East, Toronto, Ontario
M5S 2C3.

We wish to acknowledge the support of the Atlantic
Apparel Contractors Association, offered in memory of
Mariano C. Saveri.

Cover photo: Immigrant workmen on railroad site, ca.
1910. (Photo courtesy of the Western Reserve Historical
Society, Cleveland, Ohio)

PANE E LAVORO: THE ITALIAN AMERICAN WORKING CLASS

Proceedings of the Eleventh Annual Conference
of the American Italian Historical Association
held in Cleveland, Ohio, October 27 and 28, 1978
at John Carroll University

edited by
George E. Pozzetta

1980

The Multicultural History Society of Ontario

Toronto

Contents

Preface

It hardly seems possible that the conference on "The Italian American Working Class" represented the beginning of the second decade of annual meetings dedicated to discovering, preserving, and disseminating information on the Italian experience in North America. When AIHA president Professor Rudolph J. Vecoli introduced the proceedings in 1968, he wrote that the story of millions of Italian immigrants "is still by-and-large an unexplored dimension of American history," and added, "The AIHA proposes to stimulate and facilitate scholarship in this long-neglected field of study." The AIHA is living up to the challenge he presented.

The steady growth of a core of scholars interested in a multitude of topics relating to the Italian experience in America has been reflected in our meetings over the years. The eleventh annual meeting was no exception. Participants came from diverse institutions such as the University of California, Berkeley, the University of Florida, Valencia Community College, Brown University, the University of Northern Colorado, Appalachian State University, the University of Toronto, and Michigan State University. Though our meetings have always been marked by cooperative efforts between scholarly and lay people—indeed, our association has been built on those foundations—the contributions of the latter group were, as never before, an integral part of the 1978 conference. From the start, people such as Alphonse D'Emilia were involved with the planning, especially of local arrangements. And though it seemed to some that we needed better liaison in integrating and making relevant the social and scholarly programs, the results on balance were favorable. It is my hope that the camaraderie exhibited between the scholarly and lay community will continue. Since much remains to be done, such warmly cooperative action should make it possible for the AIHA to reach its potential.

Thanks are due to the History Department of John Carroll University, to the university itself, especially President Henry F. Birkenhauer, S. J., and to many others, among them, Professor George Pozzetta, who had the difficult task of assembling scholars from around the country, Professor Charles Ferroni, and Mr. Alphonse D'Emilia.

A final word—when it seemed that our efforts to meet in Cleveland would founder on the rocks of traditional Italian American divisiveness, our members rose to the occasion, set aside personal considerations, and acted in the best interests of the association. It is this kind of selfless action, as well as the ever-growing, solid interest in the Italian American experience, that should carry the AIHA through many decades of dedicated, effective service.

Luciano J. Iorizzo
President, AIHA
State University College, Oswego, New York
August, 1979

Introduction

Attracted to America in search of *pane e lavoro* (bread and work), Italians have long held a significant place in the American working class. As hard-calloused laborers, both organized and unorganized, they have played important roles in shaping the American encounter with unionism and working-class culture. As citizens and residents of numerous communities, Italian immigrants have added their own unique flavor to the world about them as manifested in their distinctive neighborhoods, value systems, and family life. Large numbers of these hard-working immigrants arrived in this country with limited job skills and a culture which, though adaptable, often handicapped them in the race for rapid upward mobility. Historically, they have been slow to shed their blue-collars. The complex and fascinating story of how Italian immigrants arrived in the New World, merged into the North American economy, and coped with the various challenges inherent in these processes is still largely untold. The American Italian Historical Association devoted its eleventh annual meeting to continuing the scholarly dialogue on these open-ended topics.

The bulk of the published volume resulting from these deliberations, like the majority of the papers presented at the conference itself, focuses on the theme of Italians and the labor movement. What emerges is a multifaceted picture. No one region of the nation or single profession laid claim to the loyalties of Italian immigrants. Bringing with them a willingness to work and sacrifice, these travelers spread themselves widely. With the possible exception of the Jewish merchant and peddler, Italians were the most ubiquitous foreigners in America. They were distinguished not only by their geographic distribution, but also by the diversity of trades they pursued. Italians proved ready to engage in any kind of employment in order to provide for the essential needs of the family (always the family!). Some members of this vast working army came for only a short, temporary stay; others remained and established roots that have endured to this day. All of them, however, placed their distinctive stamp on the American work experience.

We learned from Philip Notarianni that Italians were a significant factor in the unionization of the southern Colorado and Utah coal mining industry. Italians became intertwined with the efforts of the United Mine Workers of America to organize miners at the turn of the twentieth century. A major strike in 1903 – 04, featuring martial law, deportations, and press censorship, severely tested union solidarity. Though the strike was lost, Notarianni claims that Italians gained valuable lessons in unionism. The mines also served as the setting for Betty Boyd Caroli's investigation of the Cherry, Illinois, mine disaster of 1909. When fire swept through a giant midwestern coal mine, several score Italians lost their lives. Caroli used this event as a focal point to analyze less well-known aspects of the Italian immigrant experience. "Chains of Little Italies looped across the Midwest," she wrote, "and some of them provided worse housing, more dangerous jobs, more hostile neighbors and fewer supportive organizations than could be found in urban centers."

The states of the American South contained significant concentrations of Italian workers. George Pozzetta examined Italian cigarworkers in Tampa, Florida, and the role they played in the 1910 general strike, which paralyzed the cigar industry. During this labor stoppage, Italians joined with Cuban and Spanish cigarworkers and engaged in a seven-month walk-out against factory owners. As in the western mining districts, immigrant militancy provoked vigilante activities and harsh repression from opponents, eventually forcing the union to its knees. In the textile industry of Lawrence, Massachusetts, Italian leadership, in the person of Anthony Capraro, was a decisive factor in leading workers to the streets in 1919. Rudolph Vecoli placed the man and his times in historical perspective. Paul Buhle isolated the little understood, but important, influence of Italian American radicals in the Rhode Island labor movement during the first three decades of the twentieth century.° Shifting focus, Robert Harney addressed the important story of the sojourner, the precursor of the effective union members pictured in many of the previous papers, and examined those temporary migrants who came to the rugged territories of the Canadian North.

Italian immigrant women who worked often lagged behind their male counterparts in joining unions, but when they became members, they showed a firm attachment to union principles. Colomba Furio traced the cultural and organizational problems that needed to be overcome before Italian women entered the New York City garment industry in large numbers. Jean Scarpaci followed the long career of Angela Bambace, union member, organizer, and ultimately, vice-president of the International Ladies Garment Workers Union. These varied accomplishments were analyzed through the prism of Bambace's ethnicity.

Conference participants also concerned themselves with the nature of life outside of the workplace. Vincent Lombardi discussed the attraction of Mussolini's brand of fascism for working-class Italian Americans. He found that the fascist message spoke to many of the intellectual and emotional needs of the Italian in America. Not all, however, were willing to wear the brown shirt. Charles Killinger examined the "involuntary" immigrant in the form of those anti-fascist exiles who fled the homeland in opposition to the excesses of Mussolini's regime.° Native Americans noticed the strength of these conflicts and added them to the list of complaints laid at the feet of Italians. Clifford Reutter's investigation of the stormy encounter between Italian workers and nativists during the 1920s delineated these stresses.°

The contemporary American scene contained its own challenges and conflicts for working-class Italian Americans. Charles LaCerra attempted to take the pulse of Italian American political consciousness in the 1970s.° Fred Milano's analysis of the impact of the Vietnam War on Italian Americans suggested that wartime strains affected people in differing manners. His examination of Italian American veterans found that their ethnicity was enhanced by the war experience. A similar message of ethnic relevance was contained in Marianne DiPalermo McCauley's analysis of the alterations that have taken place in the Italian American family structure as a result of upward mobility.° Lucia Chiavola Birnbaum focused on the contemporary women's movement, illuminating the position of Italian American women by tracing the patterns of feminism among their sisters in Italy.°

Family, ethnic, and working-class identity were all examined in the larger context of the neighborhood. Over time, these congregations have demonstrated an amazing permanence, indicating that perhaps Italian American working-class culture has developed unique ways to cope with the urban environment. William Simons, in "Bloomfield: An Italian Working Class Neighborhood," revealed a viable, stable neighborhood existing in the eastern section of

Pittsburgh.° Phylis Martinelli's examination of the Excelsior District of San Francisco showed a neighborhood that, while in a period of transition, was still able to marshall the loyalties and affections of its residents.° Gary Mormino found similar "pride of place" among residents of "The Hill" in St. Louis.° Two sections of Chicago, Bridgeport and Chicago Heights, benefited from the researches of Rose Ann Rabiola and Dominic Candeloro respectively.° Here too Italians left evidence of job and residential stability, and the maintenance of traditions dealing with food, marriage, language, and religion.

Slide and film presentations and panel discussions added to the variety of the conference program. Herbert DiGioia presented a film detailing the life of labor leader Anthony J. Paterno,° while Peter N. Pero illustrated the role played by Italians in the Chicago labor movement through the use of slides.° Selma Appel handled with grace and skill the sensitive topic of negative stereotypes of Italian immigrants in a well-attended slide presentation.° Cleveland's Italian population was the topic of a panel, which examined the city from the perspective of religion, settlement house work, law, labor, and education.°

Volumes and conferences of this kind inevitably raise far more questions than they answer, and, in a genuine sense, this is entirely appropriate. The field of Italian American studies is still young, and much of the labor that needs to be done consists of filling gaps and stimulating debate. It is in this sense that *Pane e Lavoro* is offered. The volume is an exploratory venture into the field of Italian American labor and working-class history. As such, it lends dimension and perspective to the wider patterns of American history. Italian immigrants played a prominent role in the development of modern American society and their story cannot be ignored. The factual details and general themes which emerged from these essays are the beginnings of what has to be a much larger effort to understand the full history of these complex immigrants.

For the many labors that went into producing the conference and publishing its proceedings, there are many people who deserve special recognition. On the local Cleveland scene, Alphonse D'Emilia kept his good humor and balanced judgement through several trials, as did Carlo Ferroni. Moreover, they both invested the many long hours of work on conference arrangements that are necessary ingredients of any successful meeting. We are all in their debt. The editorial assistance provided by the Multicultural History Society of Ontario aided immeasurably in producing this volume. Robert Harney oversaw the editing and printing of *Pane e Lavoro* and substantially strengthened it at several points along the way. Finally, sincere thanks must go to the typists who worked through several drafts of this manuscript: Adrienne Turner, Peggy Lee, and Sandra Sanchez.

George E. Pozzetta
Gainesville, Florida
September, 1979

° Factors of time, budget, author preference, and editorial judgement have determined the selection of the papers appearing in this volume. Starred items are not included in the Proceedings, but authors can be contacted directly, through the offices of the AIHA, for copies of papers or findings included in the presentations.

WORK
AND THE
WORKING CLASS

Anthony Capraro and the Lawrence Strike of 1919

Rudolph J. Vecoli

Lawrence, Massachusetts, located about thirty miles north of Boston in the Merrimack River Valley, was in the early decades of this century the scene of several of the most bitterly fought labor struggles in the textile industry. These strikes captured national attention and had far-reaching significance for the American labor movement. Of these, the strike of 1912 has been the subject of extensive historical study; perhaps because of the role of the Industrial Workers of the World (IWW) and the celebrated case of Ettor and Giovannitti, it appears to hold a particular fascination for labor historians. But the strike of 1919, which in some ways was of greater consequence, has been almost totally ignored. Involving more workers and lasting longer than the 1912 conflict, it embodied the post-war spirit of labor militancy, inspired in part by the Russian Revolution, and was sustained by an established, powerful union, the Amalgamated Clothing Workers of America (ACWA). In certain respects, the Lawrence strike of 1919 prefigured the mass organizing drives of the CIO in the 1930s.[1]

The American Woolen Company, the most powerful textile corporation in the United States, which had four of its largest mills in Lawrence, dominated the life of the city. Of Lawrence's population of more than 96,000 in 1919, nearly half were immigrants, the majority of whom were employed in the woolen mills. Including some fifteen nationalities, this labor force was predominantly "new immigrant" in character, two-thirds originating from eastern and southern Europe and the Middle East. The Italians, numbering about twelve thousand and comprising more than a third of all mill workers, were by far the largest ethnic group. But Germans, Ukrainians, Syrians, Poles, and Lithuanians were also present in force, while smaller contingents of Russian Jews, Armenians, Portuguese, Greeks, and Belgians further spiced the ethnic mix. Only about ten percent of the mill operatives were designated as "English-speaking," a category which included persons of British, Irish, and French Canadian origin as well as old stock Americans.[2]

The distinction between English-speakers and non—English-speakers demarcated a basic cleavage in the social structure of Lawrence. The latter were tagged as "foreigners," a term loaded with pejorative connotations. The older immigrant stocks, formerly themselves victims of prejudice, having now achieved respectability, shunned the newcomers as pariahs. An astute observer commented:

> The English-speaking, whether British or American, whether employers or employed, have always shown a surprising degree of intolerance toward those of other tongues and other manners. The American laborer, the Irishman, and—strange to say, the French-Canadian, regard the Italian or Greek or Jew as a being who occupies in the scheme of creation a place a little higher than that of the Fiji islander, but far beneath that held by the most depraved English-speaking tramp, that was ever kicked off a freight car. The foreigner, in short, is a wop, a sheeny, or a Polack.[3]

Living in ethnic enclaves, housed in shabby, crowded tenements, providing for their needs through their own institutions, these "foreign elements" had little social intercourse with the English-speaking residents of Lawrence. This pattern of ethnic segregation was also reflected in the mills where preference for the highest paying and more pleasant jobs, such as weavers and menders, was given to the English-speaking workers, while the "dirty work" was assigned to the recent immigrants. Not only did this reflect the bias of the bosses, but also the prejudices of the older ethnic groups who refused to work with the "greenhorns."[4]

The ethnic hierarchy in work assignments translated into differentials in earnings and standards of living. Because of rapid technological developments in the textile industry, the demand for machine tenders had increased while the need for skilled workers diminished. Thus raw immigrant labor was welcomed and became the preponderant element in the work force. In 1919 the minority of skilled operatives had average weekly earnings of more than $25, while the unskilled brought home about $13 a week. True, the wages in both categories had more than doubled since the 1912 strike; however, the cost of living had also doubled during the war years, especially with respect to essentials such as food and clothing. Moreover, immediately following the armistice, a cutback in the production of textiles resulted in widespread unemployment and underemployment. The upshot was that the vast majority of the Lawrence mill workers in 1919 had annual incomes of at least

$500 less than the "minimum existence wage" for a family of four, which was estimated to be $1500.[5]

Given these economic conditions, it is not surprising that the strike was precipitated by the threat of a wage reduction. In November, 1918, the United Textile Workers of America (UTWA), an American Federation of Labor (AFL) affiliate, initiated a campaign for an eight-hour day in the industry. Only some 200 of the more than 32,000 mill operatives in Lawrence belonged to the UTWA (another five or six hundred belonged to an independent union), and in order to press the demand for a reduction of the work week from 54 to 48 hours, the support of the unorganized workers was enlisted. Since demand was in any case down, the American Woolen Company and other Lawrence firms readily agreed to the shorter work week, but with a commensurate reduction in earnings. When the non—English-speaking workers learned that the result would be a 12½ percent reduction in their already meager pay, they balked at the agreement. Despite the entreaties and threats of the UTWA officers, a general committee composed of representatives of all the nationality groups demanded a 48-hour work week, but with 54 hours pay. At a mass meeting, the textile workers voted unanimously to strike if this demand was not met by January 31. Accordingly, on February 3, practically all of the 32,000 mill hands walked out, shouting the strike slogan "48-54."[6]

The solidarity of the woolen workers, however, was short-lived for the ethnic and skill distinctions soon expressed themselves in a breaking of ranks. Gradually the English-speaking workers, including the Irish and French-Canadians, began to drift back into the mills; they were followed by some of the smaller groups, Greeks, Portuguese, and Turks. But the main body of immigrant workers remained impressively intact through the gruelling ordeal. Harvell L. Rotzell observed in retrospect: "The Italians, Poles, Lithuanians, Russians, Ukrainians, Syrians, Franco-Belgians, Germans, and Jewish [sic], numbering between fifteen and twenty thousand were the backbone of the strike and there was never a serious break among them in the 16 long weeks of the strike."[7] The conflict thus assumed the character of an ethnic as well as economic struggle, pitting the newcomers against the older groups. At issue appears to have been not only the specific matter of wages, but also the resentments engendered by the maltreatment which the "new immigrants" had received at the hands of "American" workers and bosses alike. Out of this common experience of degradation, they fashioned a pan-ethnic unity:

Clad thus in the same mantle of opprobrium, the denizens of Lawrence's Little Babel have come to see one another more or less as
comrades, in opposition both to their employers and to their English-
speaking, unionized fellow-workers.[8]

The strike divided Lawrence into two hostile camps along lines
of class and ethnicity. The city was described as in the grip of a
civil war. On one side were some twenty to thirty thousand mill
workers, foreign-born, polyglot, and unorganized. On the other was
arrayed the city's power structure, City Hall, the Chamber of
Commerce, the churches (especially the Roman Catholic Church),
the press, and the conservative labor organizations, all allied with
the Woolen Trust! The strike opponents quickly advanced the view
that "the trouble in Lawrence" was not a conflict over wages but
part of "the world wide revolution of the proletariat." No less than
Secretary of Labor William B. Wilson characterized the strike as
"a deliberate organized attempt at a social and political movement to establish soviet governments in the United States."[9] The
mill owners quickly seized upon this interpretation of the dispute.
Winthrop L. Marvin, speaking for the National Association of
Wool Manufacturers, wrote to Secretary Wilson: "Manufacturers
of the Lawrence district are in harmony with you and with leaders
of organized labor in this vicinity that Bolshevist propaganda in
Lawrence is the real cause of the continuing troubles there." In
rejecting conciliation of the strike the mill owners declared: "There
can be no arbitration between Americanism and Bolshevism." The
AFL-affiliated Lawrence Central Labor Union and the UTWA
condemned the strike as due to the influence of "alien Bolshevik
I.W.W. agitators" who had seduced the "non-English speaking
non-organized textile workers" with "un-American promises."[10]

But the person identified as "the most persistent and bitter
opponent of the strikers" was Father James T. O'Reilly, pastor of
St. Mary's Church. The General Strike Committee declared that he
"has done more than any other single individual in Lawrence to try
to discredit our cause and inflame the public mind against us by
circulating false reports to the effect that we are a body of Bolshe-
vists, anarchists, etc." O'Reilly, who had been a leading foe of the
IWW-led strike of 1912, perceived himself as engaged again in a
fight against "foreign, anti-American, revolutionary forces." A master of invective, he declared the issue in Lawrence to be:
"Whether such a combination of local and imported revolutionists,
real dyed-in-the-wool foreigners, radical socialists, avowed bolshe-

vists, shall hold this city by the throat in the name of honest labor."[11] Although O'Reilly was the most vocal clerical opponent, the evidence suggests that other Catholic priests generally shared his views.

Early in the strike, The Citizens Committee of Lawrence, composed of prominent business and professional men drawn from the various ethnic groups, was formed to seek a solution to the recurring labor troubles which were giving their city "an international bad name." Moderate and reformist in temper, the committee called for improvements which would make Lawrence "a cleaner, finer, and better city in which to live and work." Specifically, it advocated programs of Americanization, neighborliness, and civic betterment for the immigrant population. The committee advised its "foreign-born friends" that America provided abundant opportunities for them and their children, but that these could only be enjoyed through obedience to, not defiance of, American laws. Its efforts to mediate the strike were unsuccessful and despite its stance of impartiality, the committee was in the final analysis on the side of law and order and property rights.[12]

The high-sounding rhetoric of the Citizens Committee about "true Americanism" was at odds with the heavy-handed repression which was pursued by the public authorities throughout the strike. With the memory of the 1912 dispute still fresh in mind, Commissioner of Public Safety Peter Carr and City Marshall Timothy J. O'Brien determined from the beginning upon a policy of *force majeure*. Since this was not a bona fide labor conflict but part of the worldwide Bolshevik revolution, they gave the police a free hand in using arbitrary force against the strikers. Reinforced by officers from surrounding towns, mounted and foot patrols instituted a "reign of terror," assaulting, arresting, and incarcerating strike leaders, pickets, and innocent bystanders alike. Police on horseback rode their mounts down sidewalks, chasing, trampling, and clubbing pedestrians. Rights of free speech and assembly were denied the workers by city officials, who prohibited them from holding parades or open air meetings, even on private property. Protests against police brutality to President Wilson and Governor Coolidge were to no avail, but the plight of the strikers did arouse sympathy in liberal quarters.[13]

Despite the opposition of church, state, business and labor, the despised foreigners maintained an unbroken resistance through sixteen long weeks. In the early days of the strike, H. J. Skeffington and James A. Sullivan had been assigned as Commissioners of Conciliation by the U.S. Department of Labor to mediate the dispute. Their initial report embodied the view of the strike as Bolshevik-inspired and also the expectation that it would be short-lived. Summarizing their discussion with the strike leaders, Skeffington reported:

> We told them that we [sic] our judgement the strike was lost, that they had attempted to kick up a violent agitation such as obtained in Lawrence in 1912, that the State officials had organized so effectively and produced such a show that [sic] force that it was impossible for them to make any headway, that they would need at least $10,000 a week to carry on the strike and that they couldn't possibly do that. ... Surely the strike for 54 hours pay for 48 hours work will not succeed in Lawrence. The employers are as firm as a rock on that point and the City officials, and as far as we could find out the general public, are all in favor of the mills opening up on a 48-hour week for 48 hours pay.[14]

Such appears to have been the general expectation.

How then did these workers who ordinarily lived on the verge of destitution sustain the struggle for almost four months? How from their kaleidoscopic ethnic diversity did they create such an impressive unity of purpose and action? What was the source of leadership in the strike movement? Was there any substance to the charge that the leaders were "imported agitators" and Bolsheviks? And finally, did the strike succeed or fail in its objectives? This study will attempt to provide at least partial answers to these questions.

Contrary to the allegations that they were outside troublemakers, many of the strike leaders came from the rank-and-file of mill workers and local labor. The most prominent of these were Samuel Bramhall and Imre Kaplan, who respectively served as chairman and secretary of the General Strike Committee. Bramhall was an Englishman, a long-time socialist and anti-clerical, and president of the Lawrence carpenters' union. Kaplan, a twenty-seven-year-old Russian Jew, was a delegate of the Mulespinners' Union and a professed revolutionary. With customary restraint, Skeffington described them as "red-eyed socialists of the most violent type," adding that "Kaplan is the agent of the Russian bolsheviki crowd if there is any agent in Lawrence."[15] Other leaders emerged from the various nationality groups to mobilize and organize their countrymen; they served on the General Strike Committee and its subcommittees. Strategy and tactics had to be communicated, picket lines organized, rumors and fears dispelled, and relief administered to some fifteen ethnic groups diverse in language, custom, and temperament. The success of this inter-ethnic collaboration moved A. J. Muste to comment: "If the League of Nations has been realized nowhere else, it has been realized in Lawrence. Fifteen nationalities are represented on the strike committee and are working together harmoniously."[16]

Feeding the strikers and their families was the most urgent task. Each nationality elected a relief committee, and the chairmen of these committees formed a General Relief Committee. Soup kitchens and food stations were established; tickets were issued to strikers for meals and provisions. A "Strikers' Cross" provided medical care for the ill and injured. The maintenance of morale was a second pressing concern. Meetings were held daily at which speakers in various languages exhorted the strikers to remain firm and songs of resistance were sung. One labor organizer, Anthony Capraro, noted that "the struggles of the Lawrence strikers have been put into song by one of their own members," but their favorite song was the "Internationale" which they sang at the opening and closing of their meetings.[17] *Victory Bulletins* were published periodically to provide news and to bolster the spirits of the strikers. *Bulletin* No. 8, for example, reported: "Sunday was another *May Day*. We visited our comrades of other nationalities, talked with them, sang with them. National lines are disappearing. We are making our Union one solid international organization."[18] One wonders the extent to which this was wishful thinking and to what extent a fusion of ethnic elements did occur in the heat of the strike.

The leadership of the 1919 strike was distinguished by restraint, effective organization, and prudent management. These qualities owed much to the contribution of certain "outsiders" who did rally to the cause of the strikers. Among the most important of these were three former clergymen, A. J. Muste, Cedric Long, and Harvell L. Rotzell; all three had progressed during the war from radical Christianity and pacifism to social radicalism. Having formed the Comradeship of the New World in Boston in January, 1919, to combat all forms of injustice, they hastened to Lawrence the following month to put their convictions into practice. Each played an important role in the strike, but Muste soon became a key figure as chairman of the executive committee and as the major spokesman and negotiator.[19] In addition to their organizing work in Lawrence, the ex-ministers brought the strike to the attention of a larger public through their speeches and writings. *Forward*, a Boston monthly, for example, devoted several supplements to documenting "The Truth About Lawrence."[20] The "intellectual gang," as they were called, enlisted the moral and financial support of well-to-to liberals and radicals. The appearance on the picket lines of such socialites as Elizabeth Glendower Evans inspired conservative diatribes against "Parlor Socialists" and "Boudoir Bolsheviki."[21]

Muste and his colleagues also broadened the ideological scope of the Lawrence strike. Beyond the issue of "48-54" was the struggle for industrial democracy to prepare the day when "the workers of the world shall own and control their own industries." While the end was socialism, the revolution was to be bloodless. Eschewing violence, the former clergymen urged the workers to respond to police assaults with folded arms. The relative lack of violence on the part of the strikers was attributed to the teaching and example of these disciples of the Quaker principle of passive resistance.[22] The moderating influence of the former ministers was resented by the more radical element among the strike leadership who wished the struggle to take on a more direct revolutionary character. Capraro was himself troubled by the Christian rhetoric and attitudes which the ex-preachers sometimes introduced in discussions of the General Strike Committee. On one occasion he challenged Muste to refute the radical charge that he, Long, and Rotzell were really not radicals but clergymen who were seeking "to promote peace between capital and labor, capitalistic peace, of course."[23]

On February 24, the *New York Call* carried a lengthy article on the Lawrence strike which concluded:

> Despite all the powers arrayed against them, the strikers are courageously keeping up the struggle, but there is a limit to their endurance, and that limit is the hungry cry of their little children. The suffering of the little ones is the weakest point in the armor of the workers as it is the strongest weapon that the bosses can wield.[24]

Indeed, the limited resources of the workers were quickly depleted. Citing these desperate straits, Muste appealed to Sidney Hillman, president of the Amalgamated Clothing Workers of America, for organizers and money. After consultation with August Bellanca, a vice-president of the ACWA, Hillman sent two organizers to Lawrence, Anthony Capraro and H. J. Rubenstein.[25]

Twenty-eight years old at the time of the strike, Capraro was a native of Sciacca, a market town on the southern coast of Sicily.

Since his father was a dealer in wines, grains, and agricultural implements, Antonino grew up in a bourgeois family with the advantages of culture and education. Of his twelve brothers, six emigrated, not out of economic need, but for the sake of adventure. Nino himself, after an earlier sojourn in the United States with his parents, came to join several brothers in 1904. Then thirteen, he resisted his brothers' wishes that he continue his education and chose instead to learn the tailor's trade. While still in Sciacca, Nino had been influenced by the anarchist ideas of his eldest brother, Giuseppe. Having first arrived in Tampa in the 1890s, "Joe" had there learned both the cigarmaker's craft and anarchist philosophy from the Cubans in the cigar factories. Moving to New York City, Joe and another brother, Diego, became active in the anarchist movement there. Drawn to the libertarian creed by both his individualistic temperament and his admiration for his older brothers, Nino quickly immersed himself in the anarchist circles. He attended lectures, read widely, engaged in heated discussions, and participated in radical activities.[26]

Then, on July 7, 1908, young Capraro was entrapped by an agent provocateur; arrested for carrying a concealed weapon and unlawful entry, he was convicted and sentenced to a three- to four-year term in Sing Sing. After spending his seventeenth to twentieth years in prison, Capraro was released on August 12, 1911, a physical and mental wreck. Yet his years in prison had not been unproductive. A fellow prisoner and *paesano*, Michele Cerafisi, a highly educated man, became his tutor. Through almost daily correspondence, Cerafisi and Capraro carried on an intense dialogue about literature, politics, and life. In his own words, Capraro left prison a "mature revolutionary." An aspiring journalist, he worked for a time for the conservative *Il Progresso Italo-Americano* and then became a reporter for the more congenial *New York Call*. Meanwhile, he was intermittently involved in labor organizing. Since August and Frank Bellanca, leaders of the Italian garment workers, were also from Sciacca, they knew Capraro. Because he had acquired a reputation for being fearless and incorruptible, Anthony was recruited by August Bellanca as an organizer for the ACWA and given the most dangerous assignments. It was natural then that Bellanca should send Capraro to Lawrence as the ACWA's troubleshooter.[27]

During these years, Capraro had styled himself an anarcho-syndicalist, believing in the economic organization of the working class for the prosecution of the class struggle. However, with the Bolshevik Revolution, he was drawn to the teachings of Lenin, whom he regarded as "the greatest of the living true Marxists." Lenin's work, *The State and Revolution*, had a particularly profound effect upon him.[28] Capraro unmistakably aligned himself with the Communists as the true defenders of the Marxian socialist doctrines of the abolition of private property and the destruction of the state. He had little regard for the socialism of Victor Berger and Morris Hillquit. There is no question then that when he arrived in Lawrence in late February, Capraro was a Communist—or Bolshevik, if you preferred.[29]

Entrusted with the disbursement of ACWA funds, Capraro immediately assumed a central position as a member of the General Strike Committee and its executive committee, as well as chairman of the all-important finance committee. After a few weeks, he could write to Joseph Schlossberg, general secretary of the ACWA: "The whole situation is in our hands." Although often in poor health, Capraro was tireless and efficient in his strike activity, raising funds, organizing relief, supervising picketing, speaking and writing endlessly. Yet he still found time to organize the Young People's International League, an organization devoted to the radical education of youthful textile workers.[30] In addition, as correspondent of the *New York Call*, Capraro publicized the sufferings and hardships of the Lawrence strikers. Through vivid accounts of police attacks he engaged the support of New York City's socialists for the embattled workers.[31]

Shortly after his arrival, Capraro provided a grave assessment of the situation in Lawrence to the ACWA officials: "The situation here is growing more and more serious every day. The masses' morale is wonderful but the leaders are getting discouraged because of the lack of funds."[32]

Reminding them of the unfulfilled promises of ACWA aid, Capraro warned: "Whatever the reason for such inaction I must say that it has failed to kill the strike only because the mass is out for business in spite of all difficulties." Without immediate help, however, "no amount of solidarity among the workers can prevent the collapse by bankruptcy of the whole struggle." Capraro insisted that $10,000 be sent immediately to the General Strike Committee. That very day, the general executive board of the ACWA appropriated $2,000 from its reserve fund and also asked the union's 75,000 members in New York City to contribute one hour's pay a week to the Lawrence strike fund.[33] This timely intervention of the Amalgamated Clothing Workers saved the strike from defeat. Over the next two months, nearly $100,000 was contributed in support of the Lawrence textile workers' fight, the greater part of it from the members of the ACWA.[34]

Because they comprised the largest ethnic element among the mill workers, the unwavering adherence of the Italians to the strike was essential. Capraro's selection as the ACWA representative no doubt took this fact into account. Nino, as he was popularly known, quickly won acceptance as the leader of the Italian strikers. He worked closely with Frank M. Coco, a barber and socialist, and Giuseppe Salerno, a mill hand, both members of the General Strike Committee. In addition, he had the help of Gioacchino Artoni, a veteran organizer with the ACWA, and Vittorio Buttis, itinerant propagandist for the Federazione Socialista Italiana. Buttis, who was in charge of the soup kitchen for the Italian strikers, also compiled a daily chronicle of the strike, which was published in *La Notizia* of Boston. Certainly the Italian leadership was leftist, but ranged in ideology from social democracy to communism.[35]

The Italians appear to have been particularly tenacious and uncompromising in their commitment to the strike. When the threat of deportation was raised, they declared they would welcome being sent back to Italy *en masse*. At one point, when relief funds were running low, the Italians voted to waive their benefits in favor of more needy groups. In late April, they resolved to remain on strike for another twelve weeks or longer if necessary. As in 1912, families sent their children to sympathizers in other cities, smuggling them out of Lawrence in moving vans.[36] Mutual aid societies made financial contributions in support of the strike. The Tripoli Club donated twenty-five dollars and voted to expel any members who scabbed. Small merchants in the Italian colony generally supported the strike either from conviction or expediency. Reputed opponents were denounced as enemies of the working class and subject to boycotts and worse.[37] Extension of credit by small shopkeepers was an important form of assistance to the strikers. On one occasion, when relief funds ran out, Capraro called a meeting of Italian grocers and told them they had an obligation to contribute to the workers' struggle; everyone contributed.[38]

Among the well-to-do Italians of Lawrence, some took a neutral, if not hostile position with respect to the strike. Several were members of the Citizens Committee appointed by the mayor to mediate the strike. Among them were Angelo G. Rocco, who in 1912 had been the youthful leader of the Italian strikers, but was now a successful attorney, and Dr. Costante Calitri, a physician. While disassociating themselves from the radical leadership, Rocco and Calitri publicly defended the workers from charges of being Bolsheviks and anarchists; they also decried the violation of rights by the police; and called for sympathetic understanding of the strike of foreign workers for better living conditions. Yet according to Capraro, "the most bitter enemies of the striking mill workers are the priests and the class of petit intellectuals." Among the latter he included a "certain Italian lawyer" (Rocco?) and a physician (Calitri?).[39]

A major source of opposition to the strike within the Italian community was the Catholic clergy. Father Mariano Milanese, pastor of the Italian Church of the Holy Rosary since 1905, was accused of betraying the interests of his parishioners who were mainly workers. As in 1912, it was rumored that he had been paid by the woolen companies to oppose the strike, that he urged the police to beat the strikers, and that he had denounced the Italians as dangerous criminals. Given the traditional anti-clericalism rampant among the Italians, such allegations found fertile soil. Milanese felt compelled to issue a published statement in which he denied the ugly rumors and declared that the Italians had allowed themselves to be deceived by "those who are sworn enemies of the Priesthood, of Catholicism, of your faith and of your religion." Milanese complained that even "our most intimate friends look at us with rancour and disgust." Yet he admitted that he had counseled workers to return to the mills because he knew for a certainty that the manufacturers would never accept their demands. By this admission, the pastor convicted himself of the worst charge of his enemies. Not surprisingly, feelings against Father Milanese ran high. Windows in his church were broken; religious functions were boycotted; and even physical assaults took place.[40] Capraro, after witnessing an altercation involving Milanese and Salerno, commented.

> This, indeed, is a very small incident. Yet in Lawrence it may assume considerable proportions. Milanese is such a rascal that I shouldn't be a bit surprised if he was either to hire thugs to attack me or to incite the Irish Catholic element against us. Do you realize what this would mean here? The Italians are terribly anti-priest. And if the Irish took upon themselves the task to avenge the priest a race riot of the most serious character would ensue.[41]

Capraro also had to contend with a small, but extreme element among the Italians who agitated for more radical measures. *Maes-*

tra Cacici, a leader of this faction, it was said, could arouse an audience to murder with her violent rhetoric. This group demanded that Arturo Giovannitti and Carlo Tresca, the heroes of the 1912 strike, be brought to Lawrence. In response to an invitation delivered by *Signora* Cacici herself, Giovannitti and Tresca demurred on the grounds that their presence in Lawrence would impede negotiations which promised to bring a speedy settlement to the strike. However, should the strike continue, Giovannitti and Tresca assured their comrades that they would be with them "in body as we are now in spirit."[42] In this they were following the advice of cooler heads, including Capraro, who believed that such a provocation would incite the authorities to harsh retaliation. But the revolutionary element would not be appeased. Also, after twelve weeks, Capraro noted that the strikers' morale was flagging and that some dramatic event was needed to revive their spirits. He then engineered a theatrical coup which did generate renewed enthusiasm among the workers but which also placed his life in jeopardy.[43]

While Giovannitti was reluctant to return to Lawrence, Tresca was willing, although City Marshall O'Brien (whom Tresca had slapped in an encounter in 1912) vowed that he would be killed if he set foot in the city. Securing acquiescence from a reluctant General Strike Committee, Capraro demanded complete control over the timing and staging of Tresca's visit. Meeting with Tresca in Boston on May 1, Capraro was stymied by the problem of how to evade the tight police security. By chance they were dining in the North End when Dr. Calitri entered the restaurant. It turned out that he was a friend and *paesano* of Tresca; despite his personal views, Calitri agreed to take Tresca in his car to Lawrence and to harbor him in his home. Capraro then spread the news by word-of-mouth that an important meeting would be held at Lexington Hall the evening of May 2. With Tresca hidden beneath the speaker's platform and guards preventing anyone from leaving, Capraro opened the meeting before a capacity crowd of Italians. Sensing the mounting tension, he gave strict instructions that no one was to leave the hall, there was to be no fighting, and no applause until he said the word. Then he turned and said:

> "Carlo." Carlo Tresca came up and stood along beside me. Well, have you ever heard the stunning detonation of silence? Not a word was uttered, not a sound made, and yet there was a situation which was about to explode. The intensity of the emotion that was generated by the presence of Carlo Tresca ... was such that it was an

absolute pity to continue to keep these people without giving vent to their emotions. . . . I said, "Comrades, *compagni*, you may applaud if you want to." The explosion was absolutely incredible and immediately after that, I saw that they let a little steam out, so I said, "Silence." There was perfect orchestration of sound and silence, and then Carlo started to speak."[44]

Tresca gave a fiery speech urging the strikers to remain steadfast in their cause and then was spirited out of town.

The next day, the *Lawrence Telegram* carried the headline: "Tresca Smuggled In and Out of City—I.W.W. Leader Delivers a Vicious Speech Against the Police." The article, which quoted Capraro at length, described the meeting in detail and even mentioned that "a prominent Italian doctor and lawyer [Calitri and Rocco?] had been active in shielding Tresca during his stay here."[45] The Lawrence police had been made to look like fools; they responded by setting up machine guns manned by ex-soldiers. Even before the Tresca incident, the mood in Lawrence was becoming uglier. The *Leader*, on April 27, citing the example of western cities where citizens had herded IWW leaders into freight cars and shipped them away, asked in bold type: "WHERE ARE THE VIGILANTES?" On April 30, City Marshall O'Brien announced that police protection had been withdrawn from the strike leaders. On May 3, the *Lawrence Telegram* commented that if the authorities did not take steps against the radicals, "the common people of America will, even if they have to form mobs to do so." On May 5, a Liberty Loan speaker urged the use of the lamp post for foreign-speaking strikers.[46]

At two o'clock in the morning of May 6, a gang of masked men broke into Capraro's room in the Hotel Needham, kidnapped him and Nathan Kleinman, as well as an ACWA organizer, took them out of the city, and beat them. Capraro was brutally assaulted and threatened with lynching, but managed to escape his assailants. Capraro had the presence of mind to have a photograph taken of his bloodied body prior to receiving medical attention, a photograph which was widely published. Soon after the attack, he wrote a vivid account of the incident, "How the Lawrence Ku-Klux Gang Taught Me American Democracy."[47] During his night of terror, Capraro recalled that he had decided to return to Lawrence as soon as he could: "[to] wash myself of the stain that I had procured for myself when I promised my assailants that I would not if they spared my life." While still recovering from his injuries, Capraro did return to Lawrence on May 18 to a hero's welcome. In his speeches to enthusiastic crowds, he disclaimed any claim to heroism: "I am back to tell you, Comrades, that I am not a hero, but a mere victim of the capitalistic system we are all fighting."[48]

The murderous attack upon Capraro, however, appears to have backfired. After visiting Lawrence, Bellanca wrote that the "villanous act," rather than intimidating the workers, had "electrified them all, men and women, Italians, Syrians, Germans, Lithuanians, French, Irish, Armenians, and disposed them to the greatest, the most noble sacrifices." A. J. Muste commented: "These brutal tactics instead of breaking the strike have only welded more firmly together the various race elements and imbued them with revolutionary ardor." The outrage also stimulated an outpouring of financial contributions. Evelyn Bramhall comforted Capraro with the thought that "the spreading of the news of such brutality will bring us thousands and thousands of dollars to continue this war— for such it is."[49]

Capraro's near martyrdom elicited the following tribute from the General Strike Committee:

> We have found you tireless and efficient even in ill health in the work you have undertaken with your Italian comrades, on the Finance Committee and as editor of our paper. But most of all we have found you a lovable [sic] comrade and friend, and . . . we shall treasure your friendship as one of the priceless byproducts of our struggle which gives us hope that a cooperative commonwealth will come in which men shall no more be brutalized by the competitive struggle for bread.[50]

The Italians were particularly affected by the attack upon Capraro. A thousand of them visited him, pooling their pennies and nickels for a gift as an expression of their appreciation and affection.[51]

As the strike entered its fourth month, the endurance of the workers appeared to be reaching the breaking point. For several weeks in May, the strike fund was depleted, ending regular relief. Yet an effort to reopen the Everett Mill on May 19 failed with only a handful of the former 1500 employees reporting for work. The very next day the mill owners announced that a fifteen percent increase in wages would go into effect June 2 and that there would be no discrimination against strikers. Writing to Capraro, Rotzell exclaimed: "Hurrah we have a real victory and every one is jubilant." At a huge mass meeting outside Lexington Hall, the workers voted unanimously to accept the recommendation of the General

Strike Committee that the strike be declared at an end. In Muste's words:

> Thus, amid the gay shouting and singing of thousands of men, women, and little children, the weary struggle came to a glorious end. AND NO SENTIMENT WON SUCH LONG AND WILD AP-PLAUSE FROM THAT IMMENSE MULTITUDE AS THE APPEAL TO STICK TO THE AMALGAMATED TEXTILE WORKERS OF AMERICA, THEIR OWN ONE BIG UNION, BORN OUT OF THE AGONY OF THEIR STRUGGLE![52]

At a victory picnic held on May 25, Capraro was singled out for a tumultuous ovation. Speaking to the assembled Italians, he was presented with a bouquet of carnations which he returned, saying: "I am honored only in so far as I am able to honor you."[53]

For Capraro, as for Muste, Bellanca, and others, the victory in Lawrence was not the end of the struggle but the first step toward the creation of One Big Union in the textile industry—and beyond that the workers' commonwealth. The recently formed Amalgam-ated Textile Workers of America was to be the vehicle for realizing those objectives. When Capraro was sent to Lawrence one of his assignments was to establish a textile workers' union affiliated with the ACWA. Within a matter of weeks, he was able to report that "the central executive and general strike committees and the mas-ses of the workers voted unanimously and enthusiastically for affili-ation with the Amalgamated."[54] The Lawrence strike committee also endorsed the draft of a constitution for the Amalgamated Textile Workers of America which defined its purpose as follows:

> Our ultimate aim is, by whatever methods of proletarian action may be most effective, to help achieve the abolition of capitalism and the system of wage-slavery; and to establish the ownership and control of industry by the workers, for the workers.[55]

The movement for the formation of such a union culminated in an organizing convention held in New York City on April 12 and 13. Under the patronage of the ACWA, and with the particular encouragement of Bellanca, seventy-five delegates from various textile centers assembled in the Labor Temple at 14th Street and Second Avenue. Just as the ACWA had been born of a revolt against the United Garment Workers Union, so the ATWA was the product of disaffection with the United Textile Workers of Amer-ica. The Lawrence strike had demonstrated the capacity of the unskilled immigrant workers, who had been hitherto ignored by the

UTWA, to organize and wage a drawn out struggle. With Muste in the chair, the convention adopted the preamble of the ACWA constitution as its own. Based on the Marxist doctrine of the class struggle, it called for the organization of labor according to the principles of industrial unionism and for the education of the workers in preparation for the time when they would assume control of the system of production. The radical spirit of the convention was also expressed in its resolutions, which called for the observance of May First, extended greetings to Soviet Russia, Hungary, and Bavaria (the salutation concluded "Long live the Soviets!"), demanded the immediate withdrawal of American troops from Russia, and protested the political and industrial prisoners in the United States. In its "Call to Organize", the convention invited "our fellow workers in [the textile] industry to join with us in organizing a class conscious, industrial union which shall be organized and controlled by the rank and file of the workers themselves."[56]

The ATWA set up its headquarters in New York City with Muste as general secretary and Capraro, after he recovered from the beating, as editor of its organs, the *New Textile Worker* and *Il Tessitore Libero*. Capraro had nurtured the idea of a textile workers' union in Lawrence affiliated with the ACWA, but his hope was that one day the two would merge to form "One Big Industrial Union of the Textile and Clothing Workers," a vertical organization of labor from the weaving of the cloth to the sewing of the garment.[57] Although the Amalgamated Clothing Workers in its 1920 convention voted for unity with the Amalgamated Textile Workers, the merger was never consummated. One reason was that Sidney Hillman was opposed to the idea. However, there was also growing opposition to the proposed amalgamation among Capraro's old comrades in Lawrence. Some now viewed the ACWA as not sufficiently revolutionary.[58] A conflict over this issue in the Lawrence local of the ATWA led to Capraro's resignation of his position in the union. In a letter to Muste of March 1, 1920, he explained his reasons:

I was accused by Kaplan in the midst of a Central Council meeting of being an agent of the Amalgamated Clothing Workers of America. The members of this body took cognizance of the incident by various expressions but failed, as a body, to repudiate Kaplan's explicit accusations and its mean implications. . . . Now, you will understand that a lack of pronouncement on the part of the Central Council to the effect that the executive body of the Lawrence Local did not entertain the same belief with regard to my role in our organization

justifies me to believe that the opinion of that body coincides with
that of Kaplan. That being the case I could not with any amount of
dignity remain in the organization. . . . [59]

As a Sicilian, Capraro had a high sense of personal honor and this
attack upon his integrity was more than he could brook. But he
also felt out of place in the textile workers' union and wished to
return to his work as an organizer for the ACWA.[60]

What appears to have happened in Lawrence is that one Legere
had gained ascendency, particularly among the younger militants
in the union. It was said of Legere that "a great number of workers
. . . are ready to go with him wherever he decides, so great is the
confidence which they have in him as a leader of tremendous
imagination, energy, and experience in the labor movement." A
syndicalist, Legere favored One Big Union along the lines of the
Winnipeg model. He was so opposed to fusion of the ATWA with
the ACWA that he favored secession of the Lawrence Local if that
should happen.[61] Capraro viewed this development from afar with
growing displeasure: "In Lawrence the supreme need is a strong
class-conscious textile organization. Whatever fosters such an organization is good; whatever does not foster such an organization is
the work either of spies or of fools." Pursuing this logic, he concluded that Legere must either be a spy or a fool.[62]

But ideological disputes were not the major obstacle confronting
the infant ATWA. The Amalgamated Textile Workers initially
spread rapidly through the mill towns of New England, New Jersey, New York, and Pennsylvania. Using foreign-language organizers and literature, it was especially successful in attracting immigrant workers. ATWA membership reached a peak of 50,000 in
1920. However, the severe depression which struck the textile
industry beginning in April, 1920, caused widespread unemployment and mill closings.[63] Under such conditions the strength of the
union was rapidly eroded. In the textile strike of 1922, the longest
and largest such dispute in New England, the Amalgamated Textile
Workers controlled the strike only in the Pawtuxet Valley of Rhode
Island. The United Textile Workers directed the struggle in other
areas, except for Lawrence, where the majority of the strikers
followed the leadership of One Big Union (evidently Legere had
carried the day!).[64] A leading labor scholar of the day, William M.
Leiserson, observed: "While the Amalgamated Textile Workers
made rapid progress in the first year or two of its existence, it has
more recently shown it is not any more successful in organizing
and holding the unskilled foreign-born workers in the industry than

the United Textile Workers."[65] The 1922 strike was the ATWA's "last hurrah." Its final convention was held in New York City in the spring of 1923; its leaders discouraged, the organization collapsed, leaving surviving locals to fend for themselves.[66]

In the 1930s, the Textile Workers Organizing Committee of the CIO, funded by Hillman's Amalgamated Clothing Workers and David Dubinsky's International Ladies Garment Workers, succeeded where the ATWA had failed. The textile workers finally were organized into an industrial union, encompassing skilled and unskilled workers, foreign-born and native, white and black. Neither Muste nor Capraro was to play a part in the delayed realization of their dream of one big textile union. However, one might ask the extent to which the experience of the 1919 strike (and similar strikes elsewhere) contributed to the shaping of an American working class ready to make the most of the new deal of the thirties. The connections between the earlier, if largely failed, efforts of immigrant workers to redress their grievances and the mass organizing drives of the 1930s in which they and their children played prominent roles remain to be studied systematically.

Regardless of its consequences, the Lawrence strike of 1919 is in itself instructive as an episode in ethnic labor history. First, it is clear that apart from the hysteria of the Red Scare, there were real immigrant radicals afoot in the land. "Comrade Fellow Worker Anarchist Communist Radical Revolutionary Anthony Capraro," as he was addressed by one correspondent, was one of these.[67] There were others who viewed the strike in Lawrence as a battle in the class war. Not all were avowed Communists, but some were. The fear of Bolshevik influence then was not simply a bogeyman born of the conservatives' fevered imagination. Nor was such radicalism limited to "outside agitators"; rather it appears to have been widespread among the laboring people of Lawrence, and especially the "new immigrants."[68] The 1919 strike gives the lie to both Cole's assertion that the immigrants "would follow alien leaders for better conditions but would never adopt un-American [i.e., radical] views" and Rosenblum's dictum that the conservatism of the American labor movement can be attributed to the "new immigrants."[69]

What the Lawrence strike did not do was to create class conscious working-class solidarity among all wage earners. Rather it brought to the surface those cleavages of ethnicity and status which divided the workers into antagonistic, competing groups. The basic dichotomy, as indicated earlier, appears to have been between the English-speaking and the non—English-speaking. The strike then was not only a conflict between labor and capital, but also a struggle between the older established ethnic elements and the more recent arrivals. This was a struggle involving both socio-economic interests and cultural values. Capraro observed that the Irish Americans had proven to be the "greatest enemies of the strikers".[70] As a still marginal ethnic group, the strike gave the Irish the opportunity to reinforce their position by demonstrating to the Yankee establishment their utility as guardians of law and order. Father O'Reilly and City Marshall O'Brien, the leading antagonists of the immigrant strikers, personified this role. Thus, while the common struggle generated a trans-ethnic unity among the non—English-speaking groups, the conflict widened the abyss which separated them from the English-speaking portion of the working class. Certainly the heritage of the 1919 strike must have continued to influence inter-group relations, politics, social life, and economic arrangements in Lawrence for years to come.

Notes

1. The 1912 strike is extensively treated in Melvyn Dubofsky, *We Shall Be All. A History of the Industrial Workers of the World* (New York, 1969); Philip S. Foner, *History of the Labor Movement in the United States*, 4 (New York, 1965); and Donald B. Cole, *Immigrant City: Lawrence, Massachusetts, 1845–1921* (Chapel Hill, 1963). Although Cole's terminal date is 1921, he devotes less than two pages to the 1919 strike. His failure to analyze this conflict in depth and his overreliance on the English-language press lead Cole into factual errors and absurd conclusions.

   The most detailed account of the 1919 strike is to be found in the contemporary study, J. M. Budish and George Soule, *The New Unionism in the Clothing Industry* (New York, 1920), 254-69. Brief mention is to be found in Robert W. Dunn and Jack Hardy, *Labor and Textiles* (New York, 1931), 218-20; and William M. Leiserson, *Adjusting Immigrant and Industry* (New York, 1924), 204-205. Otherwise the literature of labor studies is silent regarding this strike.

2. A. J. Muste, "The Story," *The Truth About Lawrence, Forward Supplement*, (Boston), 3 (February, 1919): 2-3; Anthony Capraro, "Lawrence Textile Strikers," *New York Call*, March 14, 1919. An illuminating series of articles on the immigrant population of Lawrence by Norbert Weiner appeared in the *Boston Herald*, Feb. 23, 28, March 1, 1919. Clippings in Anthony Capraro Papers, Box 9, "Lawrence Strike," Immigration History Research Centre (IHRC), University of Minnesota.

3. *Boston Herald*, Feb. 23, 1919.

4. "Interviews with Textile Workers," Capraro Papers, Box 9, "Lawrence Strike." See for example, "Statement concerning Wood Mill of the American Woolen Company given by Rose and Grace Santora"; and "Interview with Annie Trina."

5. "Interviews with Textile Workers," Capraro Papers; *Boston Herald*, Feb. 23, 1919; Budish and Soule, *op. cit.*, 254-57; H. L. Rotzell, "The Issues," *The Truth About Lawrence, Forward Supplement*, 3 (February, 1919); James F. Hughes to Hugh L. Kerwin, January 15, 1919, "Textile Workers. Lawrence, Mass.," Federal Mediation and Conciliation Service, Case 33/2694, Record Group 280, National Archives. Hughes, Secretary of the Building Trades Council of Lawrence, wrote to Kerwin, Director of Conciliation, U.S. Department of Labor, that seventy per cent of the textile workers were working three days a week while thirty per cent were idle.

6. Budish and Soule, *op. cit.*, 257-59; Harvell L. Rotzell, "The Lawrence Textile Strike," *The American Labor Year Book 1919–1920* (New York, 1920), 172-73; Muste, "The Story," 2; *New York Times*, Jan. 26, Feb. 1, 4, 1919; *New York Call*, Feb. 2, 1919; *Boston Herald*, Feb. 28, 1919.

7. Rotzell. "Lawrence Textile Strike"; Clipping, April 29, 1919, Capraro Papers, Box 9, "Lawrence Strike."

8. *Boston Herald*, Feb. 23, 1919; "Interviews with Textile Workers," Capraro Papers, Box 9, "Lawrence Strike."

9. Demarest Lloyd to William B. Wilson, May 31, 1919, "Textile Workers. Lawrence Mass.," FMCS, Case 33/2694, RG 280, NA. Writing as Secretary of the Harvard Liberal Club of Boston, Lloyd challenged Wilson to reconcile the economic settlement of the strike with his allegation that it was revolutionary in character. This file of the Federal Mediation and Conciliation Service documents fully the interpretation of the strike as Bolshevik in inspiration. This point of view is summarized by William H. Crawford, "Three Months of Labor Turmoil in Lawrence, Mass.," *New York Times*, May 25, 1919, Section 4.

10. Winthrop L. Marvin to William B. Wilson, April 12, 1919; James R. Menzie and others, Lawrence Central Labor Union, to Frank Morrison, Secretary, AFL, February 10, 1919; John Golden to William B. Wilson, July 9, 1919; "Textile Workers. Lawrence, Mass.," FMCS, Case 33/2694, RG 280, NA. Budish and Soule, *op. cit.*, 259. The standard work on the anti-radical nativism of this period, Robert K. Murray, *Red Scare: a Study in National Hysteria, 1919–1920*, (Minneapolis, 1955), totally ignores the Lawrence strike.

11. General Strike Committee, Lawrence, Mass., to William B. Wilson, April 24, 1919; The Roman Catholic Strikers of Lawrence to Cardinal William O'Connell, May 2, 1919; Letter to the Editor, James T. O'Reilly, March 1, 1919 (Clipping), Capraro Papers, Box 9, "Lawrence Strike."

12. The Citizens Committee of Lawrence, *Circular No. 1*, Capraro Papers, Oversize 2; Clippings, Capraro Papers, Box 9, "Lawrence Strike"; *New York Call*, March 27, May 16, 1919.

13. Crawford, "Three Months of Labor Turmoil,"; *New York Call*, March 27, April 8, 15, May 7, 8, 1919; *Truth About the Lawrence Police*,

Forward Supplement (Boston), 3 (April, 1919). The latter includes affidavits and photographs documenting police brutality.

14. H. J. Skeffington to H. L. Kerwin, February 14, 1919, "Textile Workers. Lawrence, Mass.," FMCS, Case 33/2694, RG 280, NA.

15. Ibid.; *Boston Herald*, February 28, 1919; *New York Call*, March 14, 1919.

16. *New York Call*, May 14, 1919.

17. *Loc. cit.*, March 14, 15, 1919; General Strike Committee, *Victory Bulletin*, nos. 5-8, Capraro Papers; Budish and Soule, *op. cit.*, 260-61.

18. General Strike Committee, *Bulletin No. 8*, May 7, 1919.

19. "Autobiography in Miniature of Cedric Long,"; "Biographical Sketch of A. J. Muste," Capraro Papers, Box 9, "Lawrence Strike"; *New York Call*, May 23, 1919; Interviews with Anthony Capraro, April 19, August 11-12, 1975; *New York Times*, February 17, 1919. See also A. J. Muste's brief memoir in Rita J. Simon, ed., *As We Saw the Thirties* (Urbana, Ill., 1967), 123-50; and *The Reminiscences of A. J. Muste* (The Oral History Office, Columbia University, 1965).

20. *Forward* (Boston), 3 (February, April, 1919).

21. Crawford, "Three Months of Labor Turmoil,"; *New York Call*, March 24, May 8, 27, 1919; *Truth About the Lawrence Police; The Leader* (Lawrence), March 30, 1919; Clipping, April 6, 1919, Capraro Papers.

22. "Biographical Sketch of A. J. Muste"; Budish and Soule, *op. cit.*, 260; Crawford, "Three Months of Labor Turmoil,"; *The Truth About Lawrence*, 8; *Reminiscences*, 407.

23. Capraro to A. J. Muste, October 18, 1919, Capraro Papers, Box 2, "Lawrence Strike"; Vittorio Buttis, *Memorie di Vita di Tempeste Sociali* (Chicago, 1940), 105.

24. *New York Call*, February 24, 1919.

25. Capraro Interviews; Buttis, *op. cit.*, 108.

26. Capraro Interviews. Because Giuseppe and Diego Capraro came to the attention of the Italian police for their anarchist activities, dossiers were compiled on them: Ministero dell'Interno, Direzione Centrale di Pubblica Sicurezza, Casellario Politico Centrale, Archivio centrale dello Stato (Rome). The Consul General of Italy in New York reported in 1911 that the Capraro brothers were very active propagandists, especially of the theories of Francisco Ferrer. Il R. Console Generale al On. Ministero dell'Interno, Direzione Gen. P.S., New York, November 18, 1911.

27. Capraro Interviews; Board of Parole for State Prisons, State of New York, Anthony Capraro's Parole, August 10, 1911, Capraro Papers, Box 5, Prison Record and Pardon. The Capraro Papers also contain an extensive file of correspondence between Capraro and Cerafisi.

28. Capraro Interviews. A copy of *The State and Revolution* was given to Capraro by "Arthur Adams," the representative of the Russian Soviet Government in New York City. One of Mr. Adams' cards is in the Capraro Papers.

29. Anthony Capraro, "Communism versus Victor Berger's Socialism" (typescript), Capraro Papers, Box 9, "Capraro's Writings." This essay appears to have been written in 1921. Capraro was editor of *Alba Nuova* (New Dawn), the organ of the Federation of Italian Workers of

America of the Workers (Communist) Party of America. Vol. 1, n. 2/3 (Oct., Nov. 1921) and vol. II, n. 1/2 (Feb. 15, April 15, 1922) are in the IHRC.

30. Capraro to Joseph Schlossberg, March 19, 1919; Mrs. John Bateman and others to Capraro, May 8, 1919, Capraro Papers. The activities of the Young People's International League can be followed in the letters from Bert Emsley to Capraro, October 20, 1919–July 28, 1920, Capraro Papers, Box 9, "Lawrence Strike"; Capraro Interviews.

31. Among the articles appearing under his byline were "Lawrence Strikers Shed Their Blood; Murdered and Maimed in Labor's Cause," March 27, 1919, and "Police Clubs Used in Vain to Break Textile Strikers' Solidarity in Lawrence," April 15, 1919.

32. Capraro to Schlossberg, March 19, 1919.

33. *New York Call*, March 20, 22, 1919.

34. *Loc. cit.*, March 27, May 22, 1919; Rotzell, "Lawrence Textile Strike."

35. *Reminiscences*, 379-380. According to Muste, Capraro was a "very eloquent, persuasive talker in Italian." Buttis, *op. cit.*, 104-108; *New York Call*, March 14, May 19, 27, 1919; Capraro Interviews; Capraro to "My Dear Maria" (Bambace), August 4, 1919, Capraro Papers, Box 3, "Nino's Letters to Maria."

36. Skeffington to Kerwin, February 14, 1919, "Textile Workers. Lawrence, Mass.," FMCS, Case 33/2694, RG 280, NA; *New York Call*, March 29, April 9, 1919; *Lawrence Telegram*, April 25, 1919, Clipping, Capraro Papers, Box 9, "Lawrence Strike"; Budish and Soule, *op. cit.*, 261.

37. Letter of Tripoli Club di Mutuo Soccorso, n.d.; Società di Mutuo Soccorso della Basilicata to Comitato Generale dello Sciopero di Lawrence, Mass., March 2, 1919; Società Mutuo Soccorso (Duke of Abruzzi) to Comitato generale sciopero, March 3, 1919; Carlo Vespasiano to Comitato dirigente lo Sciopero, March 7, 1919. Vespasiano, the proprietor of a pharmacy, refutes the charge that he is an enemy of the working class and signs himself "L'amico del popolo."

38. Capraro Interviews. According to the *Leader*, "in the foreign quarters, the milkmen, grocers and provision dealers, whose customers were almost wholly among the foreign peoples ... trusted out many thousands of dollars. Some of this they may eventually get back, but what will happen to the grocers and milkmen who confidingly accepted orders from the strike committee for supplies to the amount ... of 16,000 to 18,000 dollars?" April 6, 1919.

39. *New York Call*, March 27, April 9, May 16, 1919. Rocco and Calitri expressed their views in a letter to the editor, *Lawrence Sun American*, March 13, 1919. Calitri also published and distributed a handbill objecting to the gossip that he was an enemy of the workers; to the contrary, he declared, he was not opposed to the strike, but wished victory to the workers in the struggle. *A tutti gli Italiani di Lawrence*, Capraro Papers, Oversize 2.

40. Cole, *op. cit.*, 187-88; M. Milanese, *Agli Italiani di Lawrence, Quaresima 1919; New York Call*, April 15, May 20, 1919.

41. Capraro to "My Dear Maria" (Bambace), August 1-2, 1919, Capraro Papers, Box 3, "Nino's Letters to Maria."

42. Arturo Giovannitti and Carlo Tresca to "Compagni Scioperanti di Lawrence, Mass.," n.d., (on *Il Martello* letterhead).
43. Capraro Interviews; Buttis, *op. cit.*, 105-106.
44. Capraro Interviews; Capraro's retrospective account conforms closely to contemporary reports.
45. Clipping, May 3, 1919, Capraro Papers, Box 9, "Lawrence Strike."
46. *Leader*, April 27, 1919; *New York Call*, May 7, 11, 1919; Crawford, "Three Months of Labor Turmoil."
47. *New York Call*, May 23, 1919; Capraro Interviews.
48. *New York Call*, May 19, 23, 1919.
49. *Il Lavoro* (New York), May 10, 1919; *New York Call*, May 14, 1919; Bramhall to Capraro, May 19, 1919, Capraro Papers, Box 9, "Lawrence Strike"; Budish and Soule, *op. cit.*, 261-62; *Reminiscences*, 399.
50. Mrs. John Bateman and others to Capraro, May 8, 1919, Capraro Papers, Box 2, "Lawrence Strike—Rotzell."
51. *New York Call*, May 12, 1919.
52. Rotzell, "Lawrence Textile Strike"; *New York Call*, May 19, 22, 23, 1919; *Boston American*, May 19, 1919; *New Textile Worker* (New York), May 24, 1919; H. L. Rotzell to Capraro, May 20, 1919, Capraro Papers, Box 2, "Lawrence Strike—Rotzell."
53. *New York Call*, May 27, 1919.
54. Capraro to Schlossberg, March 19, 1919; *New York Call*, March 14, 1919.
55. "Meeting of Executive Committee of General Strike Committee of Lawrence, March 10, 1919," Capraro Papers, Box 9, "Lawrence Strike." This draft appears to be in Capraro's hand; it bears the notation, "Telegraph of this resolution to Bellanca, March 10, 1919."
56. *New York Call*, April 9, 12, 14, 15, 1919; "Minutes of the First Convention of the Amalgamated Textile Workers of America," Capraro Papers, Box 9, "Lawrence Strike."
57. Capraro to Muste, March 1, 1920, Capraro Papers, Box 2, "Lawrence Strike"; Capraro to Schlossberg, July 31, 1919, Capraro Papers, Box 9, "Lawrence Strike."
58. Budish and Soule, *op. cit.*, 269; *New Textile Worker*, May 22, 1920; Bert Emsley to Capraro, June 8, 1920; Capraro to Emsley, June 22, 1920, Capraro Papers, Box 9, "Lawrence Strike"; Capraro Interviews.
59. Capraro to Muste, March 1, 1920, Capraro Papers, Box 2, "Lawrence Strike." One of the "insinuations" which offended Capraro was that he favored affiliation with the ACWA in order to secure an increase in organizers' wages. A sympathetic correspondent wrote to Capraro: "You have made great sacrifices for Lawrence, and almost lost your life here, and the Lawrence workers listen in apathy while you are calumniated." Bert Emsley to Capraro, February 27, 1920, Capraro Papers, Box 9, "Lawrence Strike."
60. Capraro to Muste, March 1, 1920, Capraro Papers, Box 2, "Lawrence Strike"; Capraro Interviews.
61. Bert Emsley to Capraro, June 8, 1920, Capraro Papers, Box 9, "Lawrence Strike." This might have been Benjamin J. Legere, an IWW

organizer, who was active in the Little Falls, N.Y., textile strike of 1912. Foner, *op. cit.*, 4: 351.

62. Capraro to Emsley, June 22, July 9, 1920, Capraro Papers, Box 9, "Lawrence Strike."

63. Budish and Soule, *op. cit.*, 263; Dunn and Hardy, *op. cit.*, 204; Robert W. Dunn, "Unionism in the Textile Industry," *The American Labor Year Book 1921–1922*, 4 (New York, n.d.): 155-162; Leiserson, *op. cit.*, 204-205.

64. Dunn and Hardy, *op. cit.*, 220-221; *The American Labor Year Book 1923–1924*, 5 (New York, 1924): 104-106.

65. Leiserson, *op. cit.*, 206.

66. Dunn and Hardy, *op. cit.*, 203-204.

67. Bert Emsley to Capraro, October 20, 1919, Capraro Papers, Box 9 "Lawrence Strike."

68. Expressions of radicalism are common in "Interviews with Textile Workers," Capraro Papers, Box 9, "Lawrence Strike." Muste attributed "a good deal of working class solidarity" and "revolutionary fervor" to the strikers, *Reminiscences*, 398, 410.

69. Cole, *op. cit.*, 202; Gerald Rosenblum, *Immigrant Workers: Their Impact on American Labor Radicalism* (New York, 1973).

70. *New York Call*, May 23, 1919.

Italians and the Tampa General Strike of 1910

George E. Pozzetta

Historians have only recently begun to turn their full attention to the role that organized labor and immigration played in the development of the southern United States. For years scholars and laymen alike simply dismissed the region as an area where foreigners and/or unions did not exist or where they failed to find a receptive environment. A few studies have begun the necessary reassessment of these conceptions—Jean Scarpaci's investigation of Italians in Louisiana comes immediately to mind. Yet, there are many unfinished chapters to be completed in the larger story. A case in point involves the labor history of Italians in Tampa, Florida.

During the years 1885–1910, thousands of Cuban, Italian, and Spanish immigrants came to the small coastal village of Tampa, and transformed this settlement into a thriving commercial and manufacturing center. Drawn primarily by the magnet of cigar manufacturing, these "Latins" underwrote the success of the city and its major industry.[1] Indeed, within a remarkably short period of time, they made Tampa into the nation's leader in the production of high quality, hand-rolled cigars. This success, however, was not achieved without substantial labor strife. By the end of this century's first decade, cigarworker unions in Tampa participated in two general strikes and numerous lesser walk-outs. The purpose of this brief paper is to examine Italian participation in the general strike of 1910, a labor struggle lasting seven months and involving twelve thousand workers, against the backdrop of Tampa's labor and immigrant history.

Italians were the last of Tampa's three major immigrant groups to achieve a sizeable presence in the city. Cubans and Spaniards had come in large numbers when the cigar industry made its move to Tampa in 1886. Though clusters of Italians arrived in the very early 1890s, serious migration did not begin until later in the decade.[2] Handicapped by a lack of cigar-working skills and blocked to a certain extent by ethnic animosities, Italians were not able to move immediately into the cigar factories. Their involvement began for the most part by starting with the most menial jobs and slowly moving into apprenticeship positions. Several small factories provided important additional access routes in the early years by catering almost exclusively to Italians because of dissatisfaction with other Latin workers. On several occasions, Italians exploited the rivalry between Cubans and Spaniards over the events of the Cuban Revolution to acquire the necessary job skills and entrées.[3] By 1902, although they were still a decided minority in the industrial workforce, Italians were firmly entrenched in the factories.

Italians sat at factory benches with co-workers who had already determined to a large extent the character of labor-management relations in the city. Cuban and Spanish cigarworkers brought with them to Tampa a well-developed proletarian consciousness and a long tradition of trade union militancy which frequently put them in an adversary role with their employers. Although the roots of this tradition can only be sketched in this paper, they are worth examining briefly.

As early as 1866, cigarworkers in Havana Province (from which came nearly all of Tampa's Cubans) had organized a number of workers' associations, including the Workingmen's Mutual Aid Society of Havana, the Brotherhood of Santiago de Las Vegas, and the Workingmen's Society of San Antonio de los Banos. In 1878 these same workers founded the Worker's Guild and the Workmen's Center, and in 1892 cigarmakers held the first workers' convention in Havana. With a heightened sense of class consciousness often supplied by radical spokesmen, cigarworkers occupied a vanguard position in the proletarian struggles of nineteenth-century Cuba.[4] Within the ranks of these workers were many Spaniards, the bulk of whom had emigrated to Cuba from the provinces of Asturia and Galicia. Both areas were economically backward and had suffered from the peasant unrest that characterized late nineteenth-century Europe. Galicia in particular was racked by rent strikes, boycotts, cattle maiming, and arson. Both provinces contained strong centers of socialist and anarchist activity and many immigrants had been infused with these ideologies.[5] When they sought employment in the Havana cigar industry, they found a congenial environment for their radicalism. So contentious and militant did cigarmakers become that Havana owners listed labor problems as the primary reason for moving the industry to Florida.

Almost from the first, radical militants were active in the Tampa factories. In January, 1887, less than a year after the first cigar factory opened its doors, the *Tampa Journal* blamed anarchists for a local strike, labeling them "evil men, agitators, revolutionists" who sought to "gratify their morbid ideas of distinction, heroism and fame by imposing upon the ignorant prejudices of the masses."[6] The man most responsible for the popularity of radical doctrines among Cuban immigrants was the anarchist Carlos Baliño, a friend of the patriot José Marti. Baliño worked as an *escogedor* (packer), a tobacco selector, and published the radical journal, *La Tribuna del Pueblo*. He founded at least six clubs in the city and surrounding towns, and was instrumental in creating the Centro de Propaganda Obrera, an agency that regulated the distribution of anarchist literature among the city's Spanish-speaking people.[7] Pedro Esteve, an anarchist who had been banished from Spain, emerged as the Spanish radical of greatest stature. He was a printer by trade, who owned his own press, La Poliglota, and published widely on the philosophies of anarchism and socialism. He founded Antorchia, a center open to freethinkers of all nationalities, which attracted the membership of many Italians.[8]

The Italians of Tampa were not altogether out of place in an environment of this sort. They had emigrated from a cluster of five small villages in mountainous west-central Sicily. This portion of the island figured prominently in a wave of peasant uprisings that swept through Sicily in the early 1890s. In village after village, including those that sent their sons and daughters to Tampa, workers' leagues, or *fasci dei lavoratori*, had a vigorous history.[9] Santo Stefano Quisquina, the village that alone supplied nearly sixty percent of Tampa's Italians, possessed a *fascio* which was organized and led by a noted socialist teacher and author, Lorenzo Panepinto. When the *fasci* were suppressed after 1893 and the government of Premier Francesco Crispi struck out at all "subversives," many radicals fled. A number of these emigrés came to Tampa in the resulting exodus. As one Stefanesi wrote shortly after arriving, "I found myself in a world of radicals for which I was prepared. . . . In those days in Tampa, anarchists and socialists were many."[10]

Italian radicals soon structured a subcommunity that rivaled in variety and activity those of their Latin comrades. By 1900 radical speaking clubs and debating societies existed in all parts of Ybor City and West Tampa. Leftists also published newspapers, engaged in political activity, and established cooperatives. Tampa's best known Italian anarchist, Alfonso Coniglio, established a group named Risveglio and held meetings in his home.[11] Two societies called La Voce dello Schiavo and L'Alba Sociale met regularly, and, for a time, published newspapers of the same names. Socialists exhibited similar behavior, and by 1911 two "Italian locals" of the Socialist Party of America existed in Ybor City and West Tampa.[12]

Latin cigarworkers who chose not to join these organizations or read their publications could receive an education in radical ideologies and labor militancy through the *lector* system. The practice of hiring a person to read to cigarworkers as they performed their day's labor was imported directly from Cuban factories. The lector served as an important disseminator of labor news, radical polemics, and general information. As one lector reminisced, "The *lectura* [practice of reading] was itself a veritable system of education dealing with a variety of subjects, including politics, labor, literature, and international relations."[13] In Tampa the tradition was expanded somewhat to include more extensive readings from the labor and radical press. That the system worked to energize workers with a spirited sense of militancy during labor troubles was unquestioned. The anarchist Alfonso Coniglio began as a poorly educated fourteen year old in La Rosa Espanola, a small factory utilizing lectores. "Oh, I cannot tell you how important they were," he remembered, "how much they taught us. Especially an illiterate boy like me. To them we owe particularly our sense of the class struggle."[14]

Despite the unquestioned popularity of radical ideologies in the work place and the extreme militancy of cigarworkers, one must be cautious in attempting to assess the number of committed radicals in the labor force. Available evidence suggests strongly that they never approached a majority. Even while listening to socialist and anarchist tracts being read from the lector's platform, many workers were pulled by work patterns, attitudes, and traditions in Tampa that led them away from radical conversion. Cigarmakers were skilled artisans who often had numbers of apprentices working under them and regarded themselves in many ways as "a class apart."[15] Men at the bottom of the cigar trades aspired to the top—and beyond. Workers could, and often did, become bosses and owners in their own right. A recurring pattern in Tampa saw industrious cigarworkers leave the factories to establish their own small shops or factories. Because the trade required no expensive machines or buildings, scores of enterprising individuals made the attempt. These one-or two-man operations, called buckeyes or *chincharreres* (bed bugs) by locals, gave graphic evidence of an entrepreneurial spirit. One Italian, Val Antuono, followed just such a rags-to-riches path to own one of the city's largest factories in 1908.[16]

Both of these divergent influences seem to have existed together in an uncomfortable balance. During times of labor strife, radicals frequently emerged to play important roles in shaping the destinies of cigarworker unions. At these times socialist and anarchist workers joined with their fellow cigarworkers, occasionally in leadership positions, and struggled against the forces of management. Their appeals to class consciousness and worker solidarity were often effective in aiding union efforts. During periods of tranquility, the influence of radicals waned. In these circumstances, cigarworkers may have listened with interest to polemics about the class war, but many were apparently making plans to become factory owners themselves.

Tampa's cigarworkers followed the direction of their own independent union, popularly known as La Resistencia, in the general strike of 1901. This organization, created and led by immigrants and closed to native American membership, was able to capture the loyalties of cigarworkers despite the presence of several other unions in the city, including locals of the Cigar Makers International Union (CMIU).[17] La Resistencia's goals represented a repudiation of the American Federation of Labor's (AFL) brand of trade unionism. Its very formation rejected the AFL's injunction against dual unionism, and much of its rhetoric was syndicalist in nature. La Resistencia's ideas of the class struggle and the general strike made it particularly attractive to the anarchists of Tampa. Alfonso Coniglio, for example, joined La Resistencia and remembered with pride that he held union card number 245 out of an organization of well over five thousand members. Italian anarchist papers also gave La Resistencia their warm support. As *L'Alba Sociale* proclaimed, "We are not partisans of partial strikes anyway, it is our conviction that the general strike is a revolutionary motto."[18]

The major issue in 1901 involved efforts of manufacturers to open branch factories in Pensacola and Jacksonville. La Resistencia interpreted these moves as an attempt by owners to maintain an open shop policy and struck to force a closing of these operations.[19] Strike leadership was in Spanish and Cuban hands, but Italians were active in the ranks, both in supplying street-corner oratory, which helped to maintain worker morale, and in molding strike strategy. Late in the struggle, for example, Italians devised a plan to extend slender union resources. A committee was formed to visit Italian families in the city and persuade them to refuse union food supplies if not absolutely necessary. According to one account, the spirit of sharing engendered by these acts induced Ybor City grocers and landlords to extend further credit and prolong the strike.[20] The Italian anarchist press gave consistent support to the strike, with *L'Alba Sociale* taking the lead in announcing the necessity of establishing communal kitchens to feed striking workers.[21]

The strike's most dramatic episode occurred in early August when a self-appointed Citizens' Committee induced the police to seize thirteen union leaders, some of whom were radicals. These men were put aboard a steamer, warned never to return to Tampa on pain of death, and dropped off on a stretch of deserted Honduras coastline. One contemporary claimed that Tampa's businessmen paid ten thousand dollars for the favor. The radical press was quick to condemn this vigilante justice, labeling the action "monstrous and arbitrary" and predicting that "the bourgeoisie of Tampa are not accomplishing anything but injecting in the minds and souls of the workers a most tenacious and long lasting resistance."[22] Yet, within a matter of weeks, the strike ended and La Resistencia was crushed.

Authorities increased their assault on the union by using health ordinances to close communal kitchens and by pressuring landlords to refuse credit to striking cigarworkers. Police began wholesale arrests of strikers under a city vagrancy law. Manufacturers sealed the doom of the union by threatening to bring in German cigarworkers (who allegedly would increase productivity and reduce labor needs by working in teams of two), while simultaneously importing large numbers of strikebreakers from Havana. Within Tampa itself owners were apparently able to induce a few Italians to return to work as they emerged from the strike with a reputation as strikebreakers. The CMIU played a far more important role in breaking the stalemate by refusing to aid or amalgamate with La Resistencia and offering to supply workers for the factories. On November 28, La Resistencia, out of funds and beseiged from all sides, capitulated.[23]

The defeat and rapid dissolution of La Resistencia left the AFL locals alone in the Tampa labor field, and they were not long in capitalizing on the situation. In 1902 organizer James Wood arrived to plan a campaign for unionizing unaffiliated cigarworkers. He found that they had not abandoned unionism as the answer to their problems. His efforts succeeded by 1905 in organizing about three thousand workers into the AFL locals, although a small, but vocal minority of those CMIU president George Perkins termed "the old 'died in the wool,' 'never-say-die' remnant" of La Resistencia remained opposed to the AFL union.[24] One year later, local union officials launched another effort among Italian and Cuban workers and asked the International for the services of an experienced worker, adding the entreaty, "The IWW [Industrial Workers of the World] organizer will be here next week so send us a good organizer."[25]

Italians made impressive gains in the cigar industry work force during the years 1902–1910. Though they still failed to occupy any of the most highly skilled positions, they were solidly represented in the ranks of cigarmakers and very numerous in the lower paying positions. Indicative of their increased presence were the practices of the union newspaper, *El Internacional*. The paper began publication in January, 1904, and consistently augmented the space devoted to Italian-language articles as the years progressed. The incidence of Italian names mentioned, not only in connection with union activities but also in general industry news, increased appreciably as well.[26] These are important indicators as local membership lists and union records have apparently not survived.

The CMIU experienced its greatest successes among Tampa's cigarworkers during a 1909 membership drive. For a period of three months ending in November, a special dispensation granted by the International allowed cigarworkers to join for a membership fee of only one dollar. President Perkins himself visited Tampa to coordinate the drive and, from November 17 to November 30, he made numerous speeches before Italian, Cuban, and Spanish groups. A highly publicized promise by Samuel Gompers to join Perkins in Tampa (which was never kept) added a further stimulus to membership efforts.[27] By December 9, 1909, Perkins reported that 5,540 cigarworkers had signed with the union and that "they were still coming in every day up to the time [he] left."[28]

These accomplishments were not achieved without considerable opposition. Perkins himself spoke of the "aversion of the cigarmakers there [Tampa] to our movement," and he frequently mentioned the unsettling effect that "radicals" had on workers. They were constantly disrupting meetings, attacking International leaders, and urging workers to follow different directions. Some of the most radical were attracted to the IWW, which had profited from a visit in 1908 of William Haywood. Their numbers were small but Perkins admitted that "they have a rather formidable following."[29] Despite difficulties with the radical elements, the union attracted sizeable numbers of socialists to its ranks after 1901. This is borne out again by the practices of the union paper, which gave over considerable line space to socialist authors and socialist group activities. When available, published membership lists of socialist clubs and attendance reports of picnics, banquets, and the like have correlated well with known union members. This evidence appears consistent with the socialist tactic then in practice of "boring from within."[30] As the general strike of 1910 approached, factions both within and without the union seem to have subordinated their differences to the cause of worker unity, at least temporarily.

Cigarworkers claimed that owners precipitated the strike of 1910 as a means of testing their open shop demands and squelching the growing union strength. The first direct confrontation came in June, 1910, when manufacturers belonging to the Clear Havana Cigar Manufacturers Association (the "Trust") began dismissing selectors who were members of International Local 493. Grievances intensified after owners violated provisions of the *cartabon*, an agreement equalizing price and wage scales among association factories. When workers began a walk-out, owners responded with a lock-out policy of their own. By the end of August, nearly twelve thousand men and women were out of work and the city was paralyzed.[31]

The greater economic resources of the International allowed workers to plan for a longer strike period, and, at the outset, the unions were confident of victory. Representatives of the International, including Italian interpreter Antonio Cabrera, arrived on August 1 to aid in strike preparations and report on developments. As in 1901, numerous cigarworkers left voluntarily for Cuba and locations in the Northeast in search of employment. These individuals sent back funds to the city in support of the strike cause. Relief payments of money, food, and clothing quickly began flowing to those who remained in Tampa.[32] Unlike the earlier confrontation, however, the level of violence in the city was high.

As economic dislocations brought on by the strike became widespread, the Anglo community reacted angrily. Many citizens were unsympathetic with the union demand for recognition and were frightened by manufacturers' frequent threats to move the cigar industry elsewhere. The *Tampa Morning Tribune*, for instance, termed the point of union recognition "merely nominal" and derided the union's Joint Advisory Board (JAB) for its "sophomoric declaration that recognition of the union means life and liberty." In addition, most local natives believed that the vast majority of cigarworkers were anxious to return to work but were prevented from doing so by labor radicals. In reaction to the alleged influence of these socialist and anarchist "agitators," another Citizens' Committee came into being. Tampa's business and professional elite claimed that such an organization was particularly necessary after the September 14 shooting of James F. Easterling, an American bookkeeper employed at Bustillo Brothers and Diaz Company. The shots that struck Easterling came from a crowd of Italian and Cuban strikers gathered at the factory.[33]

Authorities soon arrested two Italians on suspicion of complicity in the shooting, but before they could be tried, a mob seized them from police officials and lynched both. The two individuals, Castenzio Ficarrotta and Angelo Albano, were pictured in the English-language press as hired assassins, "tools of anarchistic elements in the city."[34] In fact, both possessed rather unsavory reputations. Both had been accused of numerous crimes in the preceding years, including murder, arson, poisoning, and dynamiting. Even in the Italian colony, there were those who agreed with Sheriff R. A. Jackson's assessment that "they should have long ago have [sic] either been sent to the penitentiary or hanged."[35] Their connection with the cigar unions is not entirely clear. Albano belonged for a time to Local 462, and members of that union eulogized him expansively in the press and staged an impressive funeral. At the time of his death, however, he appears to have been making his living selling insurance. Ficcarrotta never worked in the cigar factories; his occupation is listed in several places merely as "laborer."[36] Gaetano Moroni, Italian vice-consul at New Orleans, on orders from the Italian ambassador, visited Tampa and conducted an extensive investigation of the lynching. His confidential report probably comes as close to the truth as possible. It concluded that

> the lynching itself was not the outcome of a temporary outburst of popular anger, but was rather planned, in cold blood, to the most trifling detail, by some citizens of West Tampa with the tacit assent of a few police officers, and all with the intention of teaching an awful lesson to the strikers of the cigar factories who had passed from quiet protest to acts of violence against the manufacturers and, at the same time, of getting rid of two 'terrible ruffians'.[37]

Whatever its intent, the lynching failed to cower strikers, and violence continued to accelerate. On October 4, Balbin Brothers' factory was burned to the ground by arsonists and the Tribune Building narrowly missed the same fate. Beatings of strikebreakers, scuffles at docks and railroad terminals, and random shooting incidents became fixtures of the strike scene. On one occasion, nine Italian women paraded with clubs in front of the Arguellas, Lopez and Brothers' factory in Ybor City, and threatened to beat to death any who reported to work.[38] The Tampa press published emotional editorials decrying the "presence in this community of an anarchistic, law-defying element who stop at nothing to accomplish their hellish purposes."[39] José de la Campa, president of the union's Joint Advisory Board, received several lynch threats in the mail after being publicly branded as an anarchist. He and four other strike leaders were soon arrested on charges of "inciting a riot and being accessories before the fact to the murder of Easterling."[40]

While preparations for the trials were underway, the Citizens' Committee organized patrols of special police recruited largely from the rural areas surrounding Tampa. These men, some three to four hundred in number, utilized a force of fifty cars, each containing three to five heavily armed officers, to patrol Ybor City and West Tampa. Their purpose was to guarantee "absolute protection" to workers who desired to return to the factories. Arbitrary arrests, illegal searches, routine physical assaults, and flagrant violations of civil rights characterized the actions of the citizen patrols. As a representative example, on the evening of October 18, a contingent of special officers entered the Labor Temple in Ybor City, dispersed a union meeting in progress, confiscated union records, nailed the door shut, and placed a sign overhead reading, "This place is closed for all time." So distrustful of constituted authorities had strikers become that eleven Italians armed themselves and paraded in front of the jail as a "guard" for the arrested JAB members.[41]

Branded by socialists in the city as the "Cossacks of Tampa," these patrols remained active even after two of the arrested strike leaders were convicted and sentenced to a year on the chain gang. Their efforts to induce workers back to the benches, however, met with little success. Among Italians this was particularly true. One November 10 article in the local press, which enthusiastically, but erroneously, reported "great numbers of cigarmakers" returning to work, added a revealing postscript. "It is notable that among those returning to work there are no Italians, and in many quarters this is construed as representing the Italian as being the backbone of the strike. Many in a position to know," the account continued, "say that were the Italians to resume employment at the factories, workers of all nationalities would follow at once, and within two weeks there would not be a man or woman in the cigar trades idle."[42] Responding to the rallying cry of *"morire di fame, ma vincere!,"* Italians had emerged as the shock troops of the strike forces.[43]

When the union newspaper continued to print articles critical of the Citizens' Committee, the offices of *El Internacional* were raided, presses smashed, and employees beaten. On December 23, police went a step further and arrested editor J. M. Gil on two counts of conspiracy to prevent cigarmakers from working.[44] At the same time citizen patrols stepped up their campaign of vagrancy arrests. One member saw the matter clearly: "Whenever a woman or a child is found begging—and there have been many in the past few weeks—able-bodied men who are not at work should be arrested. There would soon be no vagrants [as] they would prefer the factories to the street squads."[45] Yet, repeated claims by manufacturers that strikers would soon return to work continued to ring hollow in the face of empty work rooms.

Owners frequently attempted to split workers along ethnic lines in an effort to divide and conquer, and they viewed Italians as the key to their campaigns. On November 18 *El Internacional* reported that "our worthy comrades, the Italians," had been addressed by manufacturers in an open letter, which warned that they would have no work after the strike if they continued to follow union leadership. It urged them to reject the advice of "agitators" and return to work. Late in December another approach was tried. Manufacturers circulated a bogus manifesto, allegedly signed by Italians, which proclaimed their intention of returning to work on the owner's terms on January 2. They hoped that this news would begin a stampede back to the work benches. Italian cigarworkers hurriedly distributed a counter-manifesto, signed by 460 of their number (lack of space reportedly required leaving off several hundred additional names), which labeled the first claim as "utterly without foundation in fact."[46]

With citizen patrols guarding docks and railway stations and physically intimidating picket lines, the flow of strikebreakers into the city increased substantially during January. By the first of the year approximately two hundred cigarmakers per week, most of them black Cubans imported from Havana, were being placed in the factories. This was accomplished with at least the tacit complicity of federal immigration officials in Tampa. During the strike's first months, a number of cigarworkers had been deported as contract laborers. The Citizens' Committee complained bitterly of this "overzealous application" of immigration laws and presumably intimidated officials.[47] On January 20 a large group of Cuban blacks arrived and took their places at the benches. Four days later, 200 more stepped off a steamer at Port Tampa and local papers observed that "every boat coming in from Havana and Key West" brought more. Finally, on January 26, 1911, the JAB called off the strike with the prophetic words, "We simply give up the fight."[48]

Tampa's cigarworkers thus lost their second major strike in a decade. Dispirited, but not humbled, they returned to work. In the end, workers were unable to withstand the onslaught of powerful forces arrayed against them. Manufacturers were able to enlist the support of Tampa's business and professional community, its municipal authorities (police, board of trade, mayor's office, etc.), and the state's court system and government; they apparently intimidated the only federal agency in the city able to check their policies, the immigration office.[49]

The strike had important consequences for Italians. The front line role played by Italians removed permanently any stigma remaining over their identification as strikebreakers in the 1901 strike. It also ensured a prominent position for Italians in union affairs. Unlike La Resistencia, the International did not disappear following its defeat in 1911. Instead, it remained and slowly rebuilt its fortunes. In 1920 it would once again lead Tampa's cigarworkers in a general strike; this time in a struggle lasting ten months.[50]

The strike also had an impact on the position that radicals occupied in the union and the immigrant community. Many radicals had been disappointed with AFL management of the strike. While consistently supporting the need for worker solidarity, they criticized the unwillingness of the International leaders to adopt a more radical approach to the situation. With the strike only days old, George Perkins reported that the "more radical, hot-headed members dropped out of the union" because they were opposed to the "conservative manner" in which the Joint Advisory Board was conducting matters.[51] Socialist members had urged, as early as September, that the unions establish their own factories in the city as a method of settling the conflict. Such a move, they contended, would ensure steady employment, union wages, and the general welfare of the community without reliance on the manufacturers' association. The plan received little attention from International officials. Related requests called for the socialization of the entire industry, but met with even less favor.[52] Before long, some socialists were openly critical of the union. As one disgruntled Tampan urged, "Now it appears to me that the American Federation of Labor ought to be a power in a broader sense than it has so far been."

> The fault of labor is that it is afraid to be called radical: afraid to overthrow a system of graft and corruption.... How can you then regard a man within your trade union who constantly advocates compromises with manufacturers and capitalists, whose interests are against the principles of the Union? Organized labor must stop begging for political favors of this or that individual.... In Tampa, labor chooses to put its neck under the heel of Capitalist political power.[53]

Many cigarworkers were impressed with the level of support tendered by the International during the strike, and attacks such as these served to discredit socialists in their eyes. The union listed debts in excess of $13,000 and claimed that it had spent more than $100,000 supporting non-union cigarworkers in Tampa.[54] The high level of violence worked to turn the immigrant community against the more militant radicals. This was even more true of the wider Tampa community, which reacted to the strike with nativist charges and vigilante justice. Thus, the leftist subsociety of Tampa, in which Italians occupied a conspicuous place, suffered a major blow to its position and prestige well before the events of World War I.

Viewed against the wider patterns of development in Tampa, the strike of 1910 can be seen as a further step in a process of grudging accommodation to the demands of modernity. Early labor conflicts involving cigarworkers in the city were frequently sparked by real or imaginary threats to traditional, pre-industrial privileges or work styles. One nineteenth-century walk-out, for example, began in reaction to owner demands mandating the use of scales to weigh out the filler tobacco given to workers at the beginning of each day. The strike of 1901 saw the establishment of a formal union structure and the use of tactics which recognized the existence of the modern corporation. La Resistencia can be seen, however, as a transitional organization, with its restrictive immigrant membership and its reliance on Old World radical ideologies. By 1910 Tampa's cigarworkers were still in a situation of flux, with competing cultural, ethnic, and union loyalties contending, but the majority appear to have accepted the lure of American big labor by joining the CMIU and supporting its organizational tactics and goals. In this respect the cigarworkers who left their wooden work benches for the streets in 1910 were fundamentally different from their predecessors of twenty years earlier.

Throughout this period Italians played an important, though varying, role. They continued to be central figures in the future as cigarworkers, factory owners, and the wider Tampa community groped for satisfactory resolutions to labor unrest and ethnic tensions. The essential story of these later efforts awaits further inquiry.

Notes

Research for this essay was carried out with the support of a grant from the American Philosophical Society.

1. In 1908 cigar factories employed approximately 10,500 persons and generated a weekly wage of $200,000, representing seventy-five percent of the total payroll of the city. Spanish, Italian, and Cuban workmen comprised nearly ninety-five percent of the work force. U.S., Congress, Senate, *Reports of the Immigration Commission, Immigrants in Industries*, pt. 14, "Cigar and Tobacco Manufacturing," 1911, 187.

2. Small handfuls of Italians had been present in the Tampa Bay area from the early 1800s. They were joined in 1891 by several hundred Italians from New Orleans following the lynching incident in that city. Others drifted in from St. Cloud, a large sugar plantation to the east.

3. Sr. Seidenberg, a Spaniard, opposed the Cuban revolution and refused to hire Cuban workers. He proved willing to accept Italians and constructed residences for these workers even before completing his first factory in 1890. Other reports cited instances of Italians being taught cigarmaking skills by Cubans as an act of defiance against the specific orders of Spanish owners not to do so. See L. Glenn Westfall, "Don Vicente Martinez Ybor, the Man and His Empire" (Ph.D. diss., University of Florida, 1977), 116-17.

4. Louis A. Pérez, Jr., "Reminiscences of a Lector: Cuban Cigar Workers in Tampa," *Florida Historical Quarterly*, 53 (April, 1975): 443-44; Pérez, "Cubans in Tampa: From Exiles to Immigrants, 1892–1901," *Florida Historical Quarterly*, 57 (October, 1978): 131; Gaspar M. Jorge Garcia Gallo, *El tabaquero cubano* (Havana, 1936).

5. Raymond Carr, *Spain, 1908–1939* (Oxford, 1966), 414, 421, 440-43, 515; Salvador de Madariaga, *Spain: A Modern History* (New York, 1958), 136, 151; Gerald Brenan, *The Spanish Labryinth* (Cambridge, 1964), 131-201.

6. *Tampa Journal*, January 21, 1887.

7. Joan Marie Steffy, "The Cuban Immigration of Tampa, Florida, 1886 –1898" (M.A. thesis, University of South Florida, 1975), 63-69; *Tampa Tribune*, May 25, 1894; October 24, 1896. For more on the Cuban community, see Evelio Tellerias Toca, "Los tabaqueros cubanos y sus luchas en Cayo Hueso y Tampa," *Bohemia*, April 28, 1967, 13-23.

8. Angelo Massari, *The Wonderful Life of Angelo Massari* (New York, 1965), 107; George E. Pozzetta, "An Immigrant Library: The Tampa Italian Club Collection," *Ex Libris*, I (Spring, 1978): 12. Esteve had been expelled for, among other things, denouncing Spain for turning Cuba into a mere "hacienda."

9. Santo Stefano Quisquina, Alessandria della Rocca, Bivona, Cianciana, and Contessa Entellina accounted for nearly ninety-five percent of the Tampa community. On the *fasci*, see E. J. Hobsbawm, *Primitive Rebels* (New York, 1959), 93-107; Shepard B. Clough, *The Economic History of Modern Italy* (New York, 1964), 152-53.

10. Massari, *Wonderful Life*, 56; Calogero Massina, *S. Stefano Quisquina: Studio Storico-Critico* (Palermo, 1976), 82-85; Angelo Massari, *La Comunita Italiana di Tampa* (New York, 1967), 477-535; Dennis Mack Smith, *A History of Modern Italy*, 2 vols. (London, 1968), 2: 484-86.

11. *El Internacional* (Tampa), March 10, 1916; "Casellario Politico Centrale," dossier on Alfonso Coniglio, xerox, Immigration History Research Center, University of Minnesota, St. Paul, Minnesota.

12. *El Internacional* (Tampa), September 23, December 30, 1910; March 31, April 14, 21, 1916; *Tampa Morning Tribune*, August 18, 1910; Massari, *Wonderful Life*, 56-57, 68, 91, 106-07. Copies of these two anarchist papers are available on microfilm at the Immigration History Research Center. The P. K. Yonge Library of Florida History, University of Florida, contains several Italian-language socialist papers printed in Tampa, including *L'Aurora* and *La Voce della Colonia*.

13. Quoted in Pérez, "*Reminiscences*," 445. On the antecedents of the lector system in Cuba see, José Rivero Muniz, "La lectura en las tabaquerias, " *Revista de la Biblioteca Nacional*, 2 (October-December, 1951): 102-22; "La lectura en las tabaquerias," *Hoy*, May 1, 1948, 78.

14. Jose Yglesias, *The Truth About Them* (New York, 1971), 209. Yglesias was born and raised in Ybor City, and many of his writings deal with themes from his youth. Though nominally a work of fiction, this work contains an autobiographical reminiscence of a Tampa radical which was the product of an interview with Alfonso Coniglio.

15. There were also well defined divisions of skill and status within the cigar industry. At the top rested the selector, of which two variations existed. The *resagadores* (those who selected the leaves of tobacco to be used as wrappers) and the *escogedores* (those who selected the finished cigars by color and packed fifty uniform cigars in a box). These men had their own work areas, coffee shops, and privileges which they guarded jealously. In the middle rested the cigarmakers, who in turn had many variations defined largely by the kind of cigar produced. Below them were those workers who dealt in some way with the handling of tobacco—strippers, clerks, banders, etc. At the bottom was the mass of unskilled, manual labor jobs that any industry possesses.

16. Federal Writers Project, "Trade Jargon of the Cigar Industry of Tampa," P. K. Yonge Library of Florida History; Tony Pizzo, "The Italian Heritage in Tampa," in *Back to Ybor City Day* (Tampa, 1976), 21-23; *Builders of Florida* (Jacksonville, 1924), 221.

17. Details of the 1901 strike are recounted in Durward Long, "'La Resistencia': Tampa's Immigrant Labor Union," *Labor History*, 6 (Fall, 1965): 193-213, although this article almost totally overlooks the radical dimension of the strike.

18. *L'Alba Sociale* (Tampa), August 15, 1901; Long, 196. *La Federacion*, the newspaper published by La Resistencia, proclaimed its desire to work for the eventual conversion of society into a "free federation of free workers." Its successor, *El Federal*, called for a world-wide general strike. "Proyecto de bases," *La Federacion* (Tampa), n.d.; *El Federal* (Tampa), March 28, 1902.

19. Long, 203. These events are also reported in *L'Alba Sociale* (Tampa), July 15, August 1, 1901.

20. Long, 210-211; Massari, *Wonderful Life*, 104.

21. *L'Alba Sociale* (Tampa), August 15, 1901.

22. Ibid. This issue contains a long editorial entitled "The Seizures," which describes the kidnappings.

23. Long, 105-212. The perception of Italians as scabs was held far more widely in the Anglo community than in ethnic quarters.

24. Samuel Gompers to D. G. Sanford, April 1, 1903; Frank Morrison to Samuel Gompers, July 12, 1906; George Perkins to Samuel Gompers, June 27, 1910, Cigar Makers International Union Papers, "National and Internationals File," AFL-CIO Headquarters, Washington, D.C. Wood left his duties in Tampa and went to Palatka, Florida, where several small cigar factories existed. He was followed by two men from Tampa who shot and wounded him so severely that he lost his left arm.

25. Jacob Brodie to Frank Morrison, September 30, 1906, CMIU Papers.

26. This is based on a close reading of the newspaper for the years indicated and a nine-page typewritten report on conditions in Tampa sent by CMIU president George Perkins to Samuel Gompers in December, 1909, CMIU Papers.

27. Perkins to Gompers, October 26, 1909; Gompers to Perkins, October 28, 1909; G. P. Bradford to Gompers, November 20, 22, 23, 1909, CMIU Papers.

28. Perkins to Gompers, December 7, 1909, p. 4, CMIU Papers.

29. Perkins to Gompers, July 27, 1910, CMIU Papers.

30. *El Internacional* (Tampa), January 30, 1904; March 24, 31, 1911; David A. Shannon, *The Socialist Party of America* (Chicago, 1967), 44, 261.

31. *El Internacional* (Tampa), June 3, August 5, 12, 1910; *Tampa Morning Tribune*, June 30, July 13, 14, 28, August 3, 1910. The manufacturer's position is outlined in *United States Tobacco Journal* (New York), July 16, 1910. The union's position is seen in JAB to Gompers, June 27, 1910; December 11, 1910, CMIU Papers.

32. *United States Tobacco Journal* (New York), August 6, 1910; *Tampa Morning Tribune*, August 2, 12, 15, 23, 1910; *El Internacional* (Tampa), August 5, 12, 26, 1910. On August 3 the Tampa unions received a telegram from President Perkins pledging the "entire treasury of the International" if needed.

33. *Tampa Morning Tribune*, September 10, 14, 15, 16, 17, October 5, 1910.

34. *Tampa Morning Tribune*, September 21, 22, 1910. Frantic editorials in the English-language press pointed out that Easterling was the "first American to be attacked," and, according to the *Tribune*, city leaders pledged that he would be the last.

35. R. A. Jackson to Governor Albert W. Gilchrist, October 8, 1910, Records of the Department of State, State Decimal File, 1910-1929, "Tampa Lynching Incident," Box 3671, National Archives, Washington, D.C.

36. *El Internacional* (Tampa), September 23, 30, 1910; *Tampa Morning Tribune*, September 21, 22, 23, 1910. For reactions to the lynching outside of Tampa, see *Il Progresso Italo-Americano* (New York) September 23, 24, 25, 27, 1910; *La Parola dei Socialisti* (Chicago), October 1, 1910. Most outside newspapers reported that the men were cigarmakers.

37. Gaetano Moroni to Marquis Cusani Confalonieri, October 11, 1910, 1. The Italian government initially claimed that the men were Italian citizens and demanded an indemnity for both. Eventually, an investigation concluded that only Albano was of Italian citizenry and after considerable squabbling, the United States paid the sum of $6,000 to his relatives.

38. *Tampa Morning Tribune*, September 15, October 1, 4, November 15, 1910. Police arrested all but three of the women who were each fined fifty dollars after a quick trial. Reports indicated that they were not able to use their clubs, but did "scratch and bite" arresting officers. For reactions of the ethnic community to the arrests see *El Internacional* (Tampa), November 18, 1910.

39. *Tampa Morning Tribune*, October 4, 5, 6, 8, 1910. Cigar manufacturing journals pictured Tampa as being completely in the grip of anarchist labor leaders. See *United States Tobacco Journal* (New York), August 27, 1910; *Tobacco Leaf* (New York), September 15, 1910; *Tobacco World* (New York), September 19, 1910.

40. *Tampa Morning Tribune*, October 18, November 25, 1910. The *Tribune* referred to de la Campa as a "youthful anarchist whose career in Tampa has been characterized by the most flagrant disregard of the rights of life, person, and property." Although the extent of de la Campa's attachment to anarchism is not known, he was a close friend of Pedro Esteve, a fellow Spaniard.

41. *Tampa Morning Tribune*, October 17, 18, 19, 20, 1910; *El Internacional* (Tampa), October 21, 1910. Union officials repeatedly wrote to the United States Department of Justice in an effort to enlist federal aid in stopping these abuses. The Justice Department responded that "no federal intervention is justified." See, J. M. Cheney to Attorney General, October 6, 1910; Amos L. Hill to William Howard Taft, January 11, 1911; Ernest Bohm to J. A. Foroler, January 13, 1911, Records of the Department of Justice, "Strike File-Cigarmakers, 1911," Records Group 60, National Archives, Washington, D.C.

42. *Tampa Morning Tribune*, November 10, 1910.

43. *Il Progresso Italo-Americano* (New York), November 8, 1910, quoted in *Il Martello* (New York) of same date.

44. *El Internacional* (Tampa), December 23, 30, 1910; *Tampa Morning Tribune*, December 23, 1910.

45. *Tampa Morning Tribune*, October 18, 1910; *El Internacional* (Tampa), December 16, 1910.

46. *El Internacional* (Tampa), November 18, 1910; December 30, 1910; *Tampa Morning Tribune*, November 19, December 30, 1910.

47. T. V. Kirk to Commissioner General of Immigration, February 10, 1911, Records of the Bureau of Immigration and Naturalization, Record Group 85, National Archives, Washington, D.C.; *Tampa Morning Tribune*, January 10, 24, 1911.

48. Kirk to Immigration Commissioner, January 28, 1911, Immigration Records; *El Internacional* (Tampa), January 20, 27, 1910; *Tampa Morning Tribune*, January 24, 25, 26, 1911.

49. Governor Gilchrist of Florida made a week-long visit to Tampa to investigate the strike. He was pressured into this action by nationally publicized criticism of the situation made by Samuel Gompers at the 1910 AFL national convention. Gilchrist issued a report at the end of his visit which completely exonerated city officials and laid the entire blame for strike violence at the union's feet.

50. The fortunes of the union can be followed best through the pages of *El Internacional*, which continued publication until 1946, and the CMIU records. For the 1920 strike see, Durward Long, "The Open-Closed Shop Battle in Tampa's Cigar Industry, 1919-1921," *Florida Historical Quarterly*, 47 (October, 1968): 101-121.

51. Perkins to Gompers, July 5, 1910, CMIU Papers.

52. For divisions among cigarworkers, see "Diary of a Tampa Cigar Worker [A. Litapia]," ca. 1911, Special Collections Department, University of South Florida Library, Tampa, Florida; *El Internacional* (Tampa), September 9, October 7, December 23, 1910; January 24, 1911. Ironically, during Samuel Gompers' first general strike in 1877, his New York local bought a building and set up a factory. Harold C. Livesay, *Samuel Gompers and Organized Labor in America* (Boston, 1978), 50.

53. *El Internacional* (Tampa), September 23, 1910. For an extended analysis of anti-AFL union activities undertaken by socialists, see David A. Corbin, "Betrayal in the West Virginia Coal Fields: Eugene V. Debs and the Socialist Party of America, 1912-1914," *Journal of American History*, 64 (March, 1978): 987-1009.

54. JAB to Gompers, June 27, 1910; ? to Gompers, August 23, 1910, CMIU Papers; *Tampa Morning Tribune*, January 27, 1911. See also "The Attempt to Drive Union Labor From Tampa," *American Federationist*, 18 (January, 1911): 151, for further efforts to aid Tampa strikers. One source indicated that of the total number of strikers, "only about 1,700 are entitled to benefits."

Italian Involvement in the 1903–04 Coal Miners' Strike in Southern Colorado and Utah

Philip F. Notarianni

In the history of western United States labor, the ethnic element in the coal mining industry has been largely neglected. At the turn of the twentieth century, southern and eastern Europeans, especially Italians, were funnelling into the coal mining regions of southern Colorado and Utah. This time proved crucial for organized labor in these states, as it marked the beginning of attempts to organize coal miners into a cohesive body. The immigrant worker became intertwined in such efforts; thus, an investigation of this period becomes essential to an understanding of the mutual impact of labor and immigration.

The present study deals specifically with Italian involvement in the 1903–04 strike of District 15 of the United Mine Workers of America (UMWA) in southern Colorado and Utah. Because certain counties in the two states, namely Huerfano and Las Animas in Colorado and Carbon in Utah, were vital both in terms of the Italian element and union activity, they form the geographical boundaries for this investigation. The role of the UMWA, Italian union organizers, the *braccianti* (day laborers), as well as state and Italian government officials will be studied in an effort to determine how they interacted and what effect the strike had upon the lives, ideologies, and contact with an American environment of Italian coal miners.

In the late nineteenth and early twentieth centuries, the coal mining industry in the West exhibited specific characteristics. Large coal interests, specifically the Colorado Fuel and Iron Company (CF&I) and Victor Fuel Company (VFC), Colorado-based, and the Utah Fuel (UFC) and Pleasant Valley Coal (PVC) Companies of Utah,[1] strictly controlled their work force. This was accomplished by the use of Chinese contract labor to prevent union organization and to keep wages low. These companies also sought to control all aspects of their work force through company-owned land and housing, company stores, and, in the case of CF&I, education of the worker and his family.

United States census reports[2] fixed the number of foreign-born Italians in Colorado and Utah as follows:

	1890	1900	1910
Colorado	3,882	6,818	14,375
Utah	347	1,062	3,117

However, Italian laborers were part of a fluid work force often on the move, and such a "fluidity of movement" factor probably inflated the census' figures, the product of a count conducted only every ten years.

Grievances with regard to wages, the eight-hour day, semi-monthly pay periods, abolition of the scrip system, proper ventilation in the mines, reduction for contract miners from 2,400 to 2,000 pounds of coal for a "ton," and the check weighman as a representative of the men were all rising to the fore in the summer of 1903. In addition, the CF&I had created a restrictive climate for the miners which severely compromised their personal freedom.[3]

In 1901 the CF&I established the "Sociological Department" of the company with the intention of aiding the employees and their families, but functioning in a paternalistic manner, as "a means of educating the younger generation, of improving the home relations and furthering the interests of the men, making them better citizens and more contented with their work".[4] "Contentment" with the work environment was undoubtedly a key objective for the department; hence, a means of preventing unionization.

The UMWA had been attempting for three years, without success, to build the southern Colorado fields into an effective organization. However, the union's victory in the 1902 anthracite strike, which included a large immigrant labor force, undoubtedly led the organization to attempt the feat in another area. On November 9, 1903, despite reluctance on the part of members of the UMWA National Executive Board, based on poor organization in the field and the high possibility of intervention by Colorado governor James H. Peabody, a strike in District 15 was authorized by UMWA president John Mitchell after he had attempted to secure a meeting of the CF&I and VFC.[5]

Of the 8,503-man work force, Italians comprised roughly thirty-five percent, or 2,976 men.[6] Nearly sixty percent of the work force was affiliated with the union, though most men did not pay dues. Major Zepth T. Hill, of the Colorado National Guard, was sent to assess the need for troops and reported: "There are at Hastings today about a thousand unemployed people. They are principally southern Italians, and seem to be very bitter against the officers of the Victor Company. There are a large number of Southern Italians in the old town [of Segundo], and they are liable to cause trouble".[7] V. Macchi di Cellere, the Royal Charge d'Affairs of Italy, wrote the Italian Ministry of Foreign Affairs in February, 1904 that Italians were "most numerous" among the strikers of Colorado.[8]

In Utah the strike commenced on November 13 in the mining camp of Sunnyside, and spread to the Carbon County camps of Castle Gate, Clear Creek, and Winter Quarters. Grievances were similar to those in Colorado, but, unlike in Colorado, recognition of the UMWA was an *official* demand.[9] Charles Demolli, a national organizer for the UMWA, was the chief organizer in Sunnyside. He had succeeded in organizing a union with a reported enrollment of 468 members.[10] With regard to Italians, G. W. Kramer, vice-president of the Utah Fuel Company, stated: "The Castle Gate mine is what we might call an Italian mine, because of the large number of Italians to the number of other miners. At Castle Gate there are 356 Italians, 108 English speaking, Austrians 10 . . . "[11] Italians comprised nearly forty-four percent of the workers of Castle Dale, Sunnyside, Clear Creek, and Winter Quarters.

The support of Italian miners was essential for any successful strike in District 15. Attitudes toward immigrant labor, however, remained somewhat ambivalent, and in the end, John Mitchell, who reflected UMWA sentiment, asserted his belief in the fear of cheap foreign labor. On December 5, 1903, the UMWA president addressed the Denver Chamber of Commerce as follows:

Years ago in the south [Colorado] the population was largely American. In that field now I dare say there are less than 25 percent of the miners who were born of American soil. If the conditions [of work] were fare [sic], if the conditions were American, it would not be so. I do not wish to decry the laborers in the field, but when men whose standard of living is lower than the men then in the field are brought in, the standard of wages is lowered.[12]

Certain factors can be ascertained concerning the construct of the southern Colorado Italian community—here defined as a social group, with a cultural heritage, in a specific locality, with Italian institutions, voluntary organizations, and other social bodies that support the functioning of peer relationships.[13] The regionalism that existed in Italy, distinguishing northern from southern Italians, caused a fragmentation within the Italian community, estimated at almost a 50-50 split. Tensions between North and South Italians were reported by the CF&I, which assessed the situation as follows:

> Northern and Southern Italians and Sicilians are a good illustration of the feeling sometimes displayed. Not infrequently has it developed into a really war-like situation, shown on several occasions on the Hospital lawn by convalescent patients hurling at each other canes and crutches and other instruments of war. It manifests itself most frequently, however, in the less earnest battles among the school children, who forget only occasionally the traditional existing state of war.[14]

Thus, regionalism was instilled in the younger generations of Italians, preserving its character.

During the strike, the Americo Vespucci mutual aid society was functioning in Trinidad; however, none of its records have been located. That this organization was prevented from meeting by the National Guard suggests that it could have been serving as a type of labor or trade union. In addition, labor ideas and conceptions were often discussed at lodge meetings.[15]

Critical to the fragmentation within the Italian community were the *padroni*, Italian labor agents who recruited contract labor for the mines.[16] These men, predominantly bankers and merchants, induced their countrymen to come to Colorado, oftentimes under false pretences. Such activity, reportedly practiced by Giovanni Aiello, a Trinidad banker, enraged many of his countrymen, who labeled him a "Judas."[17] *Krumiri* (strikebreakers) became an important aspect of the strike because coal operators wished to replace striking miners, thus breaking the walk-out.

Italians of Colorado exhibited no communal relationship with those of Utah, but both areas were part of UMWA District 15, had the same Italian consular agent, and were serviced by organizers from Colorado. One important vehicle of exchange was *Il Lavoratore Italiano*, an Italian labor weekly first published in 1902 in Trinidad, whose correspondents were found in Utah as well as in Colorado. As influential agents in the transmission of philosophies and ideologies ethnic newspapers are sometimes suspect due to the historian's uncertainty with regard to circulation figures. Nevertheless, *Il Lavoratore Italiano*, espousing the cause of the worker and unionism, played an important role in the strike as the "official organ for District 15."

Il Lavoratore's editor in 1902, Charles Demolli, and its director-typesetter, Adolfo Bartoli, both founders of the newspaper, were important figures in the strike. Demolli was born in 1872 near Como and immigrated to the United States in 1895. Italian consular reports stated that Demolli immigrated in 1895 following his escape from internment where he was being held for conspiracy in passing counterfeit notes.[18] Demolli arrived in the United States where he began writing for Italian-language newspapers. He later drifted to the coal mines of Pennsylvania where he experienced a renewed interest in unionism. From the East, Demolli journeyed to Colorado and began *Il Lavoratore Italiano*.[19]

Adolfo Bartoli was born February 10, 1866, in Florence. In 1879 he worked as a printer's apprentice, having served with such papers as *Giornale di Sicilia*. Immigrating to the United States in 1893, Bartoli worked as a printer for *Il Progresso Italo-Americano* (New York), *L'Unione* (Pueblo, Colorado), and finally, *Il Lavoratore Italiano*.[20] Both Demolli and Bartoli became the subjects of intensive concern and investigation on the part of the Italian government. In July, 1902, Bartoli wrote an article in *Il Lavoratore Italiano* entitled "July 29," in which he defended and praised Gaetano Bresci.[21] Giuseppe Cuneo, Italian consul, informed the Italian Ministry of Foreign Affairs that Bartoli was under police surveillance for his "anarchistic principles."

The Italians of Carbon County, Utah, lived in a community oriented around a work environment, yet fragmented, primarily in terms of Italian regionalism. Aspects of the Utah experience, different from that of Colorado, were the high proportion of northern to southern Italians and the organization of fraternal organizations strongly resembling unions, but characterized by their membership's common regional background. At Sunnyside, where the Utah strike began, the Italian miners had founded Fratellanza Minatori in 1902. The lodge constitution explicitly stated that if any member was found working where a strike had been declared for reasons of an "increase in wages or for whatever motive," he would be subject to expulsion from the organization.[22] The society's resemblance to a labor union is a possible explanation of why the strike began in Sunnyside. Forty of the forty-seven founding members were from northern Italy (Tirolo, Austria, and Torino), the remainder from Cosenza, in southern Italy.

Stella D'America, founded in 1898 at Castle Gate, was comprised entirely of members from Trentino, Milano, and Torino. In fact, members specifically identified themselves in lodge records by their community and province.[23] Oral testimony confirms that "scabs" (strikebreakers) were always dismissed from active partici-pation.[24]

The northern Italian make-up of the lodges strongly suggests that the leadership of the strike, on the local level with men such as Joseph Barboglio, a northerner who was treasurer of the Castle Gate union, was from the North, and that northerners were in the vast majority. Oral accounts substantiate that the animosities among workers were provoked by regional bias.[25] A southern Ital-ian lodge, Principe Di Napoli, was also founded in Castle Gate some time in 1902; but in December, 1903, at the height of the strike, the organization underwent a change in name to Stella D'America.[26]

Thus, the Italian communities of southern Colorado and Carbon County, Utah, entered the 1903–04 strike somewhat fragmented. In both areas, the role of the Catholic Church proved negligible. Merchants and bankers were suspected as *padroni*, and as the strike progressed, accusations of tampering with union funds were ram-pant. The close group attachment seen by Victor Greene among the Slavic community in Pennsylvania in 1902 was not evident in Colorado or Utah.

The months of November and December, 1903, in Colorado were characterized by evictions of strikers from company property, the establishment of an employment agency by the UMWA to find work in other regions for striking miners, the use of strikebreakers, and the continued "pro-company, anti-labor" stand by Governor Peabody.[27] The coal companies acted promptly to evict miners from company property and privately erected homes on company land, and to terminate leases of company-owned housing. The VFC began such measures in Hastings, with an estimated 600 Italian strikers.[28] Major Hill reported in November that family evictions had embittered many Italian strikers in Hastings.[29] This threat to the family had struck a central nerve. The home, erected by the individual, symbolized success and security.[30]

Shortly after the strike began, arrangements were made to send approximately 3,000 miners to other regions and union camps—a move which further weakened union strength and unity. Strike-breakers were utilized by coal operators in an effort to supplant union miners. Mexican and Japanese men were the dominant groups recruited, but Italians were also used. This practice of bringing in Italians caused caustic comments to be wielded toward suspected *padroni*. The general view appeared to exonerate the men who were induced to come to Colorado and Utah and blame those responsible for the action. These agents paid the men's transportation and, in turn, were compensated by the companies.[31]

Governor Peabody played a vital role throughout the course of events. The pro-coal company and anti-labor stand that he and Major Hill took caused many Italians to distrust American institutions and question their impartiality.[32]

November and December, 1903, were also critical months for the strike in Utah. Evictions and the use of strikebreakers became company tools for handling the situation.[33] From the outset local officials and the Citizens Alliances viewed Italians as "hostile elements." Utah Governor M. Wells ordered out the National Guard on November 24, 1903. Charles Demolli, the Central UMWA organizer, responded to the Guard by saying:

> We do not intend to fight the company with violence. We have 303 men signed at Winter Quarters and Clear Creek who have gone out. Every Italian and 100 Finns in Clear Creek are out. I am glad the Militia has come because it will stop the violence on both sides, especially by the guards [company guards].[34]

Demolli addressed the strikers and led parades with an Italian brass band from Castle Gate. Women also participated actively in the meetings and parades in support of the men.

The strategy of Utah officials embodied the belief that a leaderless union would be basically powerless, and that without Demolli the Italians would cease support of the strike. In the *Salt Lake Herald*, Demolli was described as follows:

> Demolli, the silver-tongued, whose influence with his fellow countrymen is so feared by the Utah Fuel Company officials that efforts have been made to keep him behind bars, is in appearance far from being the wild-eyed anarchist he is pictured by his enemies. . . . He has a handsome face, typically Italian. . . . His voice is soft and his manner suave, although at times he fires with enthusiasm over the subject he may be discussing. . . . Demolli is eloquent with tongue and pen in the Italian language. Not only this but he can talk in their native tongues with Finlanders, Slavs, French or representatives of other nationalities. With his level head, shrewd judgment, college education, suave manner and great magnetism, he is regarded as one of the strongest men affiliated with the United Mine Workers and he is idolized by his followers.[36]

However, Salt Lake City's more conservative daily, the *Desert Evening News*, asserted:

The general [George Q. Cannon] . . . says the agitator [Demolli] is no better really than the average Italian fruit peddler [sic]; and this newspaper talk about his fine presence, fine speech, and pleasing address and smartness is all rot. General Cannon has no use for Demolli.[37]

Utah coal corporations wished to clear Carbon County of strikers. In the first months of the strike, indications were that Italian settlements in the county would be changed and affected by the course of events. A tent colony, known as Mitchelltown, was erected below Sunnyside and another between Castle Gate and Helper. In addition, Italians were returning to Italy with reduced-priced through tickets on the Denver and Rio Grande Railroad; others, eventually forced from the mines via the blacklist, settled along the Price River between Castle Gate and Helper, entering agriculture and business enterprises in Helper.[38]

Violence increased in Colorado in early 1904. The killing of an Italian striker prompted strikers to arm themselves. Peabody ordered out the National Guard, nearly 300 troops. Ironically, the action prolonged the strike because, before the use of troops, UMWA officials had decided to call off the strike.[39] Major Hill's arrival with the Guard in Las Animas County had a leveling effect upon the Italian element. From the outset Hill exhibited an anti-labor, anti-Italian bias by imposing a selective, rather than general, disarmament. Such a move, illustrating a gross inequity in treatment, caused Italian strikers to hide weapons and treat Hill and his men with intense suspicion.[40]

A broadside, written in Italian, was issued immediately after the Guard's appearance. The notice was directed to "Italian Comrades." In essence, it called for a firm, decisive stand that would result in justice for the miners, and end the attempt by the Citizens Alliance, coal companies, and soldiers to subject the workers to enforced slavery. The placard leveled heavy blasts at the Tarabino and Niccoli brothers, local Italian merchants, and Giovanni Aiello, as among those who had requested Peabody to send troops.[41] The call for solidarity among the miners was for "union" solidarity, but implied a "class consciousness," by decrying the actions of the Italian merchants.

Deportations, primarily from the state, became the policy utilized in Colorado to deal with strike leaders. In a letter to Peabody on March 25, Hill recommended the deportation of Bartoli, who had threatened Tarabino and others, including Mother Mary

Jones.[42] On March 26, the policy began with the expulsion of the above mentioned, along with Joseph Poggiani, also a UMWA organizer, who had been in the newspaper business while in Italy and, upon his arrival in the United States, had worked in Pennsylvania. Officially, fifty-two men were taken to the state line, mostly Italians whom Hill and Peabody despised, and all expulsions were made without formal charges and exclusively upon Hill's discretion.[43]

The entire deportation strategy embodied both Hill's attitude and the wider American desire to rid the United States of "undesirables." Peabody sought the aid of Italian consul Giuseppe Cuneo. Cuneo was asked to supply information on Bartoli, and replied to Peabody that he would ask the Italian government to provide all information possible. Hill, in turn, began collecting a vast amount of personal data on his Italian prisoners and supplying Cuneo with this information so that any criminal records would be uncovered.[44]

Cuneo's role is critical to this study because he served as consular agent both in Colorado and Utah and, in connection with the 1903–04 strike, was severely criticized by his countrymen. Such criticism was not new, for Cuneo had been denounced by Italians in the 1899 Lake City, Colorado, strike for not protecting or treating Italians fairly[45]—the same cries heard in 1903–04.

As early as November 29, 1903, Cuneo entered the strike scene by traveling to Utah to investigate the situation. At that time he heard the grievances of Italians only after conferring with General Cannon and other officials. Officially, Cuneo took a neutral stand, but it was suspect as he had allegedly been solicited to journey to Utah at the request of the coal companies—his unannounced arrival on a special train provided further evidence of corporate influence. Subsequent meetings with Governor Wells cast further doubt on his neutrality. In the final analysis, strong support for Italians by their consul would have given the strike a legitimacy it sorely lacked. Cuneo's lack of support seemed to indicate to the public and various officials that he viewed the strike as pointless.[46]

On February 12, 1904, Cellere, the Royal Charge d'Affairs, wrote the Italian Ministry of Foreign Affairs concerning the strike. He stated that a communiqué had arrived from Olinto Marcolina, a delegate to the special convention of the Colorado Federation of Labor, in which Marcolina denounced arbitrary acts, injustices, and abuse of power by federal and state officers against Italian countrymen. Cellere conveyed his belief, formulated from correspondence with Cuneo, that the strike was declared to obtain "certain desires of dubious importance." Cellere wrote further that Cuneo had responded to Marcolina's charges, stating that his accusations were exaggerated, and also that, if severity was used against the Italians, it was attributable to the strike, the violence, and the threats, of which the Italian strikers had also indulged.[47]

Cellere also asked about Marcolina's background, declaring that Cuneo desired information on Marcolina's conduct while in Italy, suspecting possible connections between him and Demolli. This belief was probably attributable to the fact that Marcolina contributed articles to *Il Lavoratore Italiano*, and also was secretary of UMWA Local 1970, Williamsburg, Colorado.[48] A reply arrived in April, stating that while at Udine, Marcolina had good political and moral conduct, having never maintained subversive ideas.[49]

Thus, Italian officials in the United States harbored doubts about the validity of the strike. Investigations of strikers carried on by these officials confirm that the stand for unionism was viewed by them as extremely suspect. Anti-Cuneo prose appeared often in *Il Lavoratore Italiano*, reflecting the belief that he was a "traitor," and had refused to support his countrymen.[50]

Martial law in Las Animas County resulted in press censorship that included the eventual suppression of *Il Lavoratore Italiano*. Hill suppressed the March 27 issue, wiring Peabody that its contents contained charges that the corporate interests had underwritten the militia campaign. The presses were seized, office padlocked, and deportations followed.[51] Most significant was the effect the action had on the effort to stop Demolli. A series of articles written by him were deemed of such "obscene, lewd, and lascivious a character" that he was apprehended, released on $1,000 bond, ordered to appear before a grand jury in Denver in October, 1904, for violation of postal regulations, and eventually found guilty.[52]

Martial law, deportations, and press censorship struck particularly hard at the Italian population. Hill's partiality was especially evident when he denied the request by the Americo Vespucci society to hold its monthly meeting on April 1, while allowing the Fraternal Union of America, Animas Club, and Mineral Lodge No. 91, Knights of Pythias, to continue without disturbance.[53] Military necessity provided the rationale for Major Hill's actions in the Trinidad campaign. Lists of arrests indicate that nearly fifty percent were Italians. In fact, on May 19, a group of eighty Italians was arrested for refusal to be included in a census and marched fifteen miles to Trinidad where they were put in large bull pens.[54]

January through May proved a time of stress and strain in Utah. In January evictions from the coal camps were still in progress, with Italians either settling in tent colonies, moving to other sections of the county and state, or leaving the country to return home. The lives of these immigrants again underwent changes, the realities of the time forcing many to leave mining and adapt themselves to other occupations. This willingness to change jobs instead of scabbing again illustrates an adaptability among the Utah Italians which appears to have increased as the strike progressed.

Casear Antoniono, Giuseppe Marinaro, and Joe Tedesco, of Castle Gate, petitioned President Roosevelt on January 24, 1904.[55] The timing and tone of the petition suggests that striking miners indeed had welcomed the National Guard, and an appeal to the president of the United States implied a belief in the workability of the American system of government.

Demolli left Utah in March. In April Mother Jones arrived and participated in a series of events that culminated in the arrest of 120 Italians. After conducting a meeting of strikers on April 17, Mother Jones and several Italians tried to meet with another organizer who was then in quarantine for smallpox. Because of her so-called exposure, officers attempted to place her in quarantine for the fifteen-day period. A shed was constructed for that purpose, but was burned by Italians before it could be occupied. Subsequently, Deputy Sheriff Harry World tried to arrest Jones, Tedesco, and Antoniono for violation of quarantine regulations. At the Half-Way House, between Castle Gate and Helper, owned by the Paul Pasetto family, and the site of another tent colony, the arrests were attempted but thwarted by a hundred armed Italians.[56]

In the early morning of April 24, a posse of twenty-five to forty-five men left Castle Gate for Half-Way House, concealing themselves in the rock above the colony. At dawn they charged the camp and apprehended 120 Italians who were loaded into boxcars and transported to Price, where they were put in bull pens. Women were left uncertain as to their future, and leveled verbal attacks upon the guards whom they viewed with vengeance.[57] The role of company guards proved significant in arousing Italian support before and during the strike.

A decision was made in April to "close up" affairs in District 15, followed by a message in June, sent by John Mitchell to district officials, which stated that a special convention should be convened to call off the strike, and that financial assistance from the National Guard would end June 30. Delegates met at Pueblo on June 20, but defied Mitchell by voting to remain out. However, the complete severing of financial support further doomed an already failing struggle. Strikers, predominantly Italians, "endured" until October, 1904 (Utah Italians until January, 1905), when local UMWA officials finally recognized the coal operators' victory and issued union members a clearance card permitting them to return to work without prejudice.[58]

Thus, the strike was lost without any material gain for the membership; but what of the effect upon Italian miners, with respect to both their living conditions and their attitude to unionism? The severing of funds by the UMWA left a bitter taste in the mouths of many miners, who believed the action was a "sell-out" by Mitchell to the coal companies. The concept of unionism now came under attack.

Italian miners in Colorado and Utah had access to at least one anarchist Italian newspaper printed outside both states, which presented vehement anti-union perspectives. *La Protesta Umana*, San Francisco, sympathized with the suppression of *Il Lavoratore Italiano*, but condemned its brand of unionism as coming from the "barracks of the hirelings and from traitors to the cause of the people." Giuseppe Ciancabilla, the editor of *La Protesta Umana*, further asserted that the suppression should serve as a lesson that, against the violence of capital and government, active resistance without scruples and pity is essential.[59]

In the same issue of the paper, A. Marchiori of Sunnyside, Utah, responded to the dissolving of funds by the UMWA by condemning "putrid and corrupt" unionism. He further maintained that "our prophecies confirmed themselves", the union began "our ruin."[60] Perhaps skepticism toward the UMWA was evident during the strike, but the fact remains that unionism among Carbon County Italians remained alive because such local leaders as Frank Bonacci remained committed to the union and its cause.[61] Italians, many for the first time, had tasted American unionism; this 1903–04 group was the vanguard which would educate later Italian arrivals in unionism.

Il Proletario, the New York paper of the Italian Socialist Federation, listed state locals in Scofield and Clear Creek, Utah, but none in Colorado. The locals were headed by one R. Anderlini. An Italian striker from Colorado, in a letter to the paper, stressed the need for class consciousness. He pointed to the corruption of the UMWA, which, he believed, worked against the laborer and for the capitalists. Of special importance was the writer's plea that "if we indeed desire to care for our working interests, we must organize politically and enter the files of our true worker's party and in this way combat for us and our children, and for our brothers in the holy name of Socialism."[62] These writers and correspondents must have been able to air their views at public gatherings and small meetings, which would indicate that such ideas had been bandied about and discussed. However, socialism did not become strong among Colorado and Utah Italians. Unionist ideals did not die with the 1903–04 strike, as the tragic Ludlow massacre of 1913–14 was to demonstrate.

In the final assessment of Italian participation in the strike, various conclusions can be drawn. First, the lack of a truly cohesive community comprised of workers, merchants, and the appropriate Italian government officials meant that there was no completely unified strike effort. Thus, class consciousness seemed to be determined by socio-economic level, not by nationality or ethnicity. The extreme reluctance of Cuneo to support his countrymen, who had legitimate complaints concerning living conditions, injured the cause among both Italians and the general public. This reluctance stemmed from his suspicion of labor movements—anarchists, syndicalists, and socialists—in Italy, and the adherence of Italian strikers to the UMWA and unionism.

Second, union recognition became a major factor. Some concession (i.e., wages) had been made, as in Utah, but all evidence indicates that Italian strikers, as pointed out by Demolli and Cuneo, viewed recognition of the UMWA as essential. Third, the UMWA had miscalculated its organizational abilities. Mitchell exhibited an ambivalence and skepticism with regard to the immigrant laborers, principally Italian, of the southern Colorado field.

Fourth, the intervention of Peabody and Hill, who both harbored a disdain for Italians and labor unionism, ensured the strike's ultimate failure, and affected Hill's conduct in Las Animas County. The anti-Italian bias, evident in deportations and arrests, engendered among the immigrants strong skepticism of political and military authority and also a deep hatred for coal company guards. In Utah this sentiment was somewhat different since the National Guard was viewed as a buffer between strikers and company guards.

Fifth, the relative lack of widespread intensive violence meant that one of the tenets of unionism—the concept that things could be changed through unity and cooperative action for sustained periods rather than through anarchistic revolts—had been followed.

Yet, the strike was lost, which raises the question of why anarchistic rhetoric evident in the Italian press did not supplant the unionism of the UMWA. Even with the presence of militia, open warfare could have erupted. One possible explanation lies in the efforts of local labor leaders, such as Joseph Poggiani, Dominic Massari, Frank Bonacci, and Silvestro Tedesco, who were committed to the UMWA, and helped educate later arrivals in their brand of unionism. Most importantly, fraternal organizations, such as the Fratellanza Minatori of Sunnyside, Utah, continued to function as types of labor unions, which meant that the organizational base for unionization still remained.

Sixth, the strike produced changes within the Italian settlements of Colorado and Utah. Immigrants, in many cases, were forced to change occupations and livelihoods. In the case of Utah, Italians entered agriculture and business, which in turn enabled many of their children to enter professions. Repatriation also occurred, as well as resettlement, which caused an additional break-up of any cohesive body that might have banded together during the strike. Ethnic displacement in the coal mines was an important result of the strike. Japanese and Mexicans were imported into southern Colorado by the coal operators whereas in Utah, Japanese and Greeks arrived to replace striking Italians.

The strike of 1903–04 was lost, but unionism among the Italians did not die. It merely lay smoldering, possibly in the caldrons of the fraternal organizations, awaiting the evolution of dedicated leaders, and a regeneration of a political, social, and economic environment more conducive to the fight for the equal rights of labor.

Notes

1. The CF&I, UFC, and PVC Companies, as well as the Denver and Rio Grande Western Railway, were all holdings of the John D. Rockefeller-Jay Gould syndicate. See the *Eastern Utah Advocate* (Price, Utah), April 30, 1908; and J. Warner Mills, "The Economic Struggle in Colorado," *The Arena*, 192 (December 1905): 610-611.
2. *Abstract of the Eleventh Census of the United States* (Washington, 1894), 38-39; *United States Census Reports*, 1, Twelfth Census (Washington, 1901), clxxiv; and *Abstract of the Thirteenth Census of the United States* (Washington, 1914), 204-207.
3. George Graham Suggs, Jr., "The Colorado Coal Miners' Strike, 1903-1904: A Prelude to Ludlow?" *Journal of the West*, 12 (January, 1973): 37.

4. Colorado Fuel and Iron Company, *Annual Report of the Sociological Department, 1901-1902*, 5.

5. For complete details of the role of the Governor Peabody, the UMWA leadership, and coal operators, see George Graham Suggs, Jr., "Colorado Conservatives Versus Organized Labor: A Study of the James Hamilton Peabody Administration, 1903-05" (Ph.D. diss., University of Colorado, 1964), 441-455. In the northern field of Colorado, coal operators agreed to consult with union officials, not as UMWA representatives, but as representatives of men in their employ (refused by CF&I and VFC in the south). Consequently, by November 28, an agreement was reached in the northern field.

6. U.S., Congress, Senate, *Reports of the Immigration Commission, Immigrants in Industries*, pt. 25, "Japanese and Other Immigrant Races in the Pacific Coast and Rocky Mountain States," 61st Cong., 2d sess., 1911, 257.

7. Hill to Peabody, November 18, 1903, Colorado Archives and Records Service, Office of the Governor: James H. Peabody, Document Box (DB): 19 (hereafter cited as Peabody Papers, with DB number provided). Hill also believed that if any trouble developed in Las Animas it would occur first at Hastings. Speaking of the Trinidad area, Giovanni Perilli wrote that there were "numerous" Italians. See Giovanni Perilli, *Il Colorado e gl' Italiani nel Colorado* (Denver, 1922), 143.

8. V. Macchi di Cellere to the Italian Minister of Foreign Affairs, February 12, 1904, Ministerior degli Affari Esteri, *Archivio Storico*, Rome. Documents pertaining to Italian immigration to the United States, 1880-1913 (microfilm), Immigration History Research Center, University of Minnesota (hereafter cited as *Archivio Storico*).

9. State of Utah, *Report of the Coal Mine Inspector*, 1903, 63-64. In Alan Kent Powell, "Labor at the Beginning of the 20th Century: The Carbon County, Utah Coal Fields 1900 to 1905" (M.A. thesis, University of Utah, 1974), 182, the author states: "The 1903-04 strike in Carbon County was fought primarily over the issue of union recognition."

10. Powell, *The Carbon County, Utah Coal Fields*, 114.

11. *Eastern Utah Advocate*, December 3, 1903.

12. U.S., Congress, Senate, *A Report on Disturbances in the State of Colorado, from 1880 to 1904, Inclusive, with Correspondence Relating Thereto*, 58th Cong., 3rd sess., 1905, 339 (hereafter cited as *A Report on Disturbances*).

13. Perilli, *Il Colorado*, provides a cursory view of the Italians in southern Colorado.

14. CF&I, *Annual Report of the Sociological Department, 1904-1905*, 15. The Dillingham Commission reported in 1911 that the southern Colorado field (Las Animas, Huerfano, and Fremont counties) contained 489 North Italians and 361 South Italians (foreign-born). See *Reports of the Immigration Commission*, pt. 25, 312.

15. Special Orders No. 32, March 29, 1904, Report of the Trinidad Campaign, Records of the Colorado National Guard, Microfilm copy of the Colorado Archives and Records Services, Denver (hereafter cited as *Trinidad Campaign*).

16. In the *Denver Times*, February 18, 1899, Giuseppe Cuneo, Italian consul in Denver, denounced the *padrone* system. Also, *L'Italia* (Chicago), December 19, 1903, ran a series of advertisements in which Andrea Filpi, a Chicago labor agent, gave notice that he could supply a hundred men for work in mines.

17. Vincenzo Massari, "Gli scioperi nel Colorado 1884-1915," *La Parola del Popolo* (December 1859-January 1959), 98. Vincenzo Massari, private interview with the writer held at Pueblo, Colorado, September 14, 1974.

18. The *Salt Lake Herald*, December 7, 1903; the Prefecture of Milano to the Italian Ministry of the Interior, October 3, 1902, *Archivio Storico*.

19. The *Salt Lake Herald*, December 7, 1903.

20. Peabody Papers, DB: 20. Bartoli's father was Minister of Finance, "Debito Publico," at Florence for thirteen years.

21. Giuseppe Cuneo to the Italian Ministry of Foreign Affairs, August 21, 1902, *Archivio Storico*.

22. Fratellanza Minatori, Sunnyside, Utah, *Costituzione*, 26-27. This document is located at the Italian Archives, Western Americana Department, Marriott Library, University of Utah, Salt Lake City, Utah.

23. Stella D'America, *Statuto E Regolamento*, 45-46. It may also be found at the Marriott Library.

24. Joseph J. Dalpiaz, private interview with the writer held at Helper, Utah, February 5, 1972; Joseph J. Dalpiaz, "Loggia Stella D'America, Helper, Utah," *La Parola del Popolo* (December 1958-January, 1959), 267-268.

25. Dalpiaz, private interview, February 5, 1972; and Stanley V. Litizzette, private interview with the writer held at Helper, Utah, December 18, 1971.

26. *Eastern Utah Advocate*, November 26, 1903.

27. A *Report on Disturbances*, 337-338; UMWA, *Journal*, November 12, 1903.

28. Hill to Peabody, November 18, 1903, Peabody Papers, DB:19.

29. Ibid. In the UMWA *Journal*, November 19, 1903, it was reported that "Italians and Sicilians" had to pay a dollar a month ground rent, and erect their own "shanties."

30. Phyllis H. Williams, *South Italian Folkways in Europe and America* (New Haven, 1938), 45-46.

31. UMWA, Minutes, *Sixteenth Annual Convention* (Indianapolis, 1905), 192. In the UMWA *Journal*, December 10, 1903, John Simpson wrote: "The mines working are as follows: Premero, 70 men, Japs and Mexicans; Delagua, 30 men, Japs and Mexicans; Walsen Mines, 60 men, Japs, Mexicans, and colored . . . "; see also *Reports of the Immigration Commission*, pt. 25, 259. The concern for strikebreakers was echoed in various Italian labor and radical newspapers throughout the strike. See *Il Proletario*, June 26, 1904—"La liberta' del lavoro" (the article absolved the strikebreakers themselves of any fault)—and the correspondence from R. Anderlini (Scofield, Utah) who condemned Giuseppe Giorgis "di Lucania" for persuading his brother to bring other workers to Utah from Michigan; and *Il Lavoratore Italiano*, February 21, 1904, March 13, 1904, and March 20, 1904.

32. Peabody to H. B. Brown, mayor of Trinidad, December 10, 1903, Peabody Papers, Letter Book (LB) 41. By December, 1903, the coal operators were sure of Peabody's support and refused any solution short of the destruction of the union.

33. *Eastern Utah Advocate*, November 19, 1903, reported that the coal companies were considering the importation of Japanese.

34. Ibid., November 26, 1903.

35. The *Salt Lake Herald*, December 7, 1903.

36. Ibid., December 8, 1903.

37. The *Desert Evening News*, December 9, 1903.

38. *Eastern Utah Advocate*, December 31, 1903; Suggs, *The Colorado Coal*, 44-45; Colorado, Bureau of Labor Statistics, *Ninth Biennial Report*, 1903-1904 (Denver, 1904), 195-196; UMWA *Journal*, March 17, 1904, and March 24, 1904.

39. Suggs, *The Colorado Coal*, 45. At the Sixteenth Annual Convention, Vice-President T. L. Lewis, referring to Peabody's action, stated: "We felt that we had to continue the strike then, notwithstanding the fact that we knew it was lost . . . [district officials] were trying to make the people out there believe it could be won." See UMWA, Minutes, *Sixteenth Annual Convention*, 188. An intriguing aspect of Peabody's order was the fact that the financing of the National Guard's operation was largely underwritten by the coal operators themselves. The *Denver Post*, March 23, 1904, reported *Il Lavoratore Italiano*, March 27, 1904, asserted that the $30,000 from Trinidad came from the Citizens Alliance. The papers of Peabody contain a letter from one E. B. Field regarding a "Law and Order Banquet" held February 23, 1904. Field instructed Peabody to acknowledge the "gifts" of those in attendance, primarily, American Smelting and Refining Co., Western Mining Co., Denver and Rio Grande Railway, CF&I, and VFC. See Peabody Papers, DB:20.

40. Suggs, *The Colorado Coal*, 46. From March 24 to 26, seven southern Italians were arrested for possession of arms. See Peabody Papers, DB: 20.

41. Peabody Papers, DB: 20. On March 25, Hill wrote to Peabody that Adolfo Bartoli was arrested for threatening Tarabino; Tarabino, upon receiving such threats, spoke to the military and acquired Bartoli's arrest.

42. Hill to Peabody, March 25, 1904, Peabody Papers, DB: 20.

43. Suggs, *Colorado Conservatives*, 487; UMWA *Journal*, June 30, 1904; Reports of Arrest, Peabody Papers, DB: 20; and Suggs, *The Colorado Coal*, 47. On March 27, 1904, Hill apologized to Peabody for not having secured Demolli for deportation, since Demolli's apprehension was explicitly requested by Peabody. See Hill to Peabody, March 27, 1904, Peabody Papers, LB: 43. Also, in Hill's March 25 report, he declared: "At Segundo, where there were some eleven saloons closed, the Italians were very much incensed, as they claimed they had paid license to the County, and had been advised by Demolli that they had a right to run." Again, this reflected Hill's concern for the "leadership" aspect of the strike.

44. Peabody to McParland, January 5, 1904, LB: 43; Peabody to Cuneo, March 28, and April 4, 1904 LB: 43; Cuneo to Peabody, March 29, 1904, DB: 20, and Peabody to Hill, March 25, 1904, LB: 43 (all Peabody Papers).

45. *Denver Times*, March 28, 1899, and April 1, 1899. These reports indicate that Cuneo had been charged by Italian laborers with extortion in connection with men in jail and attorney's fees. In addition cries of "lynch him" were heard, and a petition was circulated calling for the consul's removal from office. In the *Denver Times*, April 3, 1899, Pietro Albi, editor of *La Roma* (Denver), denied the intentions of Italians in Denver to lynch Cuneo, but insisted that they were serious in attempting to remove him from his position.

46. Powell, *The Carbon County, Utah Coal Fields*, 127-129.

47. V. Macchi di Cellere to the Italian Ministry of Internal Affairs, April 2, 1904, *Archivio Storico*.

48. Ibid.; *Il Lavoratore Italiano*, March 20, 1904; and UMWA *Journal*, April 7, 1904.

49. Italian Ministry of Internal Affairs to Cellere, Royal Charge d'Affaires, April 2, 1904, *Archivio Storico*.

50. Ironically, in July, 1904, Cuneo "retired" as consul, and was replaced by Pasquale Corte. See Italian Legation in the United States, Notes to the Department of State, September 17, 1904, Immigration History Research Center, University of Minnesota. Cuneo had been appointed in 1895.

51. Hill to Peabody, March 25, 1904, Peabody Papers, DB: 20; Suggs, *Colorado Conservatives*, 494; *A Report on Disturbances*, 350; and UMWA *Journal*, March 31, 1904. The *Denver Republican*, March 29, 1904, charged: "Suppressed Italian Paper Incited Its Readers to Acts of Blood in Trinidad Camps" (totally untrue).

52. For action on Demolli see Hill to Peabody, March 31, 1904, Peabody Papers, DB: 20; *Il Lavoratore Italiano*, February 21, March 13, and March 20, 1904. *L'Italia* (Chicago), April 16, and 23, 1904, described Demolli's arrest with "standard" press releases. See also report of Hill on Bartoli, Peabody Papers, DB: 20. Material relevant to the United States District Court, Colorado, Criminal Case 795, United States vs. John Simpson, William Howells, and Charles Demolli, is located at the Denver Federal Records Center, Denver. Demolli exonerated Howells and Simpson of any knowledge of the contents of the articles.

53. Letter of April 2, 1904; Special Orders No. 64, April 1, 1904, and No. 72, April 3, 1904, *Trinidad Campaign*.

54. Hill to Peabody, May 20, 1904, Peabody Papers, DB: 20. The census, labeled as "List of Idlemen registered in Las Animas County, Colorado, by the Military Authorities," listed a total of 1,223 men of which 661 were Italians, or 54 percent.

55. UMWA *Journal*, February 4, 1904. No evidence exists of a reply from Roosevelt. The president apparently deemed it advantageous to steer clear of the problem.

56. Litizzette, private interview, December 18, 1971. In Mary Harris Jones, *The Autobiography of Mother Jones* (Chicago, 1925), 104, the

"nice Italian family" which gave Mother Jones a room was the Pasetto family. See also Powell, *The Carbon County, Utah Coal Fields*, 163.

57. Powell, *The Carbon County, Utah Coal Fields*, 165-168; Jones, *The Autobiography*, 104-107; The *Salt Lake Herald*, April 26, 1904.

58. UMWA, Minutes, *Sixteenth Annual Convention*, 12-14; and *A Report on Disturbances*, 357-359. June 11, 1904, marked the full departure of the National Guard from Las Animas County.

59. *La Protesta Umana*, April 9, 1904.

60. Ibid.

61. See Helen Z. Papanikolas, "Unionism, Communism, and the Great Depression: The Carbon County Strike of 1933," *Utah Historical Quarterly* 41 (Summer, 1973): 254-300.

62. *Il Proletario*, December 18, 1904.

Italians in the Cherry, Illinois, Mine Disaster

Betty Boyd Caroli

On Saturday, November 13, 1909, the St. Paul Mine Company in Cherry, Illinois, was operating on schedule.[1] Almost five hundred men entered the mine about 6:30 that morning. Some came up at 1:30 while others stayed below to finish out the normal eight-hour day. While they worked, a wagon of hay on its way down to mules in the second vein touched a torch and caught fire. Before the two young men in charge noticed what had happened, timbers around the shaft began to burn too. Although the hay fire was extinguished in a "sump" at the bottom, the wooden portions of the shaft burned on with increasing intensity. Someone ordered ventilating fans stopped, but this cut off oxygen from the miners below. When fans were reversed, this drew the flames back, cutting off the escape route and burning out the fans. Fire hoses, once located, did not fit pipes. Miners, who were told of the fire nearly two hours after it had started, sought familiar escape routes only to learn that they had been changed. In the end, 250 men died,[2] making this one of the worst mine disasters in American history. The largest number—seventy-three—were Italians.[3]

The purpose of this paper is to examine the Cherry, Illinois, mine fire as part of the Italian American experience, to illustrate the kind of living conditions immigrants encountered in a midwest mining town at the beginning of the twentieth century, and to see how Italians across the nation reacted to the deaths of their countrymen.

Cherry, in northern Illinois, lies about one hundred miles southwest of Chicago. At the time of the 1900 census, it was not yet incorporated. Then, in 1905, the St. Paul Mine Company opened a coal mine and built one hundred and twenty-five houses.[4] Private capital added others. Perhaps "house" is an inappropriate name for the structures as photographs show them to have been small and flimsy. Contemporaries described them as "just shacks."[5] Even residents of Cherry could find little to praise in their town's appearance. Fifty years after the mine fire, one of them described what Cherry looked like in 1909: "[It was] drab with all the overtones of black or dirty gray. The houses, made of wood, were seldom painted ... Cinder paths which were the village walks converged on the colliery at the north end of town. ... A visitor might have concluded that the town had been built on a temporary basis, but, in reality, it did not differ from the average small mining town of Central Illinois."[6]

By 1910 census takers found just over a thousand residents in Cherry,[7] but newspaper accounts the year before estimated the population to be much larger, even double that figure.[8] Perhaps the latter had been made before the fire decimated the town's population. In any case, Cherry was not officially urban.[9]

Cherry's story reminds us that current emphasis on urban settlement patterns of Italians obscures the fact that many lived in small towns. In the last year or so, we have had new books on Italians in Buffalo, Utica, Rochester, and Kansas City,[10] to add to others which devoted large sections to Italians in Chicago, Omaha, Boston and New York City.[11] But many Italians in the period of mass immigration left the cities of the eastern seaboard fairly quickly and moved into the fields, the mines, and the lumber camps farther west. In the 1910 census, one in five Italians was not officially urban.[12] Cherry gives us some idea of what life was like for them.

Mining towns in the Midwest offered a grim picture; Bruna Pieracci, in a forthcoming book by Salvatore LuGumina, talks about her father's reaction to a mining camp in Iowa in 1909:

> The wooden houses were flimsy and compared badly to the 20-inch stone walls Italians had left behind. What was even more strange was the absence of trees or shrubbery for this mining camp had been built in the middle of what had been an Iowa cornfield. [Italians] were amazed at the flatness of the terrain. Among themselves, they called it the 'Sahara Desert' ... There was great nostalgia for the 'hills of home' but there [in Iowa] they had to stay for they did not have passage money to go back ... They rarely missed a day's work. They could not afford to. Nearly all had borrowed passage money and that [had to] be paid back.[13]

Cherry, Illinois, and the Iowa town Mrs. Pieracci described were among scores of villages that sprang up in the late nineteenth and early twentieth centuries to mine newly opened bituminous coal deposits in the Midwest. The Immigration Commission in 1911 called the growth of the industry "remarkable," noting that Illinois had employed only about 6,000 miners in 1870 but more than ten times that number by 1907.[14] Labor came predominantly from southern and eastern Europe. The influx was particularly obvious in Illinois and Indiana from which older immigrant groups and native-born workers fled, going to Kansas and Oklahoma farther west.[15] Bureau County, where Cherry was located, registered a large increase in immigrant miners between 1899 and 1907.[16]

Bituminous coal deposits, like those at Cherry, were tapped in isolated spots far from urban centers. Mary Anderson, director for many years of the Women's Bureau in Washington, made a detailed study of mining towns in the early 1920s.[17] She pointed out that the soft coal towns, in particular, were isolated and lacked services. Most had a church or two. Cherry had two—one Protestant and one Catholic.[18] Most had a few clubs. Cherry had a Knights of Pythias with seventy-five members, most of whom died in the fire.[19] But medical facilities, parks, and recreational opportunities were missing. Cherry was a town, one writer observed, "new and crude.... Scarcely any population [could have been] more unprepared or less resourceful in coping with disaster."[20]

The company town atmosphere gave men little choice except to leave, and old debts often removed even that option. Italians in Cherry were concentrated in the lowest paid mining jobs. Few were supervisors.[21] They averaged about $2.40 a day[22] and they worked 120 days a year.[23] Their annual earnings then came to less than $300 a year, well below that reported by their *paesani* who stuck to the large cities.[24]

Women, who might have supplemented family income, found few opportunities. Factories or canneries were not there. Nor were there many households willing to employ servants. Italian women in mining towns of the Midwest did not often work outside the home. In the sample collected by the Immigration Commission in 1911, not one Italian household reported a woman at school or at work.[25] Some took in boarders or lodgers. About one in eight of the southern Italian families reported income from this source.[26] Welcome though the dollars may have been, the resulting crowding surely complicated lives. The Immigration Commission found that mining towns in the Midwest reported more crowded conditions than did apartments in Italian neighborhoods in the large cities. In Illinois and Indiana, southern Italians averaged 2.75 persons per sleeping room, more than that reported by their countrymen in New York, Philadelphia, Chicago, Boston, Cleveland, Buffalo, and Milwaukee.[27]

Italians in the midwestern mining towns met cool, even hostile receptions from the native-born population. Herman Lantz, who wrote a book about a place he called Coal Town not far from Cherry, recounts the reactions of local people to the influx of foreigners just after 1900.[28] One farmer told Lantz,

> The character of the foreigners changed the country. Nine out of ten of them was no good. We would have been a heap better off if they had never been brought here. They couldn't get the others. They could get the foreign people. They mined well and they just suited the mining people. The old people hated it when they brought in the foreigners because they were so different. I know my father did. He said it was a sad day when they found coal here. Their way of living was so different.[29]

Another woman was more specific about her family's dislike of foreigners in that part of Illinois. She told Lantz,

> I can remember when they first brought the Eyetalians in 1902 for them to work on that bridge across Black Riber. I was a little seven-year-old girl at that time. Why, they brought them Eyetalians in by the carloads. My father told me to take a good look at that because he said, "Daughter, that's the worst thing that could have happened to this country." Well, it scared me half to death to see them strange Eyetalians.[30]

This strong dislike of Italians is documented elsewhere. The Immigration Commission's report on mining in the Midwest noted that "a pronounced antipathy exists on the part of native whites and other English-speaking races toward Southern Italians."[31] In boardinghouses Italians stayed in separate sections, and towns accepted an unofficial Italian section.[32]

In spite of antagonism and prejudice, immigrants from southern and eastern Europe poured into new mining towns of the Midwest. Bureau County, reported in 1910 that forty percent of its males had foreign birth places. Another twenty-three percent were children of foreign-born parents.[33] Most of the men who died in the Cherry mine had been in America only a few years. Twelve still listed foreign countries as their residences and six of these named Italy.[34]

Not surprisingly, the immigrant workers' ability in English was very limited. The Immigration Commission cited lack of English ability as a major cause of mine accidents. In the case of Cherry, this helped to lengthen the death list. One man who had escaped reported to an investigating committee:

I shouted, "Come out right away. The shaft is on fire," [but] the men were Italian and did not understand English well. They said, "What's the matter?" I said, "The shaft is afire; get out." And one of the fellows understood English a little better and he says, "What's the matter?" And I said, "Fire in the second vein and come out right quick, right away." I showed them out from the wall to the road ahead.[35]

To add to their confusion, most immigrant miners had little or no experience on the job. Many Italians saw a mine for the first time in America, although they may have had to swear differently to get the work. More than half of the Italians in midwestern coal fields had been farm workers in Italy (fifty-two percent of the northern Italians and sixty-three percent of those from the *Mezzogiorno*),[35] poor training for digging in four-foot high compartments hundreds of feet underground.

Mine supervisors pushed men to produce even under dangerous conditions. Although they blamed miners for overzealousness to earn dollars, it was often their own greed that caused deaths. Several of the Cherry miners testified that they were not permitted to leave their picks and shovels even when the smell of smoke warned them of danger. Supervisors did not want them to lose time. David Wright, who had escaped, testified that all the men in the second vein could have been saved if the alarm had been given earlier or if those who asked to be brought up were lifted.[37]

Andiano Muzzarelli reported that he heard about the danger from a little French boy who whispered to his father something about fire. When Muzzarelli and his co-workers rushed to the cage to be lifted, John Brown, the man in charge, refused to let them go up, saying, "What the hell are you fellows getting excited about? Ain't you got any nerve? Stick!"[38]

The first newspaper accounts of the fire blamed the men for smoking on the job.[39] F. P. Buck, chief clerk of the St. Paul Mine Company, admitted that an unprotected torch had been used for more than three weeks while the electrical system was out of order.[40]

In spite of this admission, the mine company got generally good marks from several newspapers. Even the United Mine Workers' *Journal* related, without refutation, a state mine inspector who said the mine was safe. "From what I have learned," he said, "I can only say that carelessness—criminal carelessness on the part of some of the men working in the second vein is responsible. The mine was equipped with all modern safety devices and was well planned. The blame rests entirely upon the shoulders of the men."[41]

The following week the Mine Workers' *Journal* called for plac-
ing liability on the company since it had not provided adequate
escape routes.[42] The December 2 issue went further. Illinois Mine
Workers' president Duncan McDonald called Cherry a "death
trap." Neither water nor hose was provided for fire emergencies;
the escape hatch and stairs were built and lined with timber; the
men had not received instruction in how to deal with fires.[43]

From the beginning, miners on the site placed blame squarely on
the company for using open torches and for restraining men from
leaving the burning mine.[44] The town became so agitated in the
days following the fire that the governor of the state sent in troops
to maintain order.[45] The mine had been sealed off even though
nobody knew the fate of hundreds of men still trapped down
below. Rumors of a dynamite plot to blow up mine officials and
investigators caused an inquest to be suspended.[46]

The tragedy of the 250 men killed at Cherry is multiplied by
their youth. Most of the victims were young, in their twenties and
thirties. Three were below the legal working age of sixteen.[47] Matt
Francesco, one of the two in charge of starting the hay bales on
their way that day, was only fifteen. He testified that he had been
working for some time in the mine but had never received any
instruction in mine safety or how to deal with a fire.[48]

When the first rescue squad went down into the mine late in the
afternoon of November 13 to lead out trapped men, the signals
they had agreed on became so confused that all twelve of the
rescuers died, including an Italian grocer, Domenico Fumento.[49]
Then the mine was sealed off and eight days later another rescue
squad went in. This time they found twenty-one men who had
walled themselves off from the smoke and stayed alive by eating
shoe leather and by moistening their lips against a damp outside
wall.[50] Eventually the mine was sealed again and not reopened
until a thermometer showed safe temperatures. Beginning in February, 1910, more bodies were removed and this process continued
until the summer.[51] The final death toll of 250 is questionable since
several men were never accounted for.

Miners in the early days of the twentieth century worked at jobs
long known to be among the most dangerous. In the state of
Illinois, in the period 1883–1910, an average of 180 men died each
year in the mines.[52] This worked out to 2.6 per thousand. To put
the matter in other numbers, if one mined coal in Illinois around
the turn of the century, his chances of dying on the job in any one
year were about one in four hundred.

And Illinois was a relatively good state. Historians have noted a positive connection between organization of miners and safety.[53] Chances of mine accidents significantly increased in areas where miners lacked a union. But Cherry men had joined the United Mine Workers, one of the first unions actively to organize immigrants.[54]

Cohesiveness in mine towns has been well documented. Robert Asher has noted the unity of small mining towns operated by a single employer.[55] Asher suggests that the special danger which miners shared fostered a kind of solidarity that shoemakers and textile workers never knew. Miners faced a particularly grim life. Boys typically started out as helpers or assistants, then moved up to more difficult and better-paying jobs. Eventually, as they became older or less able, they fell back into the lower ranks of assistants. This depressing cycle further tightened the bond among miners, Asher suggests.

Miners at Cherry however, do not appear to have felt strong ethnic ties on the job. Again and again, in the reports of the fire, men with non-Italian names talked of working with Italian partners or of helping Italian workers escape. The group that sealed itself off and lived for eight days with little food or water included a mixture of ethnics, two of whom were Italian brothers.[56] When the men finally came to safety, they told how one among them had cheated by taking too many turns at the water supply. Everyone knew who he was but nobody would tell.[57]

If ethnic bonds did not show up in the reports of the fire, they are just as absent from the appeals for relief. When the enormity of the tragedy became known, several newspapers and organizations rallied to help widows and children. Theirs was the most pressing need, but the entire town suffered. Sightseers blocked transportation routes so that supplies of food and medicine could not reach Cherry. Storekeepers and boardinghouse owners who had depended on the miners and their families lost income. The entire town needed help.

The day after the fire the *Chicago Tribune* donated $1,000 to start a relief fund and called on readers to send in their contributions.[58] On November 15 the *Tribune* sent six nurses to Cherry.[59] Eventually, the newspaper collected more than $41,000.[60] The American Red Cross sent another $85,000 and various mine workers' locals contributed $65,000.[61] The St. Paul Mine Company offered $56,000 in addition to the death settlements it eventually made.[62] In all, relief contributions collected from private sources totaled about $400,000 and the mine company paid an equal amount in death claims.

In none of the appeals of the *Tribune* did ethnicity become a factor. In the newspaper's list of hundreds of contributing individuals and organizations, one looks for a long time before finding an Italian name. This does not mean that Italians did not help their countrymen. Many surely contributed through their miners' locals or through their churches, but their efforts are well concealed.

Italian newspapers which I examined stressed class solidarity rather than ethnic bonds. *La Fiaccola*, the Italian Socialist Party paper of Buffalo, spoke of the "poor people killed at Cherry because of the fault of capitalists who are greedy for gold and pay little attention to human lives."[63] No mention was made that many of them were Italians.

Il Proletario, the paper of the Italian Socialist Federation published in New York City, carried several emotional tributes to widows and children of men killed in Cherry, but the newspaper did not refer to their ethnicity.[64] *L'Era Nuova*, *La Luce* (Utica, New York), and *Il Lavoratore Italiano* paid little or no attention to Cherry.[65]

The Italian government offered to pay the fare of anyone wanting to return to the homeland and one widow accepted.[65] But, for the most part, relief came from the non-Italian community: from newsboys in Columbus, Ohio, Protestant churches, and wealthy individuals across the country.[67]

Relief efforts met many obstacles. Widows in Cherry complained that local merchants raised their prices. The women requested money rather than credit so they could shop competitively. A surplus of some materials came into the town causing the *Tribune* to request money rather than supplies in order to avoid waste.[68]

Privately collected monies were allotted, under the direction of a local committee, according to the number of dependents each miner left and the ages of the children. Among the 607 dependents, many were children under the age of fourteen.[69] The committee decided that payments should be made regularly until children reached working age.[70]

The $400,000 settlement made by the St. Paul Mine Company was distributed somewhat differently. Officials of the United Mine Workers and a self-appointed mediator met with the mine owners to work out some form of compensation for families of the men who had died. Two plans of settlement were offered. One relied on a commission of men appointed by the president of the United

States. The other allotted to each man's heirs an amount based on England's Workmen's Compensation Act of 1906.[71] According to English law, the family of each worker killed on the job received a sum equal to three times his annual earnings. Representatives of the miners and of the mine owners favored the latter plan and it was adopted. Families thus received settlements of up to $1,800, although most received less. They still did far better than they would have under laws in effect in most states.

Many people evidently left town soon after payment came. The mine continued to operate until 1927. Today Cherry has fewer than 1,000 residents.[72]

Perhaps the Cherry fire speeded attempts to regulate the mining industry. A few days after the accident, President Taft announced that he would set up a federal agency to prevent recurrence of such tragedies.[73] The United States Congress established the Bureau of Mines a few months later. The Illinois legislature also passed new legislation on mines.

But, for the most part, the Cherry disaster has slipped from the record. A few years ago the United Mine Workers issued a commemorative calendar marking tragedies and progress in their ranks from 1870 to the present. Cherry was absent from the November 13 spot, which honored sixteen miners killed in West Virginia in 1954. Italian American historians rarely refer to Cherry.

Yet Cherry reminds us that not all Italians stayed in large eastern cities. Chains of "Little Italies" looped across the Midwest, and some of them provided worse housing, more dangerous jobs, more hostile neighbors, and fewer supportive organizations than could be found in urban centers.

Cherry reminds us too that ethnicity as a rallying cry for unity and action was often absent from the activities of America's immigrants seventy years ago. Italians across the country appear to have shown little interest in the deaths of so many of their countrymen.

Appropriately, the one highly visible memorial to victims of Cherry is a monument erected in the town by the miners' local in 1959. The stone bears this inscription: "To the memory of the miners who lost their lives in the Cherry Mine Disaster, November 13, 1909."[74] The monument cites no numbers, gives no details besides the date, and assigns no blame—just "miners who lost their lives in a disaster."

Notes

1. This description of the fire and its aftermath has been compiled from a variety of official and unofficial reports which, except as noted, agree. These sources include: Anton Demichelis, *The Cherry Mine Disaster*, booklet published at the fiftieth anniversary of the fire in 1959 in Peru, Illinois, and available from Rev. Pastor, Holy Trinity Parish, Cherry, Illinois; *Chicago Tribune*, November 14, 1909, to December 31, 1909, *passim*; Illinois Mines and Minerals Dept., Labor Statistics Bureau, *Coal Report, 1909/1910* (Springfield, 1911), 240-494.

2. This is the offical number. See Illinois Mines and Minerals Dept., *Coal Report, 1909/1910*, 247. Some men were never located.

3. This number is questionable since men with non-Italian names are listed as Italian while others with Italian names are categorized under other nationalities. See Illinois Mines and Minerals Dept. 3, *Coal Report, 1909/1910*, 494.

4. Demichelis, *The Cherry Mine Disaster*, 3.

5. United Mine Workers' *Journal*, December 30, 1909, 3.

6. Demichelis, *The Cherry Mine Disaster*, 3-4.

7. U.S. Bureau of the Census, *Thirteenth Census of the United States, 1910*, 11 (Washington, 1913): 443.

8. *Chicago Tribune*, November 14, 1909, I. See also Demichelis, *The Cherry Mine Disaster*, 4.

9. In 1910 the U.S. Census Bureau classified as urban "all cities and other incorporated places of 2,500 inhabitants or more." U.S. Bureau of the Census, *Thirteenth Census, Abstract* (Washington, 1913), 199.

10. Virginia Yans McLaughlin, *Family and Community: Italian Immigrants in Buffalo, 1880-1930* (Ithaca, 1977). John W. Briggs, *An Italian Passage: Immigrants to Three American Cities, 1880-1930* (New Haven, 1978).

11. Humbert S., Nelli, *The Italians in Chicago* (New York, 1970). Howard Chudacoff, *Mobile Americans: Residential and Social Mobility in Omaha, 1880-1920*, (New York, 1972). Stephen Thernstrom, *The Other Bostonians, 1880-1970* (Cambridge, 1973). Thomas Kessner, *The Golden Door: Italian and Jewish Immigrant Mobility in New York City, 1880-1915* (New York, 1977).

12. According to the thirteenth census taken in 1910, immigrants were selecting urban centers for settlement in larger numbers than previously. "While considerably less than half (46.3 percent) of the total population of the U.S. in 1910 was urban, 72.1 percent of the foreign born population was urban." The report continues: "In general the immigrants from the countries of southern and eastern Europe . . . have settled in cities to a greater extent than the immigrants from northwestern Europe." Italians in 1910 were classified as 78.1 percent urban, somewhat below French Canadians, Cubans, Irish, Rumanians, Russians, and Turks. See *Abstract of the Thirteenth Census*, 199-200.

13. Salvatore J. LaGumina, ed., *The Immigrants Speak: The Italian-Americans Tell Their Story* (Staten Island, Forthcoming).

14. U.S., Congress, Senate, *Reports of the Immigration Commission, Immigrants in Industries*, 61st Cong., 2nd sess., 1911, 581.

15. Ibid., 21-2.
16. Ibid., 585.
17. U.S. Dept. of Labor, "Home Environment and Employment Opportunities of Women in Coal Mine Worker's Families," *Bulletin of the Women's Bureau*, no. 45 (Washington, 1925).
18. E. Wyatt, "Heroes of the Cherry Mine," *McClure's*, 34 (March, 1910): 473. See also the report by Demichelis.
19. *Chicago Tribune*, November 15, 1909, I.
20. "A Mine Test of Civilization," *American Review of Reviews*, 41 (January, 1910): 102.
21. Illinois Mines and Minerals Dept., *Coal Report 1909/1910* lists, 484-493; see the names of the men who died, their ages, marital status, job titles, and number of dependents. Almost all held the lowest paid "miner" titles.
22. Ibid., 142. The average in the district was somewhat higher, with each man earning about $439 per year. The average number of days worked per year was 181.
23. Ibid.. 142.
24. The U.S. Immigration Commission canvassed southern Italian families in several large cities for its report in 1911. The average annual earnings reported by males eighteen years of age or more were: New York, $526; Chicago, $402; Philadelphia, $354; Boston, $338; Cleveland, $320. See *Reports of the Immigration Commission*, pts. 25 and 27, *passim*.
25. *Reports of the Immigration Commission*, pt. 6, 624, 643.
26. Ibid., 644.
27. Ibid., 677; and 26, 27, *passim*.
28. Herman Lantz, *People of Coal Town* (New York, 1958).
29. Ibid., 39.
30. Ibid.
31. *Reports of the Immigration Commission*, pt. 6, 653.
32. Ibid.
33. U.S. Bureau of the Census, *Thirteenth Census of the United States, 1910, Statistics for Illinois* (Washington, 1913), 617.
34. Illinois Mines and Minerals Dept., *Coal Report, 1909/1910*, 484-93.
35. Ibid., 475.
36. *Reports of the Immigration Commission*, pt. 6, 622.
37. United Mine Workers' *Journal*, January 6, 1910, 3.
38. Chicago Tribune, November 16, 1890, 2.
39. Ibid., November 14, 1890, I.
40. Ibid., November 15, 1890, I.
41. United Mine Workers' *Journal*, November 18, 1890, 2.
42. Ibid., November 25, 1909, I.
43. Ibid., December 2, 1890, 3.
44. *Chicago Tribune*, November 16, 1909, 2.
45. Ibid., November 17, 1909, I.
46. Ibid., November 18, 1909, 2.
47. Ibid., November 15, 1909, 2; November 23, 1909, 3; December 1, 1909, II.
48. United Mine Workers' *Journal*, December 16, 1909, I.

49. Illinois Mines, *Coal Report*, 472-73; Demichelis, 7.

50. Illinois Mines, *Coal Report*, 242; *Chicago Tribune*, November 21, 1909, I; Demichelis, 10-11.

51. Illinois Mines and Minerals Dept., *Coal Report 1909/1910*, 243-47.

52. Ibid., 186.

53. "Cost of Coal in Human Life," *Outlook*, 43 (November, 1909): 798.

54. United Mine Workers' *Journal*, November 18, 1909, 2, reports that 571 employees of the St. Paul Mine Company in Cherry belonged to the union. See also Morton Baratz, *The Union and the Coal Industry* (New Haven, 1955), 51. Edwin Fenton, *Immigrants and Unions, A Case Study* (New York, 1975) considers the same relationship between Italians and unions in different situations. The Fenton book is a published version of his Ph.D. dissertation (Harvard University, 1957).

55. Robert Asher, *"Union Nativism and the Immigrant Response"* (Paper delivered at Behrend College of Pennsylvania State University Colloquium of the Immigrant Experience in Urban America, April 29, 1978), 11. Asher relies on the work of Charles Leineweber, "Immigration and the Decline of Internationalism in the American Working Class Movement, 1864-1919" (Ph.D. diss., University of California, Berkeley, 1969).

56. *Chicago Tribune*, November 21, 1909, *passim*, and November 22, 1909, *passim*.

57. E. Wyatt, "Heroes of the Cherry Mine Disaster," *McClure's*, 34 (March 10, 1909): 473ff. The *Chicago Tribune* gives a similar version.

58. *Chicago Tribune*, November 14, 1909, 1.

59. Ibid., November 15, 1909, 2.

60. In the weeks following the fire, the *Chicago Tribune* listed contributors almost every day.

61. Illinois Mines, *Coal Report*, 504-5; Demichelis, 15.

62. Ibid.

63. Author's translation from the Italian. *La Fiaccola*, November 20, 1909, 3. An examination of issues until the end of March, 1910, shows no mention of the ethnicity of miners at Cherry.

64. *Il Proletario*, November 19, 1909. 1. Other issues examined until March 31, 1910.

65. *Il Lavoratore Italiano* ("generale settimanale dei lavoratori italiani uniti d'America," published in Pittsburgh, Kansas), reported on December 10, 1909, that Matt Francesco was blamed for starting the fire at Cherry. On November 20, 1909, *L'Era Nuova* (Paterson, New Jersey) made an emotional appeal to miners to stand up for their rights. *La Luce* (Utica, New York) carried a great deal of European news in November, 1909, but little on Cherry. Many more Italian newspapers published in the United States in 1909-1910 would have to be found and examined before generalization is possible.

66. Demichelis, 14.

67. *Chicago Tribune*, after establishing the fund, listed donors by name. See November 24, 1909, 4.

68. *Chicago Tribune*, December 15, 1909, 7. Ibid., December 16, 1909, II.

69. Illinois Mines, *Coal Report* lists the ages of children on page 494. Demichelis records 160 widows and 390 children plus others on page

13: "In all, 607 persons had been dependent upon the men killed in the mine."

70. If the family wanted to leave, they received a lump payment. Otherwise payment was made monthly, the amount depending on the number of children under fourteen. Maximum payment was forty dollars per month. See Demichelis, 14-15. Also see Illinois Mines, *Coal Report*, 516-17. Widows and others without children received a lump payment of three hundred to five hundred dollars.

71. Demichelis, 16.

72. Ibid.

73. *Chicago Tribune*, November 22, 1909, 2.

74. Demichelis, 16. The Starved Rock Library System, Ottawa, Illinois, has a collection of oral histories relevant to the Cherry mine disaster. Especially valuable are interviews of the following: Jule Pierard, Peter Donna, Celestino Menietti, and Mary Kolak. All lived in Cherry at the time of the fire. Their accounts substantiate, in most cases, the details given in the written reports.

The Cultural Background of the Italian Immigrant Woman and Its Impact on her Unionization in the New York City Garment Industry, 1880–1919

Colomba M. Furio

Women of all ethnic and social backgrounds in the United States have traditionally played significant roles within the confines of the family. In order to study these roles, it is necessary to understand the internal dynamics that existed within these families and the cultural forces that determined them. It is here that one will find clues to what may have encouraged women to seek certain types of work and avoid others, to engage in certain activities and ignore others. If women are to be viewed as part of the historical process and not simply as bystanders, the roles they played and the tensions that emerged in their roles as immigrants, workers, wives, and mothers must be examined. These tensions, and their eventual resolution, are the key factors in the preservation or destruction of the prevailing social norms existing within a particular cultural group. While these factors affect all women, they are especially important to Italian immigrant women because of the intensity of the Italian family structure and the strictly defined role that women played, and often still play, within that structure. It therefore becomes clear that any analysis of Italian women's behavior patterns would be incomplete without an understanding of the family. This is the first point to be analyzed in this paper.

The second point rests on the principle that women, like men, can best be defined by the work they perform. Recent studies of the experiences of working-class women have helped to shed light on the struggles against exploitation faced by women in American industry.[1] One industry consisting largely of women workers and long known for exploitation of its workers—its long hours, small pay, and injurious surroundings—is the garment industry. Large numbers of Italian immigrant women gravitated to this industry during the first decade of the twentieth century. Thus, a study of the Italian woman's role in the garment industry should help explicate the economic and social inequalities, based on traditional value systems and prejudices, faced by many of the early female entrants to industrial and other careers.

Between 1880 and 1915, four million immigrants came to the United States from Italy.[2] The majority came from the underdeveloped and overpopulated areas of the *Mezzogiorno*[3] and Sicily. These immigrants were principally *contadini*, farmers or farm laborers, who had spent their lives wresting a living from the soil. Their main reason for emigrating was economic. They came to the United States with the hope of earning enough money to return to their native villages and buy their own land. For many, what was to be a temporary sojourn in the United States often developed into permanent settlement. At first, many of these so-called "birds of passage" were in the habit of crossing and recrossing the ocean, taking their earnings back to their families in Italy.[4] Eventually, they brought their wives and children to the United States with the intention of permanent residence. When families arrived they came not simply as numbers of individuals, but rather as part of a cultural group. They often settled within ethnic enclaves which became known as "Little Italies." The distinctive quality maintained by each immigrant group in the United States is now referred to as ethnic or cultural pluralism.[5] The Italian woman who emigrated from southern Italy and Sicily was part of a cultural group transplanted to the United States. What were the foundations of this culture and what special position did it assign to the Italian woman?

It has been said of southern Italian society that "life in the South exalts the family."[6] Its members are "united like the fingers of the hand."[7] Indeed, the Italian family has always served in sociology as a classic example of familial solidarity: "The family is a small universe, an inclusive social world."[8] In this family, the father was the head of the family; he derived his prestige from his role as breadwinner. When he became too old to work, he still kept his place of honor until he died. The wife's role in the family was clearly defined. She had responsibilities which included obeying her husband, childbearing, managing the family's resources, purchasing and preparing food, mending and making clothing for her family, and supervising the children's upbringing. In short, it can be said that the Italian family was "father-dominated, but mother-centered."[9]

From early childhood, a girl was trained to fulfill certain expectations and responsibilities in her later life. Her value as a future bride depended not only on her family's status, but also on her proficiency in family chores. Because of the dowry system, every daughter represented a debt which eventually had to be paid. The father of several daughters often considered himself afflicted with a great personal calamity, and getting daughters properly married, became the central preoccupation of all who had them.

Girls began to collect items for their dowry at an early age. The size of the dowry would be estimated by the number of sheets the girl had.[10] Sheeting was bought at the market, and between the ages of twelve and fourteen, often before she was engaged, the girl began to embroider intricate patterns and designs on the sheets and pillowcases. "A girl who begins at an early age embroidering sheets, pillowcases and other linens is considered wholesome and serious, thus increasing her chances for making a good match."[11] An old proverb said, "If out the window she idly stares, she is not a girl for whom anyone cares."[12]

Great pressure was exerted on the young girl to fulfill her social expectations. Before the wedding, relatives and friends were invited to come and inspect the dowry which was put on display in the girl's home. The workmanship was appraised, and judgment was passed. Because of this public display, each girl tried to surpass herself, to make a *bella figura*, a good show, and to bring honor to her family. Even as children, girls' games reflected social values. At an early age, they learned how to hold a needle and to sew simple things.[13] As they grew older, many, especially those from well-to-do families, were taught fine hand sewing and embroidery at public and convent schools. Others were apprenticed to the local seamstress where they were taught pattern-making, cutting, basting, and sewing. This education was in keeping with the tradition that the woman, as a homemaker, should be able to make her own clothes and those of her family. Some of these girls would often become seamstresses themselves and would later take on their own apprentices. The *sarta* (seamstress) held a distinguished position in her village. The scissors that dangled at her waist were a symbol of her status.[14] Her skill and workmanship were greatly admired. The wealthy would visit her in her home for fittings, and she was often hired to work on a special piece for a dowry. This was one of the few ways women could earn money in southern Italy and Sicily and still remain in the home.

She was later sent to the home of a *sarta* who lived in the city. Here, she was taught, along with other girls, how to design, cut, and sew dresses, blouses, and coats. As she learned the trade, she helped the dressmaker fill orders for the rich *signore*, ladies, of the town who had their clothing custom made. Mrs. L. worked for five years as an apprentice. When she was fourteen, she began to stay at home and have her own girls whom she trained to be dressmakers. At the same time, she began to earn some money for the family by filling orders for outfits in her own home.[15]

Working outside of the home was looked down upon, especially in Sicily, and because few factories existed there, or in the *Mezzogiorno*, usually the only work women did outside of the home was crop harvesting. When women did work, they did not regard themselves as independent wage earners and their wages did not challenge their husbands' position as breadwinners.

Because of these and other socially sanctioned ideas, such as seclusion, chastity, and chaperonage, a girl was brought up close to the heart of the family. She was not allowed the attentions of any men except those of her fiancé. The honor and pride of the Italian man lay in the virtue of the women in his household. In the rare instances when a girl did transgress the norms set down by society, she was seldom forgiven by her family; even if she later married, she remained a marked woman for life. Because her destiny was marriage, education was not considered an important part of her preparation for the future. Until marriage, she was to do the housework and care for her younger brothers and sisters. By the time she was twelve years old, her childhood was ended, and she had to put away the things of a girl. As a young woman, she was considered useless, but her position changed when she married and became a mother. As a mother, she was placed on a pedestal and considered almost holy. "I obey my mother's word, which is like the word of God."[16]

All decisions were made by the mother when the father was at work or when he had immigrated to the United States.[17] She handled all economic problems, disciplined the children, and even parceled out weekly allowances to her husband. In the father's presence, the mother assumed a subservient position, yet still maintained enormous power by the threat of emotional outbursts. In effect, it was the mother who kept the family united. An old proverb said, "If the father should die, the family would suffer; if the mother should die, the family ceases to exist."[18]

Respect for the family and the protection of the family honor were cherished values in southern Italian and Sicilian society. To lose this honor usually meant loss of face in the community. The children were taught that membership in the family carried with it work and duty. They were looked upon as economic assets: *"Dal numero delle braccia di una famiglia depende la prosperita della medesima...*" (A family's wealth depends upon the number of hands it has).[19] The well-mannered and respectful child was considered a good child, and there was little connection between the desire for a good child and the desire for the education of one's children. Respect took highest priority; according to tradition, "He who does not respect his parents comes to a bad end."[20] There was also a strong bond between brothers and sisters: "*Frate e sore, core e core*"[21] (Brother and sister, heart and heart). Conflicts between children and parents were rare and, when they did occur, they were usually considered family business: "*Lite tra padre e figlio, non ci vuole consiglio.*" (Advice is not needed for quarrels between father and son).[22] Marriage was considered a binding contract until death, and marital fidelity was expected of the wife as a matter of duty, not choice. Its violation was a very serious offense against the family's honor. Other violations to the family's honor included illegitimacy, sterility, sexual impotency, lack of a dowry, unpaid debts, or a prison sentence. They were equally important to the rich and the poor. The men of southern Italian society tended to be more tradition bound because tradition supported their position of superiority. The women, on the other hand, were more willing to accept new ideas and social change. They were easily organized into voluntary associations, particularly church-centered groups, but for the men, no value existed in belonging to such groups.

Knowledge of the basic values and traditions of southern Italian society help in understanding the culture transplanted to the United States by the immigrants who came during the years of the great migration. Many studies have dealt with the problems faced by the immigrant Italian family when it came into contact with the American way of life. Oscar Handlin, one of the first to describe the immigrant experience, put forward the thesis that immigration from peasant to industrial society resulted in family stress. A similar conclusion was reached by Leonard Covello when he stated that "the family pattern, that is its social basis, is, for all practical purposes, one of the main sources of maladjustment in the American milieu."[23] More recent studies have supported very different conclusions. Virginia Yans McLaughlin bases her thesis on the theory that modernity and tradition are not dichotomous, but rather dialectical in nature. She suggests that the traditional family was therefore able to transform itself when it came into contact with an industrial society. "Far from discarding old family patterns, these immigrants found ways of maintaining them."[24] It follows that the Italian woman, despite restrictions placed on her by traditional values, was able over time to adapt herself to an industrial society. In fact, her improved status in American society depended on her improved position in American industry. The latter was made possible for her, as well as for all other women, by the rise of unionism in American labor.

The functioning of the American economy between 1900 and the outbreak of World War I was determined by the policy of laissez faire, or the completely unregulated operation of the market place. Given complete freedom, industrialists of the time were able to increase production enormously. This was often done at the expense of workers, whose needs were disregarded and who became the victims of gross exploitation. The years 1900 to 1909 also witnessed the highest increases in immigration to the United States.[25] The immigrants provided the unskilled and cheap labor force needed in the expanding economy. This period also saw the first major increases in union membership. In 1898 there were only half-a-million union members in the United States. By 1903 there were nearly two million.[26]

Although these figures represent rises chiefly in male membership, significant advances were made in the unionization of women workers. Outstanding was the establishment of the Women's Trade Union League in 1903.[27] It represented a great victory for women in American labor history, and its activities were to become vital in ending the many unfair practices that existed particularly where women workers were concerned. This critical period in the American labor movement was, in a sense, aggravated by the arrival of large number of immigrants. Labor greatly opposed immigration of all kinds because of the belief that the new immigrants negated the achievements of unionism. Because of discrimination in American industry, immigrants were forced by necessity to take the hardest and poorest paid jobs. Industries took advantage of this situation to advance their own interests. In New York City, for example, the garment industry expanded tremendously because of the availability of cheap immigrant labor. Its labor force was characterized by a steady displacement of old ethnic groups by new or recent immigrants. This displacement occurred not because of the superior skills of the new immigrants, but because new immigrants were willing to accept lower wages than those who had been in America longer. It was estimated that 10,000 immigrants were absorbed into the garment industry each year.[28] It therefore became a distinct 'immigrant industry'. It was also a large employer of women workers. Of 29,439 workers in dress and waist shops in 1913, 24,128 were women and 4,711 were men. This was a ratio of five to one, or eighty-four percent.[29] One-half of these workers were girls in their teens.[30] Ethnically, three-fifths of the workers were Jewish; the second largest group was Italian.[31] The nature of this industry also lent itself to the exploitation of its workers:

> Five elements, homework, the sweating system, the contract and subcontract systems, increasing the number of middlemen between producer and consumer, the exaggerated overstrain due to piece payment, and the fact that the clothing trades have served as the general dumping ground of the unskilled, inefficient, and casual women workers, have produced from the very beginning of the wholesale clothing manufacture in this country a condition of deplorable industrial chaos.[32]

Immigrant women in this industry were faced with two handicaps: they were immigrants and they were women.

It was against this background that Italian women were immigrating to the United States in the hope of securing a better life for themselves and their families. New York offered enormous work opportunities that would not have been available to them in Italy. Although the wages were probably the lowest paid to any group of women,[33] they considered themselves lucky to be working at all. They worked for a variety of reasons. They often carried full responsibility for supporting the family when their husbands were unemployed, which was quite common because many types of work engaged in by immigrant Italian men were of a seasonal nature. Even when husbands were working, their wives labored to supplement their low wages. The women's great desire to save money also encouraged them to find work. Consequently, the Immigration Commission found that wives of southern Italian men were more likely to be gainfully employed than any other.[34] Women who entered the various trades proved to be industrious and deft, and, as a Rochester manufacturer observed, "They are as cheap as children and a little better."[35] These workers found positions in industries such as candy, tobacco, artificial flowers, willow plumes, and paper box manufacturing, and, of course, in the garment industry.

During this era New York was the national center of the garment industry. In 1909 the city manufactured 69.3 percent of all women's clothing in the United States, and 38.4 percent of men's clothing.[36] Because of their training in Italy, most Italian women were immediately attracted to this industry. The nature of the work was in keeping with traditional ideas of the woman as the homemaker. Many young Italian girls were willing to learn this trade in the same way that they had been willing to be apprenticed to a seamstress in Italy, that is, in the hope of being able to use the skill in their future role as wife and mother. In her study of Italian women in industry, Louise Odencrantz found that eighty percent of a group of sixty-five women who had worked at some form of sewing in Italy were in the needletrades in the United States.[37] Studies by the Immigration Commission show that 90.9 percent of southern Italian women who worked in lace-making, embroidery, and sewing in Italy were in the needletrades in the United States.[38] For many of these young girls, whose rearing had been so sheltered within the family, being able to work in a factory was itself a concession to American conventions and, in most cases, the factory was certain to be near their home. It was not uncommon for these girls to be chaperoned to the factory in the morning and picked up in the evening by a male member of the family. The following is an example of transplanted traditional values in an industrial society:

> Mrs. M. went to work in a small embroidery and bead shop owned by the Fasanelli sisters, two immigrant Sicilian girls. They, in turn, worked for a large company, Brody Inc. Their job was to get dresses and other goods from the company, take them to their shop to do the beading, and then return them to the company. However, the girls were so strictly guarded by their family that they were not allowed to go to the shop by themselves. Someone had to chaperone them. When Mrs. M. came to work for them, they immediately saw that she was not experienced in doing the work. However, they agreed to take her on if she would act as their chaperone. Before they could seal the bargain, Mrs. M. was invited to the girls' home—their parents had to give consent and approval. Afterwards, they went to a bank in Chinatown where their brother worked—he also had to give his approval.[39]

Both the subdivision of labor in the garment industry and the existence of the contracting system lent themselves to the persistance of industrial homework. Large numbers of contractors sublet their work to small groups or families which had one room or more in the tenements. Large tenement areas in New York afforded exceptionally inviting conditions for homework in this industry, as well as in other trades. Homework was largely in the hands of older married women because young girls with no family responsibilities found work in factories much more profitable.[40] This type of work was dominated by the Italians. Government surveys in 1910 show that ninety-eight percent of all homework was done by the Italians.[41] Similarly, a Russell Sage Foundation study in 1910 found that almost all of the 110 families surveyed in this type of homework were Italian.[42] In the garment industry, the principle type of homework was "finishing," or hand sewing, required to complete the garment after the operating and the basting had been done. This consisted of felling the lining to the cloth of the garment where it was not already done so by the machine. Of the families investigated by the United States Department of Labor in 1916, 45.8 percent of the home finishers were Italians; the next largest group was the "Hebrews" who made up 17.2 percent of the finishers.[43] They were largely recent immigrants: 2,104 workers were foreign-born of foreign parents; 100 were native-born of foreign parents; and only 70 were native-born of native parents.[44] Italian women were inclined to take work home for two reasons: first, it was in keeping with the traditional Italian idea that the woman's place was in the home; and second, because Italians showed the largest proportion of married females, they had family responsibilities that prevented them from working in factories.[45] Often, all the children in the family would help their mothers with homework.

> When she was thirteen years old, she started to work. Her first job was to put ribbons on undergarments. At this time, she remembers, her mother would take in homework from the factory. All the children from the youngest to the oldest would work at this as much as they could to bring in extra money for the family. Their job was to put ribbons and buttons on ladies' corsets. Each corset had five buttons and one ribbon to be attached. They had to make one dozen of these corsets for six cents. Sometimes each child in the family would make two dozen corsets each before they went to school in the morning.[46]

It is clear how the evils of child labor were increased by this practice.[47] Homework also helped to retard unionism in the garment industry. As the scholar Edwin Fenton stated, "The major significance of the contracting system for the history of the Italians in the garment unions is that it was a deterrent to unionization among the Jews on which the organization of the Italians depended."[48]

What steps toward unionization of the garment industry were being taken at this time and what role did Italian women have in its development? In 1900 the International Ladies Garment Workers Union (ILGWU) was established. However, the industry did not receive the impetus toward unionization until the so-called "Uprising of the 20,000" among the shirtwaist makers of New York in 1909.[49] For the first time, the strike brought to public attention the intolerable conditions that existed in sweatshops. As one woman worker described,

> The shop was small and dingy. There were three windows on either side of the building. We were forced to work the whole day by electric light. The front part of the shop was used as the office; on the other side stood the cutting tables, and the operators, finishers, and pressers were crowded in the middle of the shop. This meant there was not a bit of sunshine nor air during ten hours at work daily. (This was in 1909, when we worked fifty-nine hours a week in the dress industry.) I do not care to describe the impression that the old sweatshop made on children of that age.[50]

Working hours were from 8:00 A.M. to 6:00 P.M. on weekdays and 8:00 A.M. to 5:00 P.M. on Saturdays. The "learners," who made up twenty to twenty-five percent of the shop work force were the most exploited. They earned three to four dollars a week, or sometimes six dollars. The regular workers earned seven to twelve dollars a week, or sometimes fifteen to eighteen dollars.[51] These conditions finally culminated in a strike against the major shirtwaist companies in New York City. The strike was the largest women's strike in the United States.[52] It began on November 22, 1909, and ended on February 12, 1910.

The real test of the strikers was their willingness to picket. Many strikers were looked down upon at the time for their seemingly unladylike behavior. Many were subjected to ridicule, as in the case of one striker:

> I shall never forget the bitterness and suffering of that my first strike! I had to be on the picket line to encourage and oversee the others. As we walked up and down, men and women would go into the restaurant, and as they passed us they offered insult after insult until we wanted to scream and strike someone. But we always had to be careful, for there was the law to protect the employer ... [53]

Many women, humiliated by this treatment, saw it as an excuse for not joining union activities. Traditional ideas of a woman's place were reflected in this employee's argument:

> No lady ever belongs to a union. I am a lady. I've always been a lady. You shall not stop me in the street and argue with me. I won't take

part in your street brawling. I know all about your union. I had a friend who belonged to it. She said the union never did her any good. It only took her money.[54]

The police and the law were also unsympathetic toward women on strike. From the outbreak of the strike to December 25, 1909, 723 women strikers were arrested; nineteen were sent to work-houses.[55] The attitude of the law was reflected by Magistrate Olmstead in sentencing a striker: "You are on strike against God and Nature, whose firm law is that man shall earn his bread in the sweat of his brow. You are on strike against God."[56]

Another problem faced by the union stemmed from the differences in language, habits, and culture of the Jewish, Italian, and American-born workers. Jewish women, who made up fifty-five percent of the workers, were optimistic, self-confident, and very active. They tended to look upon Italian girls as dominated by their families and therefore unorganizable. In the strike Italian women played a significant role, not as strikers, but as strikebreakers. "Scabs" not only returned to work while the strike was on, but were encouraged by their families to take the place of girls on strike. Several explanations can be found for this situation. Basically, the traditional position of women in Italian society required that they be obedient and submissive. This attitude, fostered in the home, was reinforced, in many cases, by priests in the community who wielded enormous power. An incidence of this was reported by an Italian girl interviewed by the *New York Call*. According to the reporter, "the priests tell them not to strike but to obey the boss."[57] How then could these young women revolt against all that they had been taught. Their families, of agrarian, peasant origins, were fatalistic in outlook. Even if they felt themselves exploited, they did not have confidence in their ability to change the social order. Coupled with this was the fact that many girls actually earned more than their fathers. How could their fathers be convinced in these cases that their daughters really were being exploited.

The union was also unprepared to deal with this problem. It lacked trained Italian officials who could communicate with girls in their own language. Unions at the time were very inexperienced and there was much internal fighting over various issues. The Industrial Workers of the World (IWW), for example, clashed bitterly with the American Federation of Labor (AFL) in the general effort to organize garment workers. To young girls unaccustomed to union activities, these factional conflicts proved very confusing. The Italian community also failed to encourage or to educate them in these activities, and finally, their "scabbing" became one of the major reasons for calling off the strike.

Recognizing the need for education, the United Hebrew Trades Waistmakers local asked the Women's Trade Union League to take charge of an education program. Arturo Caroti, who had been active along with Salvatore Ninfo in the organization of Italian women in 1909, was put in charge. Caroti concentrated on reaching those most ignorant of trade union activities, in other words, those who were potential scabs. During one year he visited 1,200 families. He formed the Italian Mutual Benefit Association in 1910, which gave girls medical care, but required that they attend monthly meetings.

He also formed the Italian Girls Industrial League, which enlisted fifty girls whom Caroti hoped to educate in trade unionism. They were brought together at first by social events and entertainment. Both these organizations were based on the mutual aid society, which began in northern Italy, and they later developed into unions. Caroti believed that creating a spirit of cooperation among the girls would be a binding force for later union activities. However, Caroti found that, after several serious talks on trade unionism, so many girls dropped out that the project was abandoned. Again, union organizers had failed to realize that they were dealing with the daughters of southern Italian farmers and peasants who accepted a subordinate position in society. The unions that had been successful in Italy were established in northern provinces, and were composed of men and dominated by radicals.

Significant advances, however, had already been made in the unionization of Italian women simply by recognizing the needs of this particular group. In 1913, Local 25, the waistmakers local of the ILGWU, created an Italian branch which would be the embryo of the future Local 89, the Italian Dressmakers local, which is still in existence today. It also established the union newspaper, *L'Operaia*, which was especially geared to the education of Italian women workers.[58] In 1915 Luigi Antonini, managing editor of *L'Operaia*, was elected to the executive board of the local. He did much to organize the Italian women, especially those who immigrated during the war years.

In examining the events of these years, it has become evident that two factors were responsible for the degree to which Italian women devoted themselves to the cause of unionism during strikes and other labor activities. One factor was the degree to which Italian men and the Italian community supported the cause of unionism; it was of paramount importance because the Italian woman most often acted in conjunction with her immediate family unit and with the approval and sanction of her community. Without this support and approval, it would have been virtually impossible for Italian women as a group to play any role in the radical activities unionism entailed.

Another factor which was to be important to the ability of Italian women to organize was the extent to which women workers were successful in their fight for better working conditions and better wages. Agitation by women workers throughout the nation brought to the attention of the public the intolerable conditions that existed in the industry. This, in turn, awakened in Italian women the realization that they were being exploited. Success on the part of these women workers inspired Italian women and gave them the confidence they needed to achieve similar goals. Women like Rose Schneiderman, Pauline Newman, Josephine Casey, and others did their part to encourage these aspirations among all women.

Between the years 1909 and 1913, several events occurred that had a pronounced effect on the attitudes of men and women workers toward unionism. The successful 1910 cloakmakers' strike created a solidarity between Italian men and women workers for the first time. It also united various ethnic groups within the industry against a common enemy. Strikers were viewed favorably by the Italian ethnic community. A nucleus of organized Italian workers, formed during the strike, was later responsible for educating the Italian workers and enlisting them in union activities. Most of the major activists of the time were socialists. Their militant activities were to dispel once and for all the belief that Italian immigrants were apathetic and docile. The socialists also played a vital role in helping the Italian community to understand the importance of militant trade unionism among all workers, men and women alike.

No amount of talk, however, would be as effective as a lesson learned by the workers themselves, the hard way. This lesson came in the form of the tragic Triangle Shirtwaist Company fire in 1911. This disaster, which took the lives of 145 young girls, was to be a turning point in the evolution of improved work conditions. The event shook the national conscience and made women workers realize that they had to fight back, not only for their own future, but also for the vindication of those who had lost their lives in the fire.

In the following year, 1912, the lesson was reinforced in Lawrence, Massachusetts. The Lawrence strike cut across all barriers (sex, race, religion, nationality, and language) that might divide people. It created a spirit of solidarity among workers never before seen. Women fought side-by-side with men to protect their homes and their families. News of this great struggle spread to all corners of the United States and even to Italy. The Italian communities manifested a spirit of solidarity which negated their strong provincialism. They had, at last, truly become "Italians."

It was not surprising, therefore, that 1913 saw the eruption of a strike which would involve 200,000 workers and paralyze four sectors of the garment industry. It was an event of importance in the history of unionism among Italian women in that it saw the rise and spread of militantism among them. Women had finally proved themselves strong in a time of crisis. They were organized along with men into Local 25 of the ILGWU. In the years following the strike, this local was to provide the education and the extended organization needed among new entrants into the industry. World War I would also make permanent industrial gains possible for women, as the war years saw a massive increase in union membership, both in the ILGWU and in the Amalgamated Clothing Workers of America. Women began to take their jobs and their unions more seriously; consequently, those who were inexperienced in labor agitation in 1909 became seasoned unionists by 1918.

Several other factors were instrumental in the unionization of Italian women. The establishment of Local 48, though consisting predominantly of men, was a necessary forerunner in the establishment of similar locals of mostly female membership. The development of such "language" locals also solved the problem of reaching the newly arrived Italian immigrants who entered the industry.

Because of all these factors, Italian men and women were confident of their ability to strike effectively, and most importantly, by 1918 they had the full support of the Italian community. The unions' consistent efforts at education paid off in 1919. An overwhelming majority of Italian women and girls joined the ranks of those who went on strike in that year. As reported by Edwin Fenton, "Some of these proved to be exceedingly energetic and bellicose, as the police rolls showed."[59] The newspapers were greatly in favor of the strikers and discouraged scabbing. As expressed by Arturo Giovannitti, the ability of Italian women to become faithful union members was a rough estimate of their adjustment to American society.[60] If this was so, then Italian women had certainly taken great steps toward this by 1919.

During the strike, Italian women distinguished themselves on picket lines, at strikers' meetings, and on organizational committees. According to Julius Hochman, manager of the New York Dressmakers Joint Board, "...not only did the women and the Italians especially respond to the strike, but they proved themselves capable of carrying on great and glorious battles when it was necessary, and remained true and loyal members of our union in time of peace."[61] Newspapers reported incident after incident in which Italian women proved themselves courageous in fighting for what they truly believed. In other words, they were no longer fighting for "bread" alone; they were fighting for ideals as well: "We need bread, and roses too!" *"Pane e Rose"* (Bread and Roses), became the motto of the striking women, and later of the infant Local 89. "If you have two loaves of bread sell one and buy a flower because the soul also hungers." The same idea was conveyed in the theme song written for Local 89 by Arturo Giovannitti:

All the races of the earth,
March and fight and hope with us.
Come! Let us sew a banner,
of human unity.

Come friends, March on! March on!
If we are guided by unity,
Bread and Roses, laughter and song,
Tomorrow will bring us.[62]

It was in this spirit that a charter for an independent local was at last granted to the Italian dressmakers on November 11, 1919. The local took the number "89" in commemoration of the French Revolution. In the words of Luigi Antonini, its first general secretary,

That birth was an act of faith ... faith in progressive trade unionism and faith in the supreme ideals of humanity.... At the beginning we were a few, just a patrol. Our strength was not in our numbers. It was in our hearts which cried out for Justice and Freedom.[63]

Among members of the first administration of Local 89 were several women who had shown particularly outstanding abilities during the strike. Among them were Laura Di Gulielmo, Anna

Fama, and Mary Bambace, all operators in their shops; Lina Ma-
netta, a draper; Angelina Limanti and Maria Prestianni, finishers;
Anna Squillante, a hemstitcher; and Millie Tirreno, an examiner.[64]
They all continued to work in their shops and still found time
before or after work to devote themselves to union activities. They
were perhaps the earliest pioneers and forerunners of those Italian
women who rose to hold positions of leadership in the locals'
administration. On January 1, 1920, Local 89 was established at 8
West 21st Street, where it remained for many years. In May of that
same year, it was able to report to the Chicago Convention of the
ILGWU an increase of 1,500 new members.[65] By 1934 it was to
become the single largest language local in the United States, with
a membership of over 40,000 workers.[66]

Notes

1. See Rosalyn Baxandall, Linda Gordon, Susan Reverby, ed., *America's Working Women: A Documentary History* (New York, 1976).
2. Robert Foerster, *The Italian Emigration of Our Times* (Cambridge, 1919), 43.
3. *Mezzogirono* refers to the regions of southern Italy.
4. Interview with Tina Gaeta, price adjuster and business agent for the International Ladies Garment Workers Union, New York City.
5. Milton Gordon, *Assimilation in American Life* (New York, 1964), 134-35.
6. Foerster, 95.
7. Giovanni Verga, *The House by the Medlar Tree* (New York, 1955), 201.
8. Lydio F. Tomasi, *The Italian American Family* (New York, 1972), 15.
9. Virginia Yans McLaughlin, "A Flexible Tradition: Immigrant Families Confront New Work Experiences," *Journal of Social History*, 7 (Summer, 1974): 432.
10. See Edward Banfield, *The Moral Basis of a Backward Society* (Glenco, Illinois, 1958), 183, for a listing of items included in a typical Italian trousseau.
11. Verga, 2.
12. Donald Pitkin, "Marital Property Considerations Among Peasants: An Italian Example," *Anthropology Quarterly*, 33 (January, 1960): 36.
13. Interview with Mrs. D., Greenwich House, New York City.
14. Interview, Tina Gaeta.
15. Interview, Mrs. Anna LaReddola, ILGWU, retired, New York City.
16. R. E. Park and H. A. Miller, *Old World Traits Transplanted* (New York, 1921), 10.
17. Miriam Cohen, "Italian-American Women in New York City, 1900-1950," in Milton Cantor, ed., *Class, Sex, and the Woman Worker* (New York, 1977), 3.

18. Leonard W. Moss and Walter H. Thomson, "The South Italian Family: Literature and Observation," *Human Organization*, 18 (Spring, 1959): 38.
19. Yans McLaughlin, 433.
20. Moss and Thomson, 39.
21. Carlo Levi, *Christ Stopped at Eboli* (Torino, 1956), 81-82.
22. Carlo Levi, *Words Are Stone* (New York, 1958), 208.
23. Leonard Covello, *The Social Background of the Italo-American School Child* (Leiden, 1967), 402.
24. Yans McLaughlin, 449.
25. Louise Pearson Mitchell, "100 Years of Women in the Workforce," in *Trade Union Women's Studies* (Ithaca, 1975), 3.
26. Mitchell, "Women in the Workforce," 3:5.
27. "There Once was a Union Maid," *Clarion*, March 28, 1974, I.
28. U.S. Department of Labor, Bureau of Labor Statistics, *Conciliation, Arbitration, and Sanitation in the Cloak, Suit, and Skirt Industry in New York City*, prepared by Charles H. Winslow, Bulletin No. 98 (Washington, 1912), 204.
29. U.S. Department of Labor, Bureau of Labor Statistics, *Wages and Regularity of Employment and Standardization of Piece Rates in the Dress and Waist Industry: New York City* Bulletin No. 146 (Washington, 1914), 8.
30. U.S. Department of Labor, Bureau of Labor Statistics, *Special Report of the Joint Board of Sanitary Control* Bulletin No. 145 (Washington, 1914), 7 (see Table VI).
31. Harry Best, "The Extent of Organization in the Women's Garment Making Industries of New York," *American Economic Review*, 9 (December, 1919): 780.
32. U.S. Department of Labor, Bureau of Labor Statistics, *Summary of the Report on the Condition of Woman and Child Wage Earners in the U.S.* Bulletin No. 175 (Washington, 1916), 294.
33. Foerster, 381.
34. Ibid., 380.
35. U.S. Department of Labor, Bureau of Labor Statistics, *Woman and Child Wage Earners in The United States*, 19 vols. (Washington, 1910-11), 305.
36. Louise Odencrantz, *Italian Women in Industry* (New York, 1919), 38,
37. Ibid., 40.
38. U.S., Congress, Senate, *Reports of the Immigration Commission, Immigrants in Industries*, pt. 6, "Clothing Manufacturing," 61st Congress, 2nd Session, 1911, 376.
39. Interview, Mrs. Morandini, retired member of the ILGWU, New York City.
40. *Summary of the Report on the Condition of Woman and Child Wage Earners in the United States*, 98.
41. Francesco Cordasco and Eugene Bucchioni, eds., *The Italians: Social Backgrounds of An American Group* (Clifton, 1974), 414.
42. Ibid.
43. *Summary of the Report on the Condition of Woman and Child Wage Earners in the United States*, 103.

44. Ibid.
45. Ibid., 87.
46. Interview with Mrs. R., Greenwich House, New York.
47. Lazare Teper and Nathan Weinberg, "Aspects of Industrial Homework in Apparel Trades," ILGWU Research Departmental Report (July, 1941), 22.
48. Edwin Fenton, *Immigrants and Unions: A Case Study: Italians and American Labor, 1870-1920* (New York, 1975), 469.
49. Louis Levine, *The Ladies Garment Workers*, 144.
50. Andria T. Hourwich and Gladys L. Palmer, *I Am A Woman Worker: A Scrapbook of Autobiographies* (New York, 1936), III.
51. Joel Seidman, *The Needles Trade*, 102.
52. Of the strikers, eighty percent were women and seventy-five percent were between the ages of sixteen and twenty-five. See Levine, 146.
53. Hourwich and Palmer, 106.
54. *Justice*, 1 (April 19, 1919), 2.
55. Levine, 144.
56. Ibid., 159. See also the *New York Call*, January 6, 1909, 1; Interview with Pauline Newman, retired organizer for the ILGWU and activist in the 1909 strike.
57. The *New York Call*, December 15, 1909, 1.
58. Vanni Montana, Will Herberg, Harry Crone, Bernard Seaman, and Kate Joseph, "We the Italian Dress and Waist Makers Speak," ILGWU, Local 89.
59. Fenton, 526.
60. Arturo Giovannitti was a socialist and a poet devoted to fighting for the liberation of all workers and particularly the Italian worker.
61. Julius Hochman, "Hail Local 89!" *Local 89, Fifteenth Anniversary Commemorative Pamphlet*, 1934, p. 19, Tamiment Collection, New York University, New York City.
62. See Local 89 Folder, ILGWU, Tamiment Collection, New York University, New York City.
63. *Thirtieth Anniversary and Testimonial to Luigi Antonini*, 1949, p. 2, Tamiment Collection, New York University, New York City.
64. "Amministrazione dell'Unione delle Sartine Italiane, No. 89," ILGWU: *Guistizia*, December 6, 1919, 2.
65. Serafino Romualdi, "Storia Della Locale 89," *Local 89, Fifteenth Anniversary Commemorative Pamphlet*, 1934, p. 40, Tamiment Collection, New York University, New York City.
66. *Fifteenth Anniversary Commemorative Pamphlet*, p. 19.

Angela Bambace and the International Ladies Garment Workers Union: the Search for an Elusive Activist

Jean A. Scarpaci

On April 3, 1975, the regular and labor press received news of Angela Bambace's death. Their printed obituaries attempted to do justice to her long and interesting career as a labor activist, a union officer, and a community leader. They highlighted her work experience starting in 1917 as a shirtwaist maker and ending in 1972 as a retired vice-president of the International Ladies Garment Workers Union (ILGWU). But none of the accounts did justice to the richness and depth of her life. Apparently the journalists could find little in the way of sources to fill in more than the vital statistics.

With Angela Bambace's death, her place in history was almost obliterated. Throughout her life she kept no diaries, maintained little personal correspondence, and conducted her public life in an ad hoc spontaneous manner. None of the obituaries could properly describe the character of this woman and activist, whose commitment to labor politics always co-existed with strong ethnic and family identity, and an awareness of femininity.

I met Angela Bambace in October, 1974. She was terminally ill, yet still able to radiate the energy and political commitment that had dominated her life. Fragments of Bambace's life were revealed to me during interviews with her, with her family, and with her surviving colleagues. What emerged was the picture of a woman at once feminine and militant, a woman whose life shed light on the history of immigration, the Italian left, and the labor movement. The following sketch of Bambace's life is intended less as a history of the union and more as a chance to glimpse how one woman's career was affected by a number of socio-ethnic problems.

Like the obituary writers, my major hurdle is one of sources. Bambace was an activist, a doer, and a talker, not a writer. She spoke forcefully but extemporaneously at meetings and on picket lines. She lived history with little eye to the future historical record. An active organizer, rather than an intellectual, she did not rate the attention of the labor or ethnic press. Union records of

Local 89, or later, of the Maryland-Virginia Department of the ILGWU (the latter became the Maryland District in 1942, then the Upper South Department in 1952), the organizations she headed, dealt mainly with day-to-day problems. The records do not cover the early period of her tenure from 1934 to 1940, and are confined to the official everyday business of the Upper South Department from 1940 to the present.

This account of her life relies heavily then on oral testimony, on conversations with Angela Bambace, her friends, and her relatives. Such sources obviously include only those who have survived, and so important opinions like those of her husband, Romolo Camponeschi, will never be recorded. Her friend and companion, the Italian American anarchist, Luigi Quintilliano, her associates from ihe Italian anti-fascist and labor movement, Carlo Tresca, Luigi Antonini, and Frank Bellanca, knew her well but left almost no account of their shared struggle.

Although the problem of sources may constitute a serious obstacle for the historian, the effort to reconstruct the life of an important woman labor leader without the "proper" source materials can easily be justified. First of all, we can establish the significance of Bambace's career from labor organizer to union vice-president. She was chief female officer of a union whose membership was at least eighty percent female. She was the only Italian American woman to reach such high office in the union's history; only three vice-presidents, Fannia Cohen, Molly Friedman, and Rose Pesotta, were elected before her. Angela Bambace knew who she was. Her politics and personal life, her sense of ethnic identity, her world view influenced others within and outside of the union.

How much of her life reflected her Italian immigrant origins? How much Italian American sentiment surfaced in her life and career? Should we see Bambace's career as the story of one of the union elite or as that of a woman who nurtured her ties with family, old rank-and-file colleagues, and her ethnic group? What were the problems she encountered in her rise to prominence and how did she deal with them? What follows is therefore an attempt to reconcile and explain the private and public world of a labor leader.

Angela Bambace was born in Santos, Brazil, in 1898. Her father, Antonio Bambace, had emigrated to Brazil from Cannitello in Calabria. He had served in the Italian merchant marine and, in Santos, owned a small fishing fleet. Antonio was at least fifteen to twenty years older than Angela's mother, Guiseppina Calabrese, who had immigrated to Brazil with her widowed mother from Leonforte, Sicily. Because of ill health, Antonio returned to Italy with his family, and his business in Brazil floundered without him. The Calabrian hills did not improve his health, and so the family emigrated once again, this time to North America. Settling in Portchester, New York, Mr. Bambace could find no work, so he returned to Italy, sending small amounts of money to his wife and two daughters in America. The family lived mostly on credit until his return.[1] The reunited family then moved to East Harlem. (They lived at 158 E. 103rd Street.) The father's continued frailty forced Angela's mother to take in sewing and eventually to join the factory work force, trimming plumes for ladies hats.[2]

As soon as Angela Bambace finished school in East Harlem in 1916, she went to work in a laundry as a bookkeeper and clerk. At eighteen, she and her younger sister Maria began to work in a shirtwaist factory as operators. Both joined efforts to organize the workers in the East Harlem shops. The young women attended meetings sponsored by Italian socialists and anarchists. At one such meeting Maria met Antonino Capraro, an organizer for the Industrial Workers of the World (IWW) and a fervent anarchist, whom she later married.[3]

Organizing for the International Ladies Garment Workers Union took more than strong commitment in the early days of the labor movement. Manufacturers often hired thugs to harass the young women who picketed their shops. Guiseppina Bambace not only allowed her daughters to attend union meetings and take an active role in organizing, she also accompanied them on some of their union rounds. She would bring a rolling pin with her and stand by her daughters,—and her instinct for social justice was more than maternal. Her daughter Maria recalled one occasion when a manufacturer went to an "enforcer" named Gagliano, who had "boys" working for him assigned to beat up women pickets.

When my mother heard that a young Jewish woman had been beaten up she went to this man and said, "Do you know what happened to-day in such-and-such a shop?" Mr. Gagliano replied, "What happened signora? Your daughters weren't hurt, were they?" He had respect for her, and her daughters were not to be harmed according to him. My mother said, "Not my daughters, but another mother's daughter was. So what difference does that make?" Gagliano called off his boys from their strong arm tactics. Even though he was considered a racketeer he behaved in a considerate manner towards my mother.[4]

Both Angela and Maria Bambace furthered the organizing efforts of the ILGWU in East Harlem and were cited for their work in the successful 1919 strikes. Their ability to reach the Italian female workers was useful to the union, especially since much of the leadership doubted that Italian workers, especially women, could be recruited. The widescale support of the strike proved, according to Salvatore Amico, that "the wise and militant participation of Italians shows that the Italian element was not second to anyone when it was correctly and courageously guided in the struggle for a just cause." (my translation).[5]

Contemporary labor leaders viewed Italian unionist impulses somewhat differently. Julius Hochman noted that "for a long time prejudice, deep-seated prejudice, prevailed as to the possibility of organizing women and especially Italian workers."[6] Serafino Romualdi stated that the "Italian element was far distant from achieving class consciousness."[7] In 1918 the board of Local 25 referred to the Italians as "an inconvience" and classified them as organizationally inferior to blacks.[8] Even a leading Italian unionist like Luigi Antonini had reservations about Italians as potential unionists. In 1918 he discussed Italian tailors in the union newspaper *L'Operaia* as belonging to "two groups that represent the two labor extremes, vile and repugnant strikebreakers or notorious leftists who are immoderate, infantile, and unrealistic, committed to fantasies. In the middle of these extremes, [Antonini felt] that the moderate element of Italians, that middle in which resides virtue, was too small to express itself" (my translation).[9]

Despite the reservations of male labor leaders, in 1919 more than 10,000 Italian workers constituted part of the dressmakers' organization. "This was accomplished without backroom compromise but after a period of violent and salutary struggle" (my translation).[10] The Bambace sisters illustrated that combination of militance and clever activism that helped to carry the strike.

Their method of organizing was straightforward. They would talk to the strikebreakers. Angela tended to use more violent rhetoric than her sister. She once told Maria, "Don't talk to her [a strikebreaker], punch her in the nose." They would visit young women in their homes at night. They would try to convert the girls who did the more important section work because they could cripple the manufacturer. Often they directed their appeal toward the Italian father of the house. Once he was persuaded, then his daughters would be permitted to attend meetings. The Bambace sisters' Italian identity, plus their language ability, gave them an advantage over non-Italian organizers. Maria remembers that she and her sister entered homes where Jewish organizers had not been welcome.[11]

Yet Angela Bambace's career itself reflects some of the inconstancy of Italian militants, caught between their sense of family and union fraternity. In June, 1919, at age twenty-one, she suspended her union activism to marry Romolo Camponeschi, age twenty-seven, her father's choice as a suitor and husband. Camponeschi was a waiter, born in Rome, who had traditional attitudes about family life.

Their first son, Oscar, was born in August, 1920, and their second, Philip, in June, 1923. The family moved to Flushing where they purchased a home. Angela lived on one floor and her sister Maria's family lived on the other. All the children spoke Italian as their first language and the milieu was that of the struggling Italo-American lower-middle classes, not that of the labor struggle.[12] Bambace's brother-in-law, Antonino Capraro, reacted negatively to the "traditional" family routine. He demanded constant awareness of social matters and found the atmosphere in the household oppressive. Nino, in a letter to his wife Maria, ridiculed Angela's husband for allowing her to refuse to make breakfast for him. He went on to characterize Romolo's life-style, saying

> These people are unable to understand anything outside of questions concerning tomato sauce and hand made gnocchi ... they can't see that a person may have interest in matters of personal dignity on behalf of others and become sincerely indignant when noticing an infraction of the underlying principles of such matters.[13]

Bambace did not take well to staying at home and she chose to return to work about 1925. Her decision to return to work not only reflected her husband's inadequate income, but also her need to deal with the world beyond her kitchen.

Perhaps the most telling illustration of her husband's political incompatibility is in a letter he wrote to her in 1938, when their older son was to enter college. He explained that he was unable to finance Oscar's education but would try to give him five dollars a week. He then continued: "If I could afford to finance him myself you may rest assured I would not hesitate to." Then he reminded his former wife, "If you can recollect many years ago when I made the suggestion to save for the education of our children your answer was twenty years from now there will be a revolution."[14]

Not only did Bambace's return to work suggest a drifting apart from her husband, but also it represented a reaffirmation of her political ideas. In 1925 and 1926, ILGWU Locals 2, 9, and 22, dominated by Communists, attempted to take control of the union. She immediately gravitated to the radicals as she met Charles (Sasha) and Rose Zimmerman, who were prominent figures in the take-over attempt. In the shop she met Clara Larson, an anarchist from Ukraine who had married a Danish seaman member of the Industrial Workers of the World. Becoming more involved in the union's political turmoil, Bambace spent more time at meetings than at home. She attended the Communist Party gatherings with Sasha and participated in her separate faction (section) as well. When the Communist union faction called for a general strike, she followed. The 1926 strike involved the cloakmakers; Bambace was a dressmaker but she did picket duty with others who supported the movement.[15] Luigi Antonini, the most powerful Italian labor leader, opposed this revolutionary action; and although some Italians supported the general strike, they did not speak for their locals. Zimmerman recalled that Bambace's position made her persona non grata within the Italian rank and file, and she gravitated more to her Jewish friends.[16]

Branching into the wider world of union politics brought Bambace into a non-Italian world. Here for the first time, her closest acquaintances were non-Italian, and here for the first time she was active with non-Italian workers. Yet she was aware of Italian causes such as anti-fascism and the defense activity for Sacco and Vanzetti. At one meeting she met Luigi Quintilliano. He had emigrated to America from Rome in 1910. After 1915 he became an organizer for the IWW and, in 1920, he helped to found the Italian Defense Committee to protect Italian immigrants during the Palmer raids. He served as one of the defense witnesses in the Sacco and Vanzetti trial. When Bambace first met him he wrote for *Il Martello*, the newspaper of Carlo Tresca in Lawrence, Massachusetts.[17]

Bambace's life was changing in a number of ways. Her return to work brought her away from the "traditional role" of wife and mother. The break with her husband was complete, so their children moved in with Bambace's mother. This freed her to devote more time to her union activities.[18] Her decision to return to work meant not only wages for producing dresses at a machine, but also participation in union activities. The latter suggests a commitment to activism and the labor movement, rather than just to the cash nexus of employment.

Her renewed activism sprang partly from the political turmoil of the union. Bambace joined the Communist faction and the Party, not so much from ideological commitment as from belief in its effectiveness. She consciously followed the guidance of Sasha Zimmerman, a man she always referred to as her mentor. In recalling Bambace's style, Zimmerman described her as a very intelligent woman able to grasp the kernel of truth without having either an extensive formal education or much background reading. Her major strength, he believed, was her ability to absorb the ideas of others and apply them in a practical and logical manner. She asked questions, listened to lectures, and attended meetings of her section. She was a most effective speaker, emotional and eloquent. Therefore, her involvement in the Communist Party came not because of conversion but pragmatism. Her style was to pursue a cause actively.[19]

In this respect, Bambace's career confirms what scholars from Edwin Fenton to Paul Buhle have suggested about the rank-and-file, that is, that Italian American workers chose to follow ideologies that worked or promised success. When that ideology was radical, as in the days of the Lawrence and Paterson strikes or the mill strikes in Rhode Island, Italian workers flocked to the red banners.[20] In the 1919 East Harlem strike, the "unorganizable" Italian women rallied to the ILGWU. The workers and their leaders might be seen as opportunistic—testing the waters.

Because Bambace's activism removed her from traditional family roles and brought her in contact with many non-Italians, did it undermine her ethnicity? Clara Larson, who lived with Bambace in 1927 and 1928 and remained a life long friend, believed that she cared more about humanity, about the worker's cause, than about Italian-ness. Apparently, Bambace also recognized that overt ethnic identity impeded her career ambitions. As an Italian dressmaker she belonged to Local 89. She was well liked and admired by Antonini but, given the personal prejudices of Italian male unionists, she could not count on rising beyond business manager. It is in this aspect of her life, career ambition, that Bambace's connections with Jewish unionists proved helpful. This was especially true in her later career.[21]

Bambace, in these years, often brought her Jewish union friends together with her extended Italian family. She presided and her mother cooked.[22] The occasion of her son Oscar's seventh birthday is illustrative of this combination. On that day, August 23, 1927, there was no chance that there would be a normal party. Oscar remembers that the people at the house ignored him completely and all day long the phone rang constantly. It was the date of the execution of Sacco and Vanzetti. Luigi and Angela had worked for their reprieve, and all those gathered at the Bambace household shared bitter defeat at the failure of the Massachusetts governor to grant a stay of execution.[23]

Between 1927 and 1933, Bambace's life was filled with union work. Her organizing talents took her out of East Harlem to other areas of Manhattan, where she worked for the Amalgamated Clothing Workers of America (ACWA) strike in Elizabeth, New Jersey, in 1932 and the long bitter strike of the New York garment workers in 1933.[24] Bambace recalled the tactics of that period. They were rough and unpredictable. She would get a job in a shop in order to talk with the workers. When that was not possible, she sometimes resorted to "pulling the power"—turning off the main switch that provided power for the machines. This was a signal for all the workers to leave the shop and assemble outside or go to the union hall to talk about working conditions. Manufacturers considered this action a violation of their property rights, and their anger sometimes turned to physical violence to discourage organizing efforts. On one occasion Bambace was pushed down a flight of stairs by an employer. On other occasions she was arrested while picketing. She seemed to thrive on the excitement of the cause and to appreciate the recognition she gained with success. Another tactic was to stand outside of the shop and convince workers to come to the union hall for a meeting rather than go to work. Although her style was forceful and she expected to be arrested for her activity, she did have a normal abhorence of imprisonment. Once, when the union lawyers failed to appear to offer bail, she cried all night and worried about her mother who expected her home; the martyrdom of a night in jail was beyond her tolerance.[25]

Although most of her closest union colleagues were Jewish Americans, she also had ties with Italians and Italian Americans who were activists. A friend recalls Bambace mentioning an intimate relationship with the Italian Communist Vittorio Vidali (alias Enea Sormenti), who allegedly was the comintern agent sent from Italy in the twenties to take charge of the Italian branch of the Communist Workers party, and also with Vito Marcantonio, who incidentally defended her in her divorce and child custody case. Marcantonio was employed by Fiorello La Guardia's firm—Bambace also claimed that La Guardia had once proposed marriage to her. (He had served as legal counsel during the 1919 East Harlem strikes.)[26] During these critical years of activism, Bambace's husband used the evidence of her political activism and emotional involvements to deny her the custody of their children. He hired detectives who followed her, first to her political meetings, then to the apartments of friends in Manhattan who gave her a place to sleep.[27] Sasha and Rose Zimmerman remembered the pain Bambace suffered when she lost the custody suit. Legal separation was softened by the location of her mother's residence near the one owned by her former husband. Officially, the children were under their father's care but they went to their grandmother's after school. This pattern continued until Romolo accepted a "shared" situation.[28]

It is difficult to reconstruct Bambace's brand of politics because of the scanty sources. Probably the word that best describes her association with other activists is that of "fellow traveler." Although she attended and supported the causes of anti-fascism, communism, and syndicalism, she seemed to be attracted not by ideology, but by the practical application of these positions. She supported the Communist union factions in the 1925-26 confrontation. When that struggle failed and when her close friends were expelled from the party as Lovestonites, she left too. She then embraced unionism as a force to control the evils of capitalism. Like most of her friends, she decided that Franklin D. Roosevelt and his New Deal for the working man promised to realize their revolutionary goals through the welfare state.

Bambace's activism, ambition, and sense of herself as an Italian American woman and a female trade unionist combined to irritate Italian male union officials. They generally saw women in the labor movement as auxiliaries in the struggle for social justice. This sentiment was reflected in G. Artoni's pamphlet, *Lotte Unionistiche* (1935). He exhorted women to share the struggles of their husbands, fathers, and brothers. "To you we turn because you give them help in the sacred work of redemption, emancipation and progress. Support and encourage them with your serene and sturdy faith in the success of the cause of justice and truth" (my translation).[29]

To varying degrees the male domination of the ILGWU was an obstacle for women of all ethnic groups. Although the labor force remained overwhelmingly female, its leadership remained male and predominately Jewish. Alice Kessler Harris has discussed the difficulties faced by Jewish female organizers such as Fannia Cohen, Pauline Newman, and Rose Pesotta in gaining recognition from their male colleagues and their bitter struggle to advance within the union ranks.[30] Another factor slowing Bambace's rise was the fierce competition for positions in the union hierachy in Greater New York. More union offices went to Jews because of their greater numbers in the industry the union represented.

A friend and co-worker remembers Bambace's resentment that no woman served on the union Executive Board in the late thirties and early forties. Her anger arose from a sense of disenfranchisement and a belief that such prejudices worked against her chances of advancement in the union. Perhaps her anger was justified, but a number of male union leaders thought highly of her as a woman and as a unionist. It was probably they who encouraged Dubinsky to send her to Baltimore to lead a special effort to organize, coinciding with passage of the National Recovery Act.[31]

Although Bambace's involvement in the general strike activities of 1925 – 26 removed her further from her Italian union contacts, her decision to go to Baltimore would alter her life-style once again. She moved into a labor area where workers were native white or Jewish, where union supporters and contractors tended to be Jewish. But the city did have an active Italian union element in the Amalgamated Clothing Workers of America, led by her old friend Ulysess De Dominicis, who had served as a general organizer, along with her brother-in-law Antonino Capraro, for an ACWA local in Rochester, New York. Naturally though, her immediate contacts were with ILGWU officials and members.[32]

Bambace arrived on the Baltimore scene while management and labor manouevered into position. Her first major success involved organizing a group of women cloakmakers into Local 227. She was called to help found a cloakmakers' local because women received different wages from their unionized male co-workers, who did not want them to work in the trade nor to receive equal pay. The National Recovery Administration (NRA) had established wage and hour codes for the industries, but one worker recalled that these codes were violated, the presence of the union notwithstanding. So at the time when she arrived, resentment had turned into militancy. The revocation of the NRA sent a shock wave through organized labor, especially as some shops attempted to cut wages and increase hours despite NRA goals.[33] For example, in March 1936, a large non-union firm, S. Cohen and Sons, refused to recognize the newly established local, discharging two workers for union activity. This led to a walk-out, which lasted from March until August, when the firm officially granted recognition to the union. Another major victory was won in a long and bitter strike against the American Raincoat Company of Baltimore—one of the largest firms in the East.[34]

When the New York Dress Joint Board called for sanctions against the Roberts Dress Company of Baltimore for dealing with non-union shops, Bambace introduced the "big city" tactic of a "sit down" strike. Although the occupation of the factory forced the owners to comply with the union demands quickly, some workers found Bambace too willing to accept compromises and peaceful solutions to grievances.[35]

Bambace's temporary assignment to Baltimore developed into a permanent one. It removed her from the New York political orbit, separated her from her sons, and threw her into a new kind of labor market. Her organizing skills and success with women workers contributed to her record of achievement; thus, her Baltimore activity consolidated her position as a champion of labor, not merely a spokesperson for women. She herself saw her assignment as a way of advancing in the union hierarchy. She continued to complain to her friends that the ILGWU needed female representation on its executive council, where she believed that she would be an asset. One gathers that she felt this way because whe was a woman without power, not because she was particularly sympathetic with womens' issues. Her involvement with women did not convert her to feminism.

Bambace did not operate in a world of sexual politics, but followed the same rules that governed her contemporaries. None of the male leaders thought about helping others younger than themselves to advance. Trained by men who believed they would live forever, she behaved like them.[36]

Although she was far from New York, she maintained ties with her old union contacts. Her schedule included bi-monthly weekend visits to Flushing to be with her children. She continued her close relationship with Quintilliano who was now out of work; eventually he came to live with her. During these years, 1938–40, letters between Bambace and her children reflected a mutual respect, understanding, and love. They asked her to come home, they commented on their school activities, and they asked about Luigi.[37]

Her relationship with Luigi showed her traditionalist position on women's issues. Most of her Jewish friends described him as a "typical" Italian male—possessive, jealous, stormy. He was without work and dependent upon her, and he resented this arrangement, demanding her undivided attention. The Zimmermans described him as having a dual personality—a radical in social life but a "despotic" Italian male at home, who expected Bambace to assume the traditional role of "wife" and "servant." Friends speculated that their relationship depended upon sexual compatibility and the father image that Luigi filled for the children. They also suggested that the boys liked his traditional ways as an "Italian father."[38] Luigi followed his own code of behavior and separated his private life from his political one. Once when she teased her unmarried friend Edith about a sexual matter, Luigi told Bambace that her friend was behaving properly. He applied the same code of behavior when he discussed social practices with her sons.[39]

Luigi's unhappiness over his unemployment and the travel requirements of Bambace's work increased the tension in their relationship. She described these pressures in a letter to her sister Maria, dated November 4, 1939, Norfolk, Va.

> As usual—no time, no time. That's my cry always, and maybe it is my fault. Lack of system, no conception of timing, etc., etc. All making things much harder for me to get around. I am wondering what my boy friend Luigi has done about the job offered him. I hope. I hope. Of course it really is a mess of a life. He in a Newark furnished room, I in a two-by-four apartment, and my boys in a great big house. I can and will make it my business to be home every week . . . [40]

Maria and her husband attempted to intercede by calling upon Ulysses De Demincis, the Baltimore ACWA organizer, to help get employment for Luigi.[41]

Bambace's friends also described her relationship with Luigi as loving and intense. Even when he worked for a time as a ILGWU field representative in Maryland, West Virginia, and Virginia, between 1942 and 1943 (employed by the New York office), he was operating within the power orbit of the now manager of the Maryland-Virginia District—Angela Bambace. The combination of his need for separate recognition and economic self-sufficiency emerged in a letter she wrote to her son Philip, dated April 20, 1943.

> Last night we went to Washington, had dinner with some very important people. I mention this because we hope that Luke will land a job doing some propaganda work for the government on behalf of the Italian people. Luke [Luigi] made a hit with these Washington guys who are all working for Uncle Sam. He started narrating some of his famous anti-fascist stories each detail described fully with plenty of gesticulation and emotion and had them spellbound. He had the floor all evening. Well I hope this will land him a job. Of course you know that he was the centre of attraction and action in all of his tales.[42]

Bambace juggled her roles as union official, mother, and companion. The balancing act was just as trying for Luigi who, although he raged against his lack of meaningful employment, accepted some reversal of household roles. She described the situation in a letter to Philip, dated June, 1943. "I am getting more and more tangled up in my work. As the district expands I have more to reach out and adjust grievances and labor management becomes harder. Oscar is working hard. Luke prepares meals for us both and I'm working like a trooper."[43] Conflicts between home life and the union, between conventional family bonds and the camaraderie of the labor struggle, characterized most ethnic families involved in the unions. Angela and Luigi's relationship was affected in the same way a conventional marriage would have been. She knew it but attempted to balance her own career ambitions with the needs of her family.[44]

In 1944 Luigi returned to New York where he took over as manager of the Theatrical Costume Workers Local 124. (In 1958, Local 124 and the Alteration Workers Local 177 became part of Local 38.[45] Quintilliano remained as manager.) He continued to commute to Baltimore on weekends.

As Bambace became more involved with her work, her life was dominated by the union. With the help of her educational director Dora Kaufman (also a Lovestonite), she developed an active workers' education program which included classes in literature. Union officials in Washington often addressed these forums. It gave the Baltimore group a wider perspective, and it enabled hard core trade unionists to see the daily living problems confronting a membership largely made up of women homemakers. Much of Bambace's time was spent on the road and she relied on Dora to handle the routine paper work. By 1940 the Baltimore cloak market was completely organized and additional forays were made to cities of Harrisburg, York, Waynesboro, and Chambersburg, Pa. Bambace's travels paid off as union membership increased from 1,100 in 1942 to 6,500 in 1947.[46]

Her job was further complicated by the need to negotiate contracts with individual manufacturers each year. Without manufacturers' associations there were no industry-wide contracts. Some of the shops locating in the area were "run away," companies that moved to non-union small towns where they paid lower wages. To overcome some of the handicaps involved in organizing work, especially in a state like Virginia (where state law went beyond the Taft Hartley Act to forbid contracts that included union guaranteed job protection), District Manager Bambace's policy was to offer employers a no-strike clause, if they agreed to reciprocate with union shop clauses. When such contracts were rendered, union security was added by verbal agreement in Virginia and in writing in other states. This tactic and Bambace's general reluctance to use the strike weapon sometimes frustrated the rank and file, who assumed that Bambace yielded to the pressures of the manufacturers. She would promise significant improvements to the workers, then emerge from negotiations with minimum changes. Some believed she was not forceful enough.[47]

During these years she also engaged in other labor-related activities. She handed out leaflets on street corners and outside plants for her brothers in the steelworkers and maritime unions. She participated in political action to gain election and then re-election of state and federal officials who were supporters of organized labor. She inspired rank-and-file members to join her in this work. It is interesting that most of these women were native whites. Oral testimony indicates that the few Italian women members of the ILGWU did little more than pay their union dues. Bambace's activism and broad interests served then to attract and orient newcomers in the labor fold.[48]

Despite her success in expanding the Upper South Department, the International subsidized its operations. Dues' payments did not provide adequate operational funds, and Bambace recognized how this situation lessened her independence and prestige. In 1950 the district claimed thirty locals with a membership of 8,000. She calculated that only a membership of 10,000 would make the department self-sustaining.[49]

Bambace's New York orientation, her ethnic and political identity, did little to prepare her for the issues and problems of the Baltimore market and the Maryland-Virginia District. In this region, anti-unionist attitudes, traditional anti-semitism, and the race question compounded more traditional problems of internal conflict and political differences within the ILGWU. Her style in dealing with these matters was direct, forceful, and self-protective. As a union leader, she placed compromise and harmony above economic confrontation or warfare; she placed loyalty and subordination of staff above individualism; she dealt with the race question on a practical basis. The post-war years tested Bambace's ability to adjust to these issues. Aided by a staff reflecting a mixture of newly organized native whites and experienced union members, she continued to expand the region. At the same time she increased her involvement in community matters, ranging from political activities as a charter member of the Americans for Democratic Action and a supporter of Histadrut, the federation of Jewish labor, and the medical complex of the City of Hope. Family matters altered with Luigi's permanent departure for New York in 1952 and her purchase of a home in Baltimore with her son Philip and his family in 1954.

Bambace countered the problems of distance and isolation by keeping close contact with organizers and business agents in the field. Her letters to her staff included personal support and encouragement. She acknowledged the difficulties faced as the ILGWU moved into non-union areas, where the "local, civic, social, liberal and political leaders" were not favorable to the union.[50] She attempted to create a sense of identity within the labor movement by promoting rank-and-file participation in labor conferences. District funds were used to subsidize the expenses of delegates from small locals.[51]

ILGWU expansion into small southern communities with traditions of anti-unionism and suspicions of outsiders challenged Bambace's staff. She learned how union elections could be undermined by a combination of statements from the press and Chamber of Commerce, plus a "clever pre-election anti-semitic speech in which the employer claimed that the union was a 'front' for ambitious Jews."[52]

Bambace also faced the issue of race as organizers in the field attempted to bring black workers into the union, while educating the white workers to accept these newcomers to their ranks. Organizers wrote to the home office asking for ILGWU literature that would "dispel" the belief of "Negroe members" that the AFL was "anti negroe."[53] Union officers learned to capitalize on any evidence that native white workers could accept and cooperate with black union members. On one occasion she directed her son Philip to send the report of a white unionist, Lavella Mills, of Local 420 in Huntington, West Virginia, to *Justice* for publication. She described her experience at Hudson Shore Labor School where she "learned to associate and work with people of different race and color."[54]

On a day-to-day basis organizers had to cope with the traditions imposed by segregation. Weekly reports document this situation:

Week ending January 12, 1947. Rutledge Manufacturing Company, Virginia, Tuesday got two white address. Visited them one she wasn't interested [sic] at present one was sick. Visit two colored girls got one signed cards.

Week ending February 2, 1947. Mon. to Wed. we visited colored did very good. One lady took some cards to get signed in the plant. Thurs. to Friday visited white. The white are still some afraid. Some say leave me the card, you all stop around again maybe I'll sign.[55]

Bambace also faced these racial prejudices as she traveled in the region. She never learned to drive her own car and relied upon the union chauffeur for transportation. The chauffeur, Jesse, was black and not welcomed in "white only" restaurants. Bambace often purchased sandwiches for them and they would sit on a park bench to eat. Sometimes she would be tired from a day of traveling around to meetings and she would fall asleep on his shoulder. She refused to compromise with her own sense of human justice.[56]

Although her New York experience did not prepare her for the issues of race and anti-semitism as they operated in the South, the problems of bureaucratic manouevering and internal dissension she faced in Baltimore were not a regional characteristic. Bambace's leadership style, developed during the period of labor turmoil and militancy, assumed a unilateral authority. She wanted to know and to clear everything. She delegated authority only to have it exercised in her name. This does not mean she would dictate her will without listening to the advice of others. In fact, her habit of questioning and wanting to hear all sides of the issues continued to be her hallmark. Yet it was modified by her other heritage, that of conforming to a decision handed down by a majority or a higher forum. She tended to delay making decisions and to try to hold each co-worker within her orbit. (Some suggest she used the tactic of divide and conquer.) In any case, she preferred the flow of information and power to go from each subordinate to her, or through her to the New York office. Though this preference followed bureaucratic logic, it also provided a backdrop for the personality types and organizational issues that were on the Baltimore scene.

Bambace experienced her share of bureaucratic problems, personality conflicts, and the cross currents of personal ambitions. In 1946 six members of the union resigned in protest against the field organizer/manager Irwin Jaffe, who they believed was ineffective and personally obnoxious. They complained that Bambace overlooked his failings, and they seemed to think that he had great influence over her. President Dubinsky accepted the resignations; Vice-President Kriendler intimated that their action was purposefully planned during his vacation. Bambace reacted forcefully. When letters came in from locals asking why the six had resigned, she countered by referring to them as racketeers, communists, and troublemakers. She equated their action with an attack on the organization. Her judgment proved correct. The six who resigned sent letters to each local in the district in which they questioned the democratic process followed in the organization. If any of the six appeared at a meeting that she attended, she would denounce them as not belonging to the union. She also sent letters to the rank and file to clarify the union position. Bambace did not make an issue of Irwin Jaffe—the insubordination of the six demanded stage center. Two years later Jaffe was discharged from the International.[57]

In the 1950s Bambace's organizational problems again included the personal ambitions of another assistant manager, who some observers (and Bambace) saw as wanting to ease her out. Another staff member would communicate directly to the main New York office without consulting her. She, like any of her contemporaries, had a strong sense of self-preservation and did not tolerate these challenges.[58]

During the war years and post-war years, she retained her contacts with anti-fascist groups and Italian war relief groups. In fact the Upper South Department chose to sponsor an Italian foster child.[59] Bambace was recognized as an Italian American labor leader by her co-nationalists in the movement. They were aware of her achievements, and she was aware of her position as a symbol to them. In 1951 the Italian American Labor Council elected her to its board, and although she replied that the distance between New York and Baltimore might prevent her from attending its meetings, she felt rather flattered by her election.[60]

In 1956 her election to the General Executive Board of the International Ladies Garment Workers Union filled a vacancy left open by the retirement of Salvatore Ninfo. Some suggest that the politics of ethnicity figured importantly in her election—that she filled the Italian slot. Others suggest that her work in Baltimore and on many of the International committees had been noticed and approved. The factor of sexual politics—that she filled a token female spot and conveniently was Italian—was there, but Bambace was the first non-Jewish woman ever elected to the top union hierarchy.[61]

Any effort to tell the story of Angela Bambace as an exercise in social and ethnic history must grapple with the elusiveness of the subject. Bambace, the dynamic, charming, witty, attractive, feminine member of the labor movement, a woman who led a public/private life that reflected her spontaneous personality and straightforward warmth, still eludes the biographer. Her ethnicity runs like a thread through all of her personal and much of her public life, even though after 1926 her union constituency was not Italian nor were most of her co-workers. In 1934 she ventured into a new territory by going to Baltimore; it separated her from her family. Over the years she commuted like a migrant worker back to her family. In retrospect, I can see a thread of inherited maternal strength, beginning with her widowed grandmother who had left Sicily for Brazil, continuing with her mother's support for her daughters' social causes, and climaxing with her career, in its character a combination of the traditional and the radical.

Notes

1. Interview with Angela Bambace, February, 1975, Baltimore, Maryland.
2. *Baltimore Sun*, "Area Labor Leader Cited," November 7, 1956.
3. Interview with Maria Capraro, March, 1975, Baltimore, Maryland.
4. Ibid.
5. Salvatore Amico, *Gli Italiani e L"Internationale Dei Sarti Da Donna: Raccolta Di Storie E Memorie Contemporanee* (November, 1944), 42.
6. Ibid.
7. Ibid., 43.
8. Ibid.
9. Ibid.
10. Ibid.
11. Interview with Maria Capraro, March, 1975, Baltimore, Maryland.
12. Interview with Maria Capraro, February, 1976, Northampton, Massachusetts.
13. Nino to Maria, July 12, 1921, Box 3, Capraro Papers, Immigration History Research Center (IHRC), University of Minnesota.
14. Romolo Camponeschi to Angela Bambace, October 10, 1938, New York, private family collection.
15. Interview with Rose and Charles Zimmerman, December 12, 1976, New York City.
16. Ibid.
17. *Justice*, June 16, 1969.
18. Conversation with Clara Larson, August 23, 1977.
19. Interview with Charles Zimmerman.
20. Edwin Fenton, "Immigrants and Unions, A Case Study: Italians and American Labor, 1870-1920" (Ph.D. diss., Harvard University, 1957); and Paul Buhle, "Forgotten Story: Italian American Radicalism and the Labor Movement in Rhode Island 1905-30" (Unpublished paper, 1977).

21. Conversation with Clara Larson.
22. Ibid.
23. Conversation with Oscar Camp.
24. *Baltimore Sun*, "She's a Gentile Grandmother and a Fighting Negotiator," March 18, 1968.
25. Interview with Angela Bambace.
26. Interview with Dora Feldman (nee Kaufman and alias Dorothy Dare), August, 1978, Baltimore, Maryland.
27. Interview with Charles and Rose Zimmerman.
28. Ibid., and conversation with Clara Larson.
29. Union Handbills and Literature, Springfield, Massachusetts, 1935, Box I folder II, p. 5, Grandinetti papers, IHRC.
30. Alice Kessler Harris, "Organizing the Unorganizable: Jewish Women and their Union," *Labor History*, 17 (Winter, 1976): 5-23.
31. Interview with Dora Feldman.
32. Interview with Edith and Abe Rosenfield, February 1978, Larchmont, New York.
33. International Ladies Garment Workers' Union Report, May 3, 1937; and conversation with an ILGWU retiree, who started working in 1934, October 9, 1978.
34. Ibid.
35. Conversation with ILGWU retiree, October 9, 1978.
36. Conversation with Clara Larson.
37. Angela Bambace papers, private family collection.
38. Conversation with Clara Larson and interview with Charles Zimmerman. Upon his retirement from the organization in 1968, the union gave Luigi a dinner. Both Oscar and Philip attended. (Luigi and Angela had separated during the 1950s.) On this public occasion he referred to them as his sons.
39. Interview with Edith Rosenfield; and conversation with Romolo Camponeschi.
40. Angela Bambace to Maria Capraro, Box 3 (folder marked old history correspondence), Capraro papers.
41. Letter to Angela Bambace, May 1, 1940, Flushing, New York, IHRC.
42. Bambace papers, IHRC,
43. Ibid.
44. Angela's ability to convey her maternal feelings and close personal relationships with her children, despite the conditions of divorce and separation, appeared in this letter she wrote to her son Philip from a hotel room in Norfolk, Virginia, May 29, 1943, personal family collection:

Dear Chink,

Monday will be your birthday. You will be in Mass. and I in Baltimore. Not very logical or reasonable, but that's the way we sometimes are compelled to live. If logic-reason and tolerance and understanding were the basic principles of all human beings who make up this world, you would be at school and not in a camp, and on your birthday we would all be together to celebrate and welcome again the "man," Pippio, on his twentieth birthday. As a child you had all the love care and attention despite the unpleasant break between your parents. As a youngster your school life in Flushing both in the elementary classes and in high has been a most pleasant one. Grandma with all her short comings, has filled your life with many pleasing and interesting little episodes. The house which is now empty and cold [Grandmother died in 1943], always clamored with excitement and life, babbling out of every nook. Our weekends are indelible [sic]. My constant nagging that the place must be kept clean ... Never a dull moment I could go on and on but I'm not. All I ask is that I may continue to help and do my share to enrich your life as a "man." A happy birthday darling. Love and good luck to you.

45. *Justice*, June 16, 1969.

46. International Ladies Garment Workers Union *Annual Report*, 1940 and 1944; and interview with Dora Feldman. By 1944 the Maryland-Virginia District governed twelve locals with a total membership of 1,529, located in Baltimore, Hebron, Sharptown, and Hancock, Maryland; Richmond, Lawrenceville, Appomatax, Farmville, Danville, and Petersburg, Virginia. ILGWU *Annual Report*, 1950.

47. ILGWU *Annual Report*, 1950.

48. Conversation with May Lewis, October 9, 1978, Baltimore, Maryland. May Lewis was a member of Local 106 and an active participant in labor politics.

49. Angela Bambace to David Dubinsky, June 20, 1950, Dubinsky folder, ILGWU archives.

50. Memorandum from Jaffe, Assistant Manager, January 4, 1945, Jaffe folder, ILGWU archives.

51. Angela Bambace to Irwin Jaffe, May 1, 1946, Jaffe folder, ILGWU archives.

52. Phil Camp (Camponeschi) to Max Danish, editor of *Justice*, re: Spencer Manufacturing Company of Spencer, West Virginia, July 17, 1950, ILGWU archives. Angela's son Philip served as Educational and Political Director of the Upper South Department.

53. Edith Gordon from Robert Gladnick, June 7, 1946, ILGWU archives.

54. "My Experiences at Hudson Shore Labor School," October, 1950, Hudson Shore folder, ILGWU archives.

55. Myrtle Lee, Organizer Weekly Report, week ending January 12, 1947, and week ending February 2, 1947, ILGWU archives.

56. Conversation with Margaret Frank, Angela's office secretary, and later, her living companion, November, 1975.

57. See correspondence, telegrams, and official hearings, transcripts relating to the case of the six resignees, ILGWU archives.

58. Conversation with Margaret Frank; and interview with Charles and Rose Zimmerman.

59. See letters to Girolomo Valenti, a general manager of *La Parola*, dated May 10, 1940, in which Angela Bambace enclosed a check from the Dressmakers Local 106 in Baltimore, ILGWU archives.

60. Angela Bambace to Luigi Antonini, president, Italian American Labor Council, January 2, 1951, ILGWU archives.

61. Mattie Jackson, a black American, is the second non-Jewish woman ILGWU vice-president. She is also the first black vice-president, and was elected in 1976.

The Padrone System and Sojourners in the Canadian North, 1885–1920

Robert F. Harney

On January, 23, 1904, more than two thousand Italian laborers paraded through the streets of Montreal. They were there to fête Antonio Cordasco, steamship agent, *banchista* (immigrant banker), and director of a labor bureau. Two foremen presented him with a crown "in a shape not unlike that worn by the King of Italy." The crown was later displayed in a glass case along with a souvenir sheet containing eleven columns of Italian names and entitled "In Memory of the Great Parade of January, 1904, in honour of Signor Antonio Cordasco, proclaimed King of the Workers." During February, foremen, *caposquadri*, and *sub-bossi* organized a banquet for Cordasco. Invitations to the banquet bore a seal suspiciously like the Royal Crest of Italy, and Cordasco's "kept" newspaper, the *Corriere del Canada*, reported the occasion in detail.[1]

Four months later, in June and July of 1904, the "King of the Workers" was under investigation by the Deputy Minister of Labour, about to be the center of a Royal Commission inquiry into fraudulent business practices, and excoriated by officials of the Italian Immigrant Aid Society. What emerges from the reports, testimony, and newspaper accounts about the activity of Cordasco and his competitors in Montreal is not just the picture of an exploitive and dishonest broker[2] but of a man truly in between— willing enough to put his boot into those beneath him, such as the greenhorns who depended upon him for jobs, but also forced to tug his forelock and to anticipate the wishes of the English-speaking businessmen and employers whom he served.

Antonio Cordasco, the protagonist of my story, was, in the end, a nearly perfect Italian parody of the "negro king," that peculiarly ugly phenomenon of an ethnic or colonial puppet who serves those who really control the society and the economy.[3] In 1904 his avarice combined with circumstance—a late thaw, high unemployment in the United States, and the alliance of the Montreal Italian Immigrant Aid Society with his chief competitor, Alberto Dini—to expose him to public scrutiny. He proved to be a man whose new crown rested uneasily; he had to threaten and cajole his *sub-bossi*, placate his capitalist overlords, hide from irate workers, and scheme to destroy competitors who aspired to his throne. At the same time, he carried on a complex foreign policy with padroni in other cities and with steamship and emigration agents in Italy and on Italy's borders. Cordasco stood astride a free enterprise system that brought Italian migrant labor into contact with North American job opportunity. His power lay in his control of the communications network between labor and capital, and that was not an easy position from which to carve an empire. Like the "negro king," he had neither the affection of his people, the migrant Italian laborers, nor the trust of his Wasp masters, but he served them both as intermediary and spared them both from dealing directly with the mysterious other.

The commerce of migration which Cordasco had ridden to power had grown up in the last quarter of the nineteenth century. Canadian conditions were particularly suitable for the development of a seasonal guest worker system. The need for manual labor at remote northern work sites, the attitudes of Canadian big business and of European village laborers, the climate, the difficulty of transportation, and the xenophobic immigration policy of the government meant that only a sojourning work force could reconcile the Dominion's needs and the target migrants' self-interest.[4] The three necessary components to such a system of seasonal migrant labor were the capitalist employer, the European worker, and the intermediaries and brokers who controlled the recruitment, transportation, and organization of the labor pool for the employers. All involved saw an advantage in the system. For the Canadian employer—particularly the labor intensive industries such as the railways, the mines, and the smeltering interests—there was constant need for a docile and mobile work force, a force free from the taint of unionism and willing to be shipped to remote northern sites, a work force which tolerated exploitation at those sites in order to make ready cash, and which required no maintenance on the part of the employer during the long winter months.

For the workers, the advantage of this system was that they could operate as target migrants. They had come to North America without their families, not in order to settle, but to earn enough money to change their condition of life in the old country. Their image or myth of Canada, if they had one, was of a very hostile and frozen land whose people were not well disposed toward south Europeans or toward foreign bachelors.[5] The system usually allowed them to reach Canadian job sites for the short work season without undue delay or hardship, and a single season's campaign enabled them to save money to send home; and by staying several seasons they could make a nest-egg so that they might never come back again. However, because of the necessity of arriving with the thaw in time for work and leaving before the St. Lawrence froze, or because of dishonest exploitation, target migrants were often trapped for many seasons, their savings dissipated by padroni-run boardinghouses, saloons, and provisioners.

For the intermediaries, of course, the system itself was the source of their income. Without a constant flow of labor, without being able to pose for both the village laborer and the North American capitalist as the only possible go-between, the padrone had no function. In the Canadian situation, they were helped by the problems of national boundaries, the new rigor of Italian laws, the competition between steamship companies, and the worker's lack of knowledge of the northern target. The fact that the North American employers maintained an almost wilfull ignorance of the work force made it easier for the intermediaries to manipulate the labor supply and to tie job brokerage to the network of migration, which ran all the way from the remote towns of Italy to the remote towns of northern Ontario and British Columbia.

As Italian laws against the excesses of agents and recruitment grew more stringent, the town of Chiasso on the Swiss-Italian border became the center of the illicit recruitment and flow of Italian workers to North America.[6] Unravelling the *vincolismo* (linkages) of sham immigration societies, travel agencies, steamship companies, and padroni who controlled the flow is beyond the scope of this paper, but it is significant that a major role in this unholy commerce was taken by King Cordasco. Two simple points need to be made. First, in the so-called *commercio di carne umana*, there was as much competition in earning the right to transport human cattle to the slaughter yards of North American industry as there was in running the North American holding pens. For every padroni in Montreal or Boston, there were one or two steamship sub-agents in a town like Chiasso or in the interior of Italy. These agents earned their way by the *senseria*, the bounty paid for each migrant recruited for steamship passage, and although the more responsible or clever among the sub-agents cared whether those they sent to America found work—because their reputation as agents depended on it—they were naturally not as sensitive to the fluctuations in the demand for labor as the North American padroni had to be. This made the sub-agents a sometimes unreliable part of the network for those who faced the more delicate task of maintaining a balance between the labor force and the employer in North America. One agent for Beaver Lines even boasted to the Canadian authorities that in a given year he had recruited more than 6,000 passengers from Italy, as well as Syrians and Germans and as many more as anybody might request.[7]

Before we try describing the padroni's activities in Montreal— using Cordasco and also his competitor, Alberto Dini, as models— we have to explain the rapidity of Cordasco's rise to power athwart the lines of communication. The new king of Italian labor does not really seem to have been intelligent enough to control the situation, but by its decision to place the mantle of sole agent on him, the Canadian Pacific Railroad (CPR) turned a small time hustler into a large padrone broker. Cordasco's power then derived from his felicitious relationship with one major employer and particularly with the railway's chief hiring agent, George Burns. It was Burns who made Cordasco into his "negro king." Burns operated out of an office in Windsor Station in Montreal called the Special Services Department of the Canadian Pacific Railway. Despite that euphemism, its main function was the hiring of docile foreign labor, especially Italians, Galicians, and Chinese for the railway's summer work.

Burns had made up his mind during the strike of 1901 that Cordasco offered him the easiest and surest means of maintaining an available labor pool in Montreal. The agent admitted as much on the stand during the Royal Commission hearings in 1904.

Question: What means do you take in order to obtain this extra Italian labour? Answer: I have engaged that labour entirely through Italian labour agents ... During the past three years, since the summer of 1901 I have dealt almost exclusively through Cordasco. Previous to that I had several others engaged, such as Mr. Dini, two gentlemen by the name of Schenker, and possibly one or two more. Question: But since 1901 you have dealt exclusively with Mr. Cordasco? Answer: Yes, I have Your Honour. Question: Was that the year you had the strike? Answer: It was. Question: And Cordasco got in touch with you during that year? Answer: I think the first business I had with Cordasco was in 1901. Question: In connection with the strike? Answer: In connection with supplying Italians to take the place of track men who went on strike.[8]

Cordasco, working for the Canadian Pacific Railway and Alberto Dini, on behalf of the Grand Trunk Railway, had to negotiate with the agents in Switzerland who were the immediate recruiters of manpower. A letter to Dini from the firm of Corecco and Brivio in Bodio, Switzerland, reveals the means by which North American labor agents and European steamship agents formed their alliances. The firm in Switzerland was in a covert relationship with both Frederick Ludwig in Chiasso and with Beaver Steamship Lines, and possibly even with Canadian Pacific Lines, but masqueraded as representatives of something called Societa Anomina di Emigrazione La Svizzera.

In fact, Corecco and Brivio had tried to monopolize the Chiasso Connection and the commerce of migration there. The letter to Dini in 1904 suggested the advantages of a full alliance.

> You do not ignore that a brother of Mr. Schenker, one of those who has opened an office in Montreal for the exchange of money in order to compete with you, has lately opened an office in Chiasso, Switzerland and gets passengers from Italy through the help of Schenker who is in Montreal. The latter sends to his brother in Chiasso notices and orders for the shipment of men and the brother reads the notices to the passengers mentioning the ships they are to go by. Having acknowledged this action on the part of Schenker we took the liberty of addressing ourselves to you in order to advise you and inform you thereof and to ask if it would be possible for you to do something for us in the matter.[9]

So the steamship agents and immigration agents in Italy or on the Italian borders who needed to protect their bounties sought allies among the padroni while the latter sought safe suppliers of labor. In 1903, only one season after he had gained his lucrative hold over the Canadian Pacific labor supply, Cordasco wrote to the most powerful of the agents in Chiasso, Frederick Ludwig.

> By the same mail I am sending you a package of my business cards. I ask you to hand them to the passengers or better to the labourers that you will send directly to me . . . To satisfy the Italians better here I have opened a banking office of which I send a circular to you from which you can see that I can do all that they request. Awaiting for some *shipment* and to hear from you soon. Yours truly, A. Cordasco.[10]

Cordasco apparently demonstrated both naiveté and lack of finesse in the letter to Ludwig. That gentleman, a smoother, tougher exploiter, wrote back to him within a month. Addressing himself to "Mr. Cordask," he explained that he had not answered "the letter

immediately because I wanted to get some information about you."
From the tone of the letter, Ludwig felt he had the upper hand in
dealing with a padrone *arrivato* like Cordasco. He informed Mr.
Cordask that he would "try him out and send passengers to him
and see if he acts as an honest man and then he will give his
address to most of the migrants going to Montreal." He added,
"What I especially recommend to you is not to change your address every moment like a wandering merchant. On your envelope
the address is 441 St. James Street and on your business card it is
375, now which of the two is the right address?" Ludwig went on
to remark that he had done business with Dini for years and had
found him a capable and good business associate. Mr. Cordask
finally is warned, "We shall see then if you will work with the
same conscience and punctuality."

Communication with those in the Old World who put labor on
the *via commerciale*—steamship agents, immigration agents, and
local notables—was sometimes testy to say the least. We find Cordasco complaining to a man from Udine who has sent him men
who were stone cutters not laborers. The stone cutters had expected work as skilled masons or in quarries, but Cordasco claimed
that he had distinctly warned the men before they left the old
country that everyone should understand that the railway work
available in Canada was for laborers, not artisans. A number of
these men refused to go to British Columbia to work; they claimed
that they were promised free passage on the railway, skilled work,
and better wages than those offered them when they arrived in
Canada.[11] Caught amidst the promises of the agents in the old
country, his own hyperbole in the pages of the *Corriere del Canada*, and the parsimonious approach to migrant labor of Canadian
big business, and worker demands, Cordasco's role as a go-between
sometimes reduced itself to lying to all parties involved, while
walking a very difficult tightrope.

Cordasco's networks ran from Chiasso on the Italian-Swiss border to the various padroni and labor agents in the American "Little
Italies" and the major steamship companies. The official report of
the Royal Commission listed some of the methods Cordasco used to
make contact with the labor supply in Europe. The investigators
admitted that they could only infer from the correspondence a
conspiracy to mislead workers. Mackenzie King, the chief investigator, had remarked that "there is no business relation existing
between himself [Cordasco] and these agents but I think there can
be no doubt as to their acting in direct accordance with an under-

stood arrangement which he has with them."[12] King's remark has a resonance similar to that of American investigators at a later time who became convinced that the Mafia existed because they could not find evidence of it.

The memoranda of understanding and letters of agreement that passed between Cordasco and his peers were callous documents reflecting the tenor of the commerce in human flesh. But steamship agents and labour agents of every ethnic background dealt with migrants thus, and the line between the clever use of the free enterprise system and fraud is more discernible to us now than it was then. Also, it is obvious from the testimony of Mr. Mortimer Waller that business practices did not change much as one crossed ethnic lines.

Question: Is there anything else you would like to state in connection with this investigation Mr. Waller? Answer: No sir, I do not think so. I think myself that Englishmen should have as fair a chance of supplying this Italian labour as the Italians themselves. Question: You think that an Englishman should have as good a chance to supply this labour? Answer: Yes. Question: You think that Englishmen have not that chance? Answer: No sir. Question: Why? Answer: The companies like the CPR will not go to anybody but Italians for the men.[13]

Mr. Waller had the same system of registering laborers as Cordasco, and charged approximately the same commission for unskilled workers and foremen.

In his testimony, Dini told the judge, "I have got an employment office, banker is name known to Italians." Earlier in his testimony, he had also pointed out that he was the steamship agent for North German Lloyd's Line, Hamburg–American Anchor Line, and two Italian Lines, including La Veloce. Cordasco, in turn, had extracted a promise from Mr. Burns that if he helped find strikebreakers in 1901, the CPR would help him become the agent for their steamship line, for Compagnie Generale Transatlantique, and for several others. Like Dini, he referred to himself as a banker and his newspaper announcement to the laborers in 1904 began:

To the army of the pick and shovel Italian laborers, bosses do not show a double face, do not be false but only one. Be true. Have a soldier's courage, apply to the elegant and solid Italian bank of Antonio Cordasco, if you do not want to weep over your misfortunes in the spring when the shipments of men will begin.[14]

Both men described themselves as bankers, perhaps as steamship agents and employment agents, but would not have used the word padrone. They specialized in performing as brokers between labor and capital, as transmitters of remittances and pre-paid tickets, and as travel advisors, while engaging, because of the migrants' dependence on them, in many other businesses.

Cordasco's banking, for example, included lending money to foremen so that they could pay the registration fee of a dollar a head for their work gangs. Often the faith of the workers in the *banchista* was touchingly naive. A letter of 1903 reads, "We the undersigned, signed with a cross mark because we cannot write or read, both of us, we authorize Mr. A. Cordasco to draw our wages for work done in the month of October last, 1903. And we both authorize the Canadian Pacific Railway Company to pay over our wages to Mr. Cordasco at 375 St. James Street." Cordasco himself understood the nature of his *intermediarismo*. An advertisement appearing in *La Patria Italiana* showed a rather charming, if dangerous and old-fashioned, sense of the world *patronato*: "If you want to be respected and protected either on the work or in case of accident or other annoyances which may be easily met, apply personally or address letters or telegrams to Antonio Cordasco."[15] It was protection that the padrone offered, protection against undue delay, protection against fraud by others, protection against all the dangers of an unknown world, of a world where the laborer could not cope for himself because of lack of education, lack of language skills, and lack of time to stand and fight when his cash supply was threatened.

Mr. Skinner, Mr. Burns' assistant, showed a certain sympathy for Cordasco, for the padrone who had to deal with what Skinner seemed to see as the child-like qualities of the laborers. "He has lots of trouble. He keeps an office with a waiting room, and they are the resorts where these people spend all winter. They come to smoke, he keep all sorts of conveniences for them."[16]

In a strange way, the chief power of the intermediary, just as in the old country, lay in his literacy. Cordasco's clerk on the witness stand mentioned writing over eighty-seven letters a month. When Dini was pressed as to what he actually did when people came to him seeking work, he answered, "I write to several contractors, to employers, to Grand Trunk if they want labourers and if they want them I'll ship them quickly." He was asked how many contractors he represented, and replied, "ten or twenty." "When the contractors want labourers, they have my address, they write or telegraph me, if I have any Italians to send them." So it was their ability to correspond and to communicate with the American employer which made *padroni* powerful. They played a role no different from that played by the *generetti* of the small towns of the Italian south and northeast, a role in which literacy was a form of capital and the basis of the brokerage system itself. Men who would have been brokers between *signori* and peasantry or between government and peasantry in Europe, found themselves brokers between sojourners and English-speaking employers.[17]

There is no doubt that Cordasco made a profit from both the employer and laborer. That was only fitting since he served both groups. The amount of the profit, however, was outrageous by any standard. At one point, it became clear that Cordasco was buying from his own supplier near Windsor Station and providing most of the canned anchovies (sardines) and bread for laborers at different CPR sites across northern Ontario. He made a 150 percent profit on a can of sardines, the bread was often moldy, and he clearly made a high profit on it as well. In a single season he cleared $3800 as a provisioner. The figure of a dollar a head for registration of men pales in comparison. Cordasco obviously was not only profiteering but down-right grasping. Foremen, testifying against him, pointed out that they had been forced to raise the money for the banquet that had been held in his honor and that some of that money had also mysteriously disappeared into Cordasco's pocket.[18]

If the investigators, the commissioner, and the officials of the Italian Immigrant Aid Society had understood the system a little better, had understood the degree to which the foremen and laborers were also consumers, they would have noticed that the anger of those who came to the stand was not over the fact that they had to pay tribute to Cordasco or that they had to register seasonally for work with him, but that he had not found jobs for them or their gangs that year. The foremen particularly, since they too were men in between, were galled by the fact that they had promised their gangs work, that they had often raised the dollar a head for Cordasco from their men, and then had lost both a season's work, the respect of their workers, and perhaps the possibility of exercising their own petty tyranny and corruption over the work force. One foreman, Michael Tisi, was pressed on the witness stand about the fact that he had paid ten dollars to be foreman of a gang of a hundred men and that each of the men had paid two dollars. He admitted paying that, but he felt that he had no grievance against Cordasco. He answered simply, "They went to work. I'm not complaining about that."[19]

It has always seemed illogical to speak about a large scale broker like Cordasco controlling thousands of men through ties of paesanism, kinship, or even through shared ethnicity. In 1903 the CPR hired over 3500 Italians. Cordasco could not have known them all. They came from all over Italy, from the Veneto to Sicily; few, if any, were his *paesani*, let alone his friends and relatives. It was the *sub-bossi* who organized and controlled the work gangs. Sometimes those gangs were made up of *paesani* but not always. The testimony of the *caposquadri* and foremen partially explains one aspect of the padrone's power. One of the foremen, Sal Mollo, testified to the Commission that his "men don't know him [Cordasco] at all. They know me. When I went there to his bank he would not hear me." Another foreman, Pompeo Bianco, claimed to know all of his gang of 104 men brought from the United States, except for perhaps a dozen.[20]

Sub-bossi boasted that they could move their men to any site at a moment's notice, and one foreman even came from Nova Scotia to Montreal to register his men in case work was found, leaving the gang behind in Nova Scotia. Loyalty to the bosses was functional; it had to do with their ability to operate as secondary intermediaries, in this instance between the men and Cordasco, but usually between the men and the section bosses of the CPR. If that loyalty was sometimes based on regional allegiances, such as the whole gang and the boss being Calabrese or Venetian, it was still not synonymous with paesanism.

From the ranks of these *sub-bossi* however, as well as from other small entrepreneurs, individuals came forth to try to compete with Dini and Cordasco in the lucrative trade in migrants. If Cordasco was the *generone*, then these were the *generetti*, nipping at his heels. Whatever the true basis of loyalty between *sub-bossi* and gangs—Cordasco was able to control thousands of men from his Montreal office without going into the field—it could depend not just on his own immediate employees but on the *sub-bossi* as vassals. As long as Cordasco had the support of his own liege lord, the CPR agent Burns, the *generetti* could not usurp his control of labor.

A significant aspect of the padrone's role—the deftness with which he had to manipulate the labor pool to meet the employer's hiring intentions—was not pursued. No government official wished to have the blame for the large numbers of unemployed Italian migrants loitering about Montreal come to rest squarely on the shoulders of a great institution like the Canadian Pacific Railway.

This was so, although the CPR, like other major employers, seemed to be carrying on an immigration policy of its own, favoring unskilled sojourners from southeastern Europe while the Ministry of the Interior tried to recruit agriculturalists from northwestern Europe.[22]

The hearings of the Royal Commission are marred as a source by a pervasive, if latent, nativism. The authorities and the non-Italian witnesses agreed on one thing, which an exchange between Mr. Burns and Judge Winchester put flatly: "Burns: But Your Honour must know that in investigating the Italian cases there is great difficulty in getting at the truth. Winchester: I have found that myself."[23] So, whatever the Italian labor bosses were doing, it was being done in a manner strange to the Canadian way. Mr. Waller had implied as much when he lamented how Anglo-Saxon labour bureaux had been eased out of the commerce in Italian brawn. Obviously, it was ethnicity itself, the trust, often ill-founded, and the networks it provided, that was the dark alien unknown which troubled all those outside it, from the CPR officials to the judge.

The veil lifted enough in 1904 to see how the padrone ultimately depended on his Anglo-Saxon master, the employer of laborers. Cordasco met with Burns or his assistant Skinner almost daily. No doubt the lines of communication between him and Burns were closer than those between most padroni who served a more varied clientele, but Dini's relation with the various contractors and with the Grand Trunk Railway seem to have been as intense. Much of Cordasco's power over his Italian migrant laborer clientele derived from his right to advertise himself as the only acting agent for the CPR. Although he maintained some independence from Burns and the CPR by being able to pose as the most efficient intermediary for the gathering of Italian labor, his position vis-a-vis the company was not strong. It could withdraw its patronage at any time and turn to his potential competitors or directly to his *caposquadri* and *sub-bossi*.

Burns contributed directly to the expansion of Cordasco's role from that of a minor employment agent into a *banchista*. The commerce of migration led inevitably to a variety of entrepreneurial possibilities and the CPR's agent gave his blessing.

The way it came about was this. He only had a regular office and was doing a large business but he had no steamship agencies. And of course when these Italians come back from work most of them have a good deal of money which they want to send over to their relatives and friends, some for their wives and children and they buy these steamship pre-paid tickets. Cordasco is desirous of getting a line of these tickets on the different steamship agencies. And he came to me about the matter and I told him he could easily get agencies if he made the proper representation to the agents that were in New York. Question: You recommended him? Answer: I took some steps to get these agencies for him.[24]

So from his castle in Windsor Station, George Burns protected his vassal from both do-gooders and the competition of lesser brokers because the railway found the padrone system efficient and flexible. A delegation from the Italian Immigration Aid Society had approached Burns offering to provide him with Italian laborers directly from Italy through the good offices of the Italian government. Burns replied to them,

I have taken up the question of the employment of labour with the proper authorities and have to advise you that it is not the intention of this company to change the arrangements of the employment of Italian immigrant labour which have been in effect during the past few years. Our present system has given entire satisfaction so far and I therefore regret I shall be unable to place direct with your Society any specific order for any number of men.[25]

Cordasco's sway over Italian migrant labor was reinforced by the company. For example, at the famous banquet in the padrone's honour, most of the foremen in attendance noted the presence of the chief superintendent of the CPR's Vancouver division. After all, that gentleman would be hiring five or six thousand Italians during the coming spring, and he seemed to be there honoring his friend Cordasco.

In 1904 company support, even though it showed the limits of Cordasco's independence, enabled him to thwart attacks upon his monopoly. That support came in at least four ways. First, at no point in their testimony did Skinner or Burns speak explicitly enough to compromise Cordasco. Second, they maintained throughout his exclusive right to hire Italians for the railway rather than turning to aspiring *sub-bossi*. Third, they had refused to order manpower from Alberto Dini, Cordasco's main competitor. Fourth, Burns did his best to discredit or ignore the Italian Immigration Aid Society.

With his overlords to protect him, Cordasco's lines of communication to Ludwig in Chiasso, to Stabili in Boston, to other lesser padroni in Portland, Providence, and Fall River, and to agents in New York and Buffalo were secure. Cordasco seemed as safe as a padrone could be. To raise money for the banquet in his honor he warned any man who hesitated to donate five dollars to the cause that he would publish his photograph upside down on the souvenir sheet. The real threat was that "anyone who refuses to pay will go out of my office," i.e., would be eliminated from the hiring register. In an address to labourers printed in *La Patria Italiana,* Cordasco flaunted his control.

> If you do not want to weep over your misfortune in the spring when the shipment of men will begin you will do business with me. Do not believe that with your dollar that you will be able to get work like your comrades who have been faithful. Those who had signed the book earlier. We will inspect our books, and money orders and our passage ticket books and those who will not have their names in them will in their despair tear out their hair and will call Mr. Cordasco, Lordship Don Antonio, 'Let me go to work.' 'No, never,' will be answered to them. 'Go to those to whom you have sent your money away . . . ' Forewarned is a forearmed man.[26]

Despite his parody of Christ's monopoly over salvation, Cordasco could not stifle all the competition. The same entrepreneurial spirit that brought so many of the migrants to North America led a certain number of men to see in Cordasco or Dini models for action. One could almost say that an infernal spirit of capitalism had begun to inject itself into his feudal system. Foremen, *sub-bossi,* and *caposquadri* who had been in America for a number of seasons—especially if they spoke English well—must have seen advantage in eliminating Cordasco as intermediary, even if they did not aspire to a brokerage status for themselves. The *sub-bossi* were, much like the *generetti* of the post *Risorgimento,* at once in a feudal and capitalist relationship with the padrone. The *sub-bossi* gave Cordasco his power; he gave them theirs. Each could claim to provide work to those below them. If one of them tried to by-pass Cordasco and deal directly with the employer, Cordasco could only hope that the employer would not take advantage of the situation to undermine him.

As we have seen, George Burns of the CPR did not take advantage of the situation. He found it easier to have one reliable padrone and to turn a blind eye to his corruption and unfair exactions. By 1904, with the help of the company, Cordasco had defeated non-Italian suppliers of labor and had excluded Dini from the CPR system, while he himself cut into Dini's commerce with the Grand Trunk Railway. From the padrone's correspondence, we can see how he used Burns and the sub-contractors' fear of anarchy in the supply system to thwart emerging competitors. Cordasco went so far at one point as to write a letter to Boston, interfering in the recruitment of laborers there and in the competition between the Bianco Stabili Company and Torchia and Company. He warned Messieurs Torchia that there was no point in recruiting people for the CPR in British Columbia because he, Cordasco, was the sole agent for that railway and he would only order manpower through Stabili. He ended his letter thus: "No shipment of men will be recognized but those made through Stabili and Company."[27] Despite the bravado of that letter, Cordasco pestered Burns with complaints about incidents in which sub-contractors along the right-of-way hired workers through Italian foremen rather than through Burns and Cordasco.

Thus far this paper has treated the sojourning worker—with the exception of *sub-bossi* and *caposquadri*—as the commodity in the commerce of migration, delivered by the padrone to the North American employer. Despite moral clichés about supine greenhorns in the clutches of padroni, the thoughtful historian soon sees that the migrants were as much the consumers of the padrone brokerage services as the employers were. The laborers judged Cordasco by only one measure—did he deliver? Did he provide employment for the length of time and at the wages promised, and did he do so without either delay, ancillary expenses, or hassle with North American authorities? If he did, the padroni played his assigned role in the commerce of migration. There was no doubt whatsoever that men sought other intermediaries if a padrone failed them. For example, in March, 1904, Cordasco urged Burns to begin hiring for CPR summer projects because he could not hold the men who had registered with him. Many were drifting off with construction bosses and agents of other smaller railways and street railways. The pages of the *Labour Gazette* in the 1900s were studded with accounts of short-lived revolts by Italian work gangs. Almost all of these uprisings occurred because of fraudulent wage promises or attempts to reduce pay; none seems to have been over working conditions.[28]

Employers such as the Canadian Pacific Railway section bosses had the means to resist revolt. When Italians at Crow's Nest Pass in British Columbia refused $1.50 a day, they were simply dismissed and the local labor agent began "filling orders with Galicians from the North."[29] On the other hand, Cordasco had no protection from the caprice or anger of Italian workers; he faced physical attack and verbal abuse. If men he gathered were dis-

missed or left a job site disgruntled, he could only plead for pa-
tience from *sub-bossi* or for patronage from other employers. So the
consumer power of the migrants—before they were acclimitized or
turned to North American unionism—when it was exercised, was
against the padrone, not the employer. In this, as in every aspect of
the system, a padrone like Cordasco was the man in between. Not
only did he face the anger of workmen and treason from his vassals,
but he ran the risk of being seen as an unreliable broker by big business because he supplied troublesome men.

Cordasco then was a nasty man and certainly did not deserve the
excess profits he exacted from the migrant labor force, but he did,
except perhaps in the spring of 1904, do his job. The sojourners
accepted the padrone because they reckoned that he provided
them the best alternative in their search for cash; their commitment to the system, like their avoidance of unionism or agricultural
work, reflected their desire to return home as quickly as possible
with cash and with as little North American encumbrance as possible. When an official of the Commissariat asked Italian laborers in
the Niagara Peninsula why they hadn't taken up some of the rich
farm lands in that region, the answer was simple: "We have to
think about our families in Italy."[30] In 1900 the Canadian consul in
Montreal had reported that of all the trapped migrants interviewed
there, none had come to Canada to settle. Agricultural work did
not bring in the cash which was the goal of the sojourning family
member. Some measure both of the padrone's successful delivery of
services and of the frame of mind of the Italian Canadian labor
force can be found in the fact that Canadian remittances to Italy
were the highest per unit for any part of *Italia oltremare* as late as
1908.[31]

Dini testified honestly and simply at one point to the Royal
Commission. When pressed to admit that it was the extraordinary
competition between agents like him and Cordasco that had led to
so many migrants arriving in Montreal that spring, he remarked
that that was not so. It was easy enough, he said, to understand
why men who earned the equivalent of twenty-five cents a day in
their home towns might come to a land where they could make
$1.50 a day, and twice that much if they became foremen. All of
the commissioners who investigated Canadian conditions later on
for the Canadian government concurred on one point: the sojourners were content with their margin of saving and profit. They
complained of the cold, of unsanitary and unsafe conditions, and
sometimes of a padrone's dishonesty, but, for example, in 1910

Viola found men in the mines at Cobalt saving a dollar a day. Foremen, according to Moroni, made as much as $3.50 a day—ten times the daily wages in southern Italy, and reason enough, if not justification, for Cordasco's surcharge when registering *caposquadri* in 1903 and 1904.[32]

Commissioner Attolico, in 1912, met a Calabrese youth in the bush "at a little station four hours away from Lake Superior."[33] The youngster complained to him about missing his hometown, but he had wintered over in a bunkhouse because he did not want to go to Port Arthur and spend his salary on *madamigella* (the ladies). The boy had already sent 350 lire—the equivalent of a half year's wages in Italy—to his mother back in the *paesello*. He had been in Canada less than three months when Attolico encountered him. He did not mind the deprivation but he kept repeating that, while there were many other Calabrese about, he was the only one from Mammole and had no one for company but God. Since the young Calabrese section hand worked for the Canadian Pacific Railway, he was mistaken if he thought the deity was his only companion. The latter might have heard his prayers, but it was Cordasco or one of his successors who had found him his job, remitted his money to his mother, delivered her letters to him, and would handle prepaid tickets for kinfolk or for his passage home later on. It was a padrone, not God and not the free flow of labor to capital, who had brought a man from the hills of Calabria to the northern Ontario bush.

Protest against the padrone system came more often from social workers, labor leaders, and nativists than it did from the consumers, the migrant laborers. Historians have assumed that this was so because the sojourners knew no better or had no choice. In fact, the system ended when the consumer no longer found it satisfactory. Padronism was callous, exploitive, and often dishonest, but it fulfilled a function for those migrants who chose to come to America, not as permanent immigrants, but in search of cash to improve their condition in the old country. To understand padronism properly and to give all parts of the system—employer, intermediary, and laborer-consumer—their due, we must see it not as a form of ethnic crime, but as part of the commerce of migration.

Notes

1. The chief source for this essay is the *Royal Commission appointed to inquire into the Immigration of Italian Labourers to Montreal and the alleged Fraudulent Practices of Employment Agencies* (Ottawa, 1905) (hereafter cited as *Royal Commission, 1904*). The Commission produced a forty-one page report and 170 pages of testimony.

2. The word "padrone" does not appear in the testimony. Mackenzie King, chief investigator for the Dept. of Labour and future Prime Minister of Canada, probably knew the word and its connotations from his American experience. I have used the word throughout the paper as a convenient label for the chief intermediaries, but do so on the understanding that the reader has a wary and sophisticated approach to its use. See R. F. Harney, "The Padrone and the Immigrant," *Canadian Review of American Studies* 5 (Fall, 1974).

3. The expression was popularized in Canada by Andre Laurendeau (1912–1968), the editor of Montreal's *Le Devoir*. Laurendeau claimed that Quebec was governed by *'les rois negres'* — the equivalent of those puppet rulers in Africa through whom the British authorities found it convenient to wield power. The expression in English would probably have the strength of "nigger king" not "negro king."

4. See Joan M. Nelson, *Temporary versus Permanent Cityward Migration: Causes and Consequences* (Migration and Development Group, Massachusetts Institute of Technology, 1976); and R. F. Harney, "Men without Women: Italian Migrants in Canada, 1995–1930," in B. Caroli, R. F. Harney, L. Tomasi (eds.), *The Italian Immigrant Woman in North America* (Toronto, 1978). On government immigration policy, see M. Timlin, "Canada's Immigration Policy, 1896–1910," *Canadian Journal of Economics and Political Science* 26 (1963). For popular attitudes toward the immigrant laborers, see E. Bradwin, *The Bunkhouse Man* (New York, 1928), and J. S. Woodsworth, *Strangers within our Gates* (Toronto, 1909). The latter was significant enough to have a *Bollettino* of the Italian Commissariat of Emigration devoted to reviewing its ideas and impact: "Gli stranieri nel Canada giudicati da un canadese (recensione)," *Bollettino* 19 (Anno 1909). See also D. H. Avery, *Canadian Immigration Policy and the Alien Question, 1896–1919: The Anglo-Canadian Perspective* (Ph.D. diss., University of Western Ontario, 1973).

5. There was apparently little knowledge of Canada in Italy before the mass migration of the 1900s. The only available study of Canada in Italy seems to have been E. Cavalieri, "Il Domino del Canada. Appunti di Viaggio," which appeared first in serial form in *Nuova Antologia* 43; 700–747; 44; 319–353; 44; 665–692. As late as 1914, a *vademecum* for immigrants, *Calendario per Gli Emigranti di Società Umanitaria* (Milan, 1914), although it had accurate descriptions of many parts of the world, showed Niagara Falls on its map of Canada, but not the industrial city of Toronto.

6. For the debate over emigration in Italy and the evolution of Italian laws about protection of emigrants, see F. Manzotti, *La Polemica*

sull'emigrazione nell'Italia unita (Milano, 1969); R. Foerster, *The Italian Emigration of Our Times* (Harvard, 1919).

7. Luigi Gramatica, General Agent (Genoa), to W. T. Preston, London, January 7, 1902, RG 76, vol. 129, *Immigration Branch, 1901*, File 28885, Public Archives of Canada, Ottawa, Canada.

8. Testimony of G. Burns, *Royal Commission, 1904*, 41.

9. Corecco & Brivio to A. Dini, May 7, 1904, *Royal Commission, 1904*, 50.

10. Correspondence between Cordasco and Ludwig, October, 1903, *Royal Commission, 1904*, 82.

11. On Ludwig, see Marcus Braun's supporting documents and miscellaneous related correspondence in the National Archives in Washington: RG 85, Immigration Subject Correspondence, File 52320/47 (1903–1904), Immigration and Naturalization, Dept. of Justice (hereafter cited as *Braun Report, 1903*). Cordasco to Antonio Paretti, April 26, 1904, *Royal Commission, 1904*, 82.

12. Report in *Labour Gazette* June, 1906.

13. Testimony of Mortimer Waller, *Royal Commission, 1904*, 48. Waller incidentally charged two dollars to register laborers for work and five dollars for foremen.

14. Notice in *La Patria Italiana*, *Royal Commission, 1904*, 106.

15. *La Patria Italiana*, Feb. 20, 1904, *Royal Commission, 1904*, 107.

16. Testimony of CPR agent Skinner, *Royal Commission, 1904*, 26.

17. See Harney, "Commerce of Migration," on the concept of the *borghesia mediatrice*; see G. Dore, *La Democrazia italiana e l'emigrazione in America* (Brescia, 1964).

18. Testimony of Pompeo Bianco, foreman, *Royal Commission, 1904*, 163.

19. Testimony of Michele Tisi, foreman, *Royal Commission, 1904*, 33.

20. Testimony of Salvatore Mollo, foreman, *Royal Commission, 1904*, 34; testimony of Pompeo Bianco, foreman, *Royal Commission, 1901*, 29.

21. Testimony of Pietro Bazzani, foreman, *Royal Commission, 1904*, 68.

22. For the government attitude, footnote 4 as well as W. D. Scott, "Immigration and Population," in A. Shortt and A. Doughty, *Canada and its Provinces* (Toronto, 1914), 561. The government's asserted preference for agricultural settlers over migrant workers coincided with Anglo-Saxon racialist hierarchies. The matter has received remarkably little study in Canada. Canadian Pacific records have not generally been open to scholars.

23. Testimony of Burns, *Royal Commission, 1904*, 153. It was Judge Winchester himself, the head of the inquiry, who agreed with Burns that Italian cases were murkier than others.

24. Testimony of Burns, *Royal Commission, 1904*, 41, 61. It is important to note that Burns stressed that Cordasco was sole agent for Italian labor; Cordasco had, in that sense, an ethnic monopoly but not a franchise for hiring all track crews. As Burns pointed out (p. 52), Italian labor had a specific purpose: "The Italians on our line are used to replace those men who have been employed earlier in the season on contracts, and to whom at this time of year, July and August, when the harvest starts, the farmer offers high wages and they jump their jobs, and the work is left behind, and we have to rely on anything we can get."

25. Burns to C. Mariotti, Secretary of the Italian Immigration Aid Society, March 16, 1903, *Royal Commission, 1904*, 3.
26. *La Patria Italiana* advertisement, Feb. 20, 1904, *Royal Commission, 1904*.
27. Cordasco to M. Torchia & Co., March 12, 1904, *Royal Commission, 1904*, 89.
28. See, for example, *Labour Gazette*, Reports of the Local Correspondent, vol. 7 (1906–1907). A systematic look at the various labor incidents would provide a better index of sojourning and the question of worker militance than does concentration on a few articulate leaders or on major confrontations.
29. Burns to Cordasco, *Royal Commission, 1904*, 113. Burns also informed the Italian Immigration Aid Society of this matter.
30. B. Attolico, "L'agricoltura e l'immigrazione nell'Canada," *Bollettino* 5 (Anno 1912), Commissariat of Emigration, Rome, 547.
31. See *Revista di Emigrazione*, Anno 1:6 (August, 1908). On a basis of amount per remittance, the figures were Canada, 221 lire; Argentina, 194; United States, 185; Brazil, 168. Sixty-four percent went to the South of Italy and the vast majority of remittances to Italy from Canada came through the postal savings sytem.
32. Moroni, "Le condizioni attuali," 49.
33. B. Attolico, "Sui campi di lavoro della nuova ferrovia transcontinentale canadese," *Bollettino* 1 (Anno 1913), Commissariat of Emigration, Rome, 7.

WORKING-CLASS CONFLICT AND ADJUSTMENT

Italian American Workers and the Response to Fascism

Vincent M. Lombardi

The Fascism of Benito Mussolini has been debated politically and academically for over fifty years, and the only firm agreement has been that it was, in the 1920s at least, an Italian answer to twentieth-century problems, an answer constructed out of the divergent threads of post-World War I Italian society. Because few people, even Fascists themselves, could agree on its scope, we cannot be certain it was more than a method, a broad approach to specific public problems, a political attitude, a state of mind.[1]

The pattern of history that Fascism wove among Italian Americans has been treated by several scholars in recent years, and work is still continuing. Michael Ledeen, John P. Diggins, Gaetano Salvemini, Alan Cassels, Philip Cannestraro, and others have examined various aspects of the Italian American flirtation with the Fascist myth. I hope to synthesize some of the more salient points of that flirtation, focusing more closely on the Italian American worker.

We know Fascism was, in practice, an anti-communist, anti-democratic, pro-nationalist system of authoritarian government that called all Italians to evolve a renewed sense of cultural identity, or *Italianità*,[2] through the support of Mussolini and his program of national rejuvenation.[3] After years of *Italia disprezzata*, Mussolini promised Italians everywhere respite from their cultural despair. In Fascism's early stages, Mussolini's appeal was wide,[4] as he had neither racial nor religious bias,[5] and he hoped to provide as coherent and universal a system as the disruptions and chaos of post-war Italy would allow. Once in power, the *Fascisti* projected themselves as "consensus" politicians, pragmatically accommodating a wide range of people and ideas within one political framework, revealing Mussolini's ability to synthesize and control political opinion in Italy.[6] His new state sacrificed objectivity for nationalism, political freedom for emotionalism, and economic independence for security.

Understanding the precise nature of Fascism is difficult. If we see it as an integral part of Western tradition, we can begin to explain adequately why so many countries ignored their democratic heritage; if we see it as a transitory political aberration introduced by a local demagogue, we cannot fully explain its appeal outside of Italy.[7] Our experiences with Hitler's Nazism has generally distorted what preceded him, and obscured what Italian Fascism meant to the Italian American worker. This historical fault has been a common one: though benefiting from hindsight, we distort another generation's actions, misjudge its motivations, and misinterpret its ideals, after intervening years have changed the premises. Today, "Fascist" has come to be applied to those in sympathy with extreme right-wing ideologies that reflect militant nationalism, racial and religious bias, and military-industrial collusion.[8] This is only partly true from the viewpoint of the Italian American.

Mussolini is one key to understanding Fascism's appeal to Italians within and outside of Italy. The frankly personal nature of his government helps us to appreciate the apparent sympathy with which Italian Americans responded to it,[9] while at the same time complicating our measurement of its dimensions. Part of the problem is that Mussolini was not seen as we see him: a gesticulating clown on a balcony, a sycophant of Hitler, though he was neither as obsequious nor as foolish as later commentators made him appear. His comic image was created with World War II, with cartoonists and writers transforming his tendency to overdramatize into a harlequinade. Italian Americans, frequently expressive, with a capacity for humor and over-dramatization themselves, did not necessarily see him as a superficial, arrogant rooster, crowing and prancing.[10]

There were inconsistencies in him and his program not readily apparent to those whom he mesmerized. His nationalistic panaceas treated symptoms, not causes. His zealous followers admired his courage rather than his reason; his program promised to exorcize society's "agitators and troublemakers" while ignoring the needs of justice. Mussolini appeared to be a decisive, self-styled "man of the people," and yet he was admired more for his vigor and candor than for the content or consistency of his ideas. His supporters, too, often disappointed by unprincipled democratic politicians, sought in him a consistency of principle (even if his principles were undemocratic, unjust, oppressive, or ironically, inconsistent). Eventually it became more important for them to know "where Italy and the Italians stood" than to evaluate the nature of that stand. Once again in history, justice and reason paled before charisma.

Whatever the nature of Fascism, and whatever the appeal of Mussolini, we can safely conclude that they more profoundly influenced Italian Americans than many of us care to admit. They accomplished this for reasons that are discernible beyond the obfuscation of more recent political factions, economic interests, or social movements, which now require its discreditation. To measure that influence, and the nature of the response, we should first briefly re-examine some conditions that existed among Italian American immigrants in general, and then explain workers' attitudes toward Mussolini's Fascism.

Contadino-class peasants and day laborers flocked to the United States for many reasons.[13] They assumed an "Italian" identity only after their arrival was met with disdain, discrimination, and isolation.[14] They responded defensively in turn with a new form of *campanilismo*, an Italian American provincialism that was born out of their new common problems and represented a solidarity previously non-existent in Italy.[15] Past deprivations and traditions, new exploitations, and the subsequent *campanilismo* created a host of "Little Italies." These isolated urban ghettos developed an Italianate society in the United States, neither completely Italian, nor completely American.[16]

In these ghettos, the *padrone* system[17] provided jobs for skilled and unskilled workers until 1910; by the second decade of this century, Italian American workers were more or less independent.[18] The jobs they held were monotonous and routine, and workers were more often than not both dispensable and interchangeable, consequently they suffered low self-esteem.[19] Their only refuge was their tightly structured communities which induced a personal and psychological, rather than economic or political, commitment,[20] and promoted much less class consciousness than one would have expected from such alienation.[21]

Observers would also have expected that such a large group of workers would have unionized easily for their economic advantage, but this was not so. Edwin Fenton's careful study of Italian American labor shows that Italian American workers were hard to unionize before 1920. They showed a lack of enthusiasm for unions because, he said, their wages did not instantly go up once they paid dues.[22] He found also that "the major determinants of the success or failure of unions to organize Italians were not social factors but the bargaining power of particular unions,"[23] along with Italian unpreparedness for doing the kind of work required of unionization. Furthermore, a lack of class solidarity inhibited their collaboration in unions on a long-term basis; and, needing jobs badly, they often accepted substandard wages. Officially, the American Federation of Labor, led by Samuel Gompers, considered most immigrants, including Italians, a threat to wage levels, and opposed open immigration on these grounds for many years.[24] In fact, it was believed that the southern Italian immigrant actually hindered successful organizational efforts of most national labor unions,[25] by being used, albeit unwittingly, as strikebreakers.[26] The efforts of local Italian labor leaders to organize immigrants in great numbers remained largely futile before the 1930s.[27] Considering their poverty level, and their former dependence on the *padrone* system, Italian American workers apparently felt they had little choice but to work when and where they could.[28]

A few Italian language locals, which were established to solve communication problems, eventually were absorbed or amalgamated into other local Italian unions, and were inadequate in size, numbers, or influence to affect materially the vast majority of Italian workers.[29] Thus, few jobs, ubiquitous discrimination, resistance of national unions, and weak immigrant bargaining power all added to the strains of language barriers to help keep Italian American union membership down.[30]

Whatever union leadership Italian American workers enjoyed before 1920 emanated from the work of former northern Italian intellectuals, socialists, syndicalists, and anarchists. Believing in the class struggle and collective action, they had had European experience in unionizing work, in mutual benefit societies, in cooperatives, and in other similar activities.[31] Once in the United States, these leaders tried an alliance of unions, various worker cooperatives, and new mutual aid societies, supplemented by vigorous educational programs. The social and cultural efforts of these societies were successful, but the economic (i.e., the unionizing goals) were less so. Among other things, diverse internal conflicts among left-wing leaders hindered success.[32]

Even the formation of the Chamber of Labor in 1920, after years of organizational effort among squabbling Italian locals and contentious union leaders, came too late to offset the persistence of the old ideal of individualized success. While the extreme left could galvanize workers in other countries, it had trouble doing so among Italian American workers, who remained conservative and increasingly ethnocentric.[33]

This was partly because the Italian enclave, serving as a permanent home for some and a temporary haven for others, persisted in being the center of immigrant activities, outside of which they believed they had few options. Many workers saw themselves in an intermediary state between the old life in Italy and a new one just ahead, and only a few were willing to risk losing a chance of striking out on their own. One thing seems increasingly clear: Italian American workers felt unions undermined their self-reliance and represented changes over which they believed they would have little control. Unions were "outside" organizations that could deny the right to act for oneself, to achieve the ideal of individual aggrandizement one came to America to achieve. Therefore, ostracized by the American public in general, rejected by official, organized labor, unsuccessfully led by a coterie of bickering intellectuals and leftists, Italian American workers found themselves isolated in the tubercles of the social and political lungs of American cities.

This isolation fostered political inactivity. Rarely provided with a coherent view of national politics in Italy or the United States, the southern Italian did not customarily observe democratic politics in action. The pervading sense of defeat and imposed humility in his daily life reduced his political involvement to a minimum, gaining him a deserved reputation in the United States for poor political participation.[34] Having little control over situations tends to make people face problems somewhat simplistically and pragmatically. With this attitude, the groundwork is easily prepared for authoritarian demagogues like Mussolini, whose promises of easy solutions can be quite appealing.

With their low self-esteem and sense of political powerlessness, coupled with a nostalgic nationalism that conjured up a visionary ideal of the old country, Il Duce's alluring capacity to "get things done" aroused a vicarious sense of power and self-respect. This was more fulfilling to their psychic needs than to their economic needs.[35]

One of the reasons for the appeal of Mussolini's Fascism lies in the fact that Fascism described the worker's Italianate ideal in human terms. Italian Americans' dehumanized alienation from the American mainstream made them susceptible to the ideal they believed Mussolini had raised phoenix-like out of the ashes of the *Risorgimento*. Though they recognized intuitively that Il Duce could do little to help them directly, he did offer a revitalization based on youth (*Giovanezza!*), a vigorous approach to solving public problems, a new hope of achieving the ideal; in short, a new mentality sketched in Fascist terms.

Thus, those who bemoaned the disorderly and lawless state of the local or national communities, saw in Fascism a uniform, orderly, and authoritarian society. This new order would clarify, simplify, and invigorate the "confused and complex reality," grant acceptance where others would not, create jobs where unions could not, and provide successful leadership where the leftists did not.

The new ideal was a false one, however, and it took until the late 1930s for Italian Americans to recognize this. Fascism had oversimplified the real world—conjuring up an illusion of an ideal state which dramatized accurate train schedules, obedient children, efficient governments, drained marshes, and above all, acceptance —all of which, true or not, obscured the important consequences of its real acts of oppression and brutality. We obtain a glimpse of this from Nicholas Chiaramonte, a former Fascist from the 1920s, who felt that Fascism really was a cruelty that "crystalized ferocity into a system, thereby shutting out all possibility of discussion."[36]

We cannot see the Italian American worker's response to Mussolini's Fascism in its true perspective unless we can judge it in comparison to the Italian American lower-middle class. By the 1920s some skilled manual workers had emerged from the working class into what we can call the petty bourgeoisie. Over the years, peddlers and carpenters were becoming merchants and contractors.[37] As a class, they owned little capital, and consisted primarily of various professionals, small businessmen, clerks, civil servants, and other assorted white-collar workers.[38] In local communities they had begun to assert leadership as individual notables rather than as union leaders, and this leadership opened channels outside the ghetto as their income and occupational responsibilities increased.

The lower-middle class became the only force in the settlement that took any political action, filling a power vacuum created by the unenthusiastic and politically inept workers. With its newly won, though limited, successes in American society, the petty bourgeoisie alone felt it had much to lose from the depression of the 1930s, and the chronic alienation of Italians from the American mainstream. In other countries the lower–middle class was security conscious. The Italian American counterpart sought opportunities to overcome class and ethnic barriers, even if it meant taking a political chance, or embracing Fascism, as the "act of coercion to which one must submit with resignation in anticipation of better things to come."[39] Out of social resentments and political ineptitude within the ethnocentric ghetto, support for Fascist operations burgeoned, championed and led by the relatively new, smaller petty bourgeoisie, and resting on the sympathetic shoulders of workers.[40] The middle class remained the smaller force in the ghetto, differing from the workers in skill, prestige, and political action, but otherwise coalescing with them in a nebulous, ethnic amalgam. It is the complex nature of this amalgam that has obscured an accurate view of the Italian American worker's response to Fascism.[41]

Having partially surveyed conditions among Italian American workers, we should examine some Fascist operations in the United States in the 1920s and thirties. In order to perpetuate the fantasy that Italy was now a beacon for Italians everywhere, Mussolini instituted a special press office to propagate information to journalists, politicians, workers, etc. that would "exploit everything that might be used to further the cause" of Fascism.[42] Pragmatism, considered to be the essence of the Fascist method,[43] permitted him to rationalize solicitations to Italian Americans through this press office for money, moral support, and allegiance. These short-term activities were always justified in the name of the long-term nationalistic ideal.

As pragmatic as Fascism was in the 1920s, a newly formed youth-based International Movement offered a long-term "universal" theory based loosely on a mixture of corporate statism and selected Christian doctrines. It was a theory designed, in part, to gain the moral (and financial) support of foreign Fascist movements.[44] In 1930 Mussolini himself boasted that the "struggle is now being carried on all over the world." He established the Italiani all'Estero in 1933 to act as foreign branches of the party, watching Italians abroad, spreading propaganda, inculcating Fascist ideals,[45] and raising money.[46]

Work among Italian Americans was conducted through a multiplicity of programs, clubs, newspaper propaganda, and subtle personal pressures calculated to enhance the image of "the fatherland." The first American club, or *fascio*, was introduced in 1923 soon after Mussolini came to power, when several groups, noted for their anti-communist bent, declared for the new Duce.[47] By 1925 he expressed an interest in seeing many such "Italian Centers" throughout the world stress the concept of "double citizenship"[48] for Italians, an obvious device for gaining political obligations and information without having to involve Italy directly in local issues.[49]

In the November, 1929 issue of *Harpers*, Marcus Duffield revealed the expanding activities of Fascist groups in the United States.[50] He complained that the Fascist League of North America, the umbrella organization for Fascist activities since 1924, was unabashedly subverting Italians in America. The article reported that the league had enrolled 12,500 members in ninety-three local chapters. These figures have never been proven, but the article's influence among government officials effectively destroyed the league. It did not, however, stop Fascist activity in the local Italian American communities. Indeed, as their activities accelerated, they became more subtle and more ubiquitous among Italian Americans. Membership in ghetto fasci skyrocketed, with a network of societies, programs, and clubs radiating out of the metropolitan New York center. There were active groups in Philadelphia, Boston, San Francisco, and several Connecticut towns along the coast. By 1940 *Fortune* reported hundreds of such organizations, although this figure has not been proved.[51]

In 1930 the Fascist League was succeeded by the Lictor Federation, which worked along with a whole catalogue of subordinate groups: the Association of Italians Abroad, the National United Italian Association, and others.[52] In addition, there were over fifty *dopolavoro*[53] clubs featuring sport, drama, recreation, and educational programs.[54] Proselytizing efforts had been quite successful, to judge by the quantity of activity.

The number of organizations and members was larger than we today have suspected: in 1937 there were 100,000 blackshirts in the United States with another 100,000 sympathizers participating in rallies and meetings across the country. Once Fascism had become identified in the Italian American mind with Italy or with Mussolini, with a real or imagined victory for Italians, they cheered and lent their support, joined the clubs, and, during the Ethiopian war, even gave their wedding rings.[55]

For years clubs and lodges had been a refuge for Italians from the loneliness and stresses accompanying the urbanization process.[56] Many Italian clubs were non-political and strictly independent; some were in debt to local notables, some were cultural and literary organizations, and others were true fascios. The variety was manifold within Italian American communities as each group served a different social, cultural, or political purpose—yet each one held up the ideal of *Italia apprezzato*.[57] With membership sufficiently dissatisfied with different aspects of their American life, and eloquently expressing their discontent and alarm, they easily inclined toward authoritarianism, and revealed pro-Fascist tendencies. By the late 1930s some of these organizations had begun to concern Congress, which, in part, accounted for the creation of the House UnAmerican Activities Committee in 1937. But the real "threat" they posed seems to have been based on their support of undemocratic doctrines. The fear that they were training militant "cadres" for direct action against the United States in case of war was seriously overestimated, because after the attack on Pearl Harbor, there was no evidence of "unAmerican activities" during the war. Their allegiance was, ultimately, to the United States.[58]

During all this time, Italian American newspapers were the ligatures that helped bind immigrants within their ethnocentric communities. They focused on common internal problems, illustrated and publicized club activities, and tried to create whatever awareness Italians had of the outside society in their otherwise insular world. The papers worked at two ostensibly contradictory tasks: to promote Americanization of the Italian, and to preserve and enhance Italian ethnicity.[59] It was this latter task that was a lonely and thankless job until Fascism appeared. As though suddenly injected with adrenalin, papers were aroused to action in 1923, quickly taking sides for or against Mussolini and his Fascist programs. There is still no proof that Italian American papers were ever under Fascist "control," as charged by Duffield in 1929,[60] although by the mid-1930s the preponderance of journals favored Il Duce and his Fascist program. Led by *Il Progresso Italo-Americano* of New York, they often used unsavory tabloid tricks to present Fascism's best image.[61]

Support of the Italian press (and of most Italian Americans for that matter) for Mussolini and Fascism began to fade after his alliance with Hitler, his energetic anti-semitic campaign (which had been noticeably absent from his regime for fifteen years), and his invasion of France. An informal survey of newspapers at the end of the 1930s showed few Italian American journals openly supporting Mussolini, although most were guarded about criticizing him. Their prompt expressions of loyalty to the United States after Pearl Harbor may indicate an Italian American sympathy for nationalist symbols, rather than any ideological support for Mussolini's totalitarian doctrines.

Fascism touched the Italian American as other movements had not. It strengthened peer identity through a common ethnic heritage. Parades, rallies, meetings, and the ever-growing number of clubs nourished themselves in urban Italian ghettos where no other economic or political organization had ever secured a hold.[62] The ghetto protected the insularity of the Italian American worker's mind, and now that insularity was being breached through a planned campaign of nationalist propaganda emanating from Italy, faithfully executed by a supportive cadre of Italian American lower –middle–class *Fascisti*. The result was sentimental identification with a sympathy for Italy by the workers, though there is still some question whether they held any deep ideological convictions other than those informed by nationalism or ethnic pride.[63]

In the 1920s Italian American workers were not alone in their admiration of Mussolini and his *Fascisti*. Many non-Italians were added to a list which included Lincoln Steffens, Ida Tarbell, Charles Beard, George Santayana, Henry Miller, and Ezra Pound. They were not all supporters of dictatorial systems, but, given the conservative and anti-Bolshevik temper of the 1920s, it seems plausible that many found his theories of corporatism, anti-communism, law and order, and nationalism quite attractive. In the years before Hitler turned Fascism into Nazism, with all its racist horror, the term was synonymous with Mussolini and his unique political experiment in Italy.[64]

What is more, the United States witnessed a mushrooming of its own homegrown Fascist-style groups, parading, saluting, promising, and threatening. The list is extensive (and frightening!) if we recognize they were all native to the American system, neither an import nor an extension of foreign governments.[65] They came from a discontented segment of lower–middle–class America, creating artificial enemies ad infinitum, promising cure-all programs, and copying, in some way, the method, approach, state of mind, and political attitudes pioneered by the *Fascisti* of Italy. While it is true that no American Fascist party existed at this time, many quasi-military extremist groups copied the style and verve of Mussolini's *Fascisti* with varying success. They based their programs on a church, a business group, a nationality, or some vague and distorted American ideal. Most of these groups flourished in the 1930s, with Chicago and Indianapolis being the chief breeding ground, of these sundry movements.[66]

The official policy of the United States government toward the *Fascisti* was not always clear during the 1920s, but seems to have been generally favorable until Duffield's article drew attention to some of the Fascist League's activities. The State, Justice, and Labor Departments, on the other hand, considered the *Fascisti* in Italy (despite their early and occasional rowdiness) to be genuine believers in law, order, and anti-Bolshevism, particularly at a time when the Red Scare was sweeping the country. Moreover, Fascists actually enjoyed the admiration of the police and general public opinion throughout the United States until the 1930s, when war clouds in Europe began to suggest Fascism's more realistic military threat.[67]

In the 1930s Franklin D. Roosevelt's domestic policies prompted some people to compare him and his programs to Mussolini— claiming that the New Deal was really an American form of Fascism, with the National Recovery Administration NRA being a prime example of corporatism.[68] Although these comparisons had little basis in fact, in California a pattern of genuine 'fascistic' activity was present. In that state there were reports of armed squads of hired "guards" formed into vigilante groups to "protect" the wine growers against so-called "leftist agitators." What they actually did was to use groups of thugs (like the Italian *Squadristi* in the 1920s) to harass vineyard workers who did not submit to the owners, and make violent attacks on incipient labor organizations. It had been thus so in northern Italy, just as Mussolini came to power in 1922.[69]

By the time World War II came, all outward manifestations of Italian American Fascism (and American fascism as well) evaporated. Pressure on the workers, as well as on the Italian American lower-middle class, by Fascist organs ended when the United States government closed Italian consulates, suspended the pro-Fascist press, deported or interned known agents, and saw to the disbandment of all Fascist organizations.[70] Surprisingly, after all the uproar, of 660,000 Italians designated as "enemy aliens" on December 11, 1941, 1,600 were taken into custody by the Federal Bureau of Investigation, and only 140 were actually interned by the Enemy Alien Hearing Board. Throughout the first year of the war, there was not a single instance of Italian American espionage against the United States,[71] while at the same time, 300,000 Italian Americans served in the armed forces. On October 14, 1942, Attorney-General Francis Biddle declared that the 600,000 Italian citizens residing in the United States at the time would no longer be considered "enemy aliens" by the government. Italians were finally being accepted.[72]

We have seen how for years many Italian Americans were generally insensitive to political and economic issues that were neither personal nor local. Isolated as they were in their ghettos, Italians developed a deep-seated resistance to any inculcation of ideology, clinging mostly to a dream, a half-imagined ideal, whose achievement demanded personal ability and hard work rather than political action or collectivization. Workers in particular were accustomed to making decisions on the basis of images and feelings about social, political, and economic processes. They responded readily to Fascism as it was represented by Mussolini more in an intuitive than overt way. He won their sympathy, their respect, and their moral support; but to say they went out en masse to join the Party, the fascio, and the marching parade because they were ideologically committed is an overstatement. They were too politically naive and passive, and far too suspicious of outside organizations to lean too heavily on Mussolini's promised actions, regardless of his appeal.

The years in the ghetto made the working class conservative, self-interested, ethnocentric, and prone to authoritarian solutions, while remaining ideologically aloof from Fascist doctrine. Only because Fascism was personalized by charismatic Mussolini in a sort of nostalgic nationalism did they respond sympathetically to his promises of self-esteem, of understanding, of belonging, and of status. The true key to understanding Italian American Fascism is to understand, not the Italian American worker, but the lower–middle class; for it was this class that formed the backbone of the Fascist organizations. It emerged among Italians as a distinct political force, articulating social resentments and deploring the political vacuum.[73] By actively working for Mussolini, this petty bourgeoisie class was unwittingly turning its members into chauvinists and teaching that military glory was the only worthwhile glory. In seeking acceptance, they found regimentation; in fighting anarchy and revolution, they met militarism; in achieving order, they were killing democracy and free speech; in arousing their latent Italianism, they flirted with treason to their new country.

The Italian American worker, on the other hand, as best as can be ascertained, only gave his heart (and some of his money) to Mussolini until Il Duce betrayed him. When Il Duce destroyed his own image in the shadow of Hitler and in the wake of miserable military fiascos, he destroyed the one thing Italian American workers supported: the promise of a dream fulfilled, of an ideal achieved.

With World War II, Italian Americans' alienation was coming to an end as unions began accepting them, as their children moved into the suburbs, and as the war effort finally transferred nationalistic sentiment wholly toward the United States. By the late 1940s Italian Americans had begun to participate in the political life of the American community, as they were absorbed into the mainstream that had rejected them for a hundred years.

Notes

1. See Renzo DeFelice, *Interpretations of Fascism*, trans. Brenda Huff Evertt (Cambridge, 1977), 67, 141, 128, 170, for views of Nolte, Salvatorelli, Nanni, and Cantimori. See Martin Kitchen, *Fascism* (New York, 1976), 83-87, who says it was a phenomenon only of developed industrial states, a response to class demands from industry and the bourgeoisie, a sense of "better black than red." Michael Ledeen, *Universal Fascism: Theory and Practice of Fascist International, 1928-1936* (New York, 1972), also discusses a definition that relates it to a social disease, or a "fever of the body politic."
2. Alan Cassels, "Fascism for Export in Italy and the U.S. in the 1920s," *American Historical Review*, 69 (April 1964): 707-08.
3. "Giovanezza," *The Century Monthly*, 115 (December 1927): 185-94.
4. Ledeen, 158.
5. No information on Jewish membership in the Fascist Party was available, but purportedly, there were many who supported Mussolini until well into the 1930s.
6. Ledeen, 159.
7. Denis Mack Smith, *Italy: A Modern History* (Ann Arbor, 1959), 339.
8. Marcus Duffield, "Mussolini's American Empire," *Harpers*, 150 (November, 1929): *passim*. See also *Harpers*, 181 (September, 1940): 382.
9. Stewart Hughes, *The United States and Italy* (Cambridge, 1965), 352.
10. John P. Diggins, *Mussolini & Fascism: The View from America* (Princeton, 1972), 66.
11. This was in the tradition of the nineteenth-century "Know-Nothings." See Oscar Handlin, *The American People in the 20th Century* (Cambridge, 1954), 93.
12. In 1850 there were 3,679 Italian foreign-born in the United States; by 1940 the figure was 1,623,580. Of eleven million foreign-born whites, in 1940, almost two million were of Italian origin. See U.S. Bureau of the Census, Department of Commerce, "Sixteenth Census of the United States, 1940: Population," vol. 11, part 1, 42-43. With the Immigration Quota Laws of the 1920s putting an end to mass migration, only a small number trickled in from Italy.
13. Harry Jerome, *Migration and Business Cycles* (New York, 1926), 196, shows a relationship between economic conditions in Italy and the United States, including congruent business cycles.
14. Frank Femminella and Jill S. Quadagno, "The Italian-American Family," in C. Mindel and Robert Habenstein, *Ethnic Families in America: Patterns and Variations* (New York, 1976), 61; M. J. Parenti, *Ethnic and Political Attitudes* (New York, 1975), 32-33.

15. Leonard Covello, "Italian-Americans," in *Our Racial and National Minorities*, ed. Francis J. Brown and J. S. Roucek (New York, 1937), 364; four of the five million Italians settled in six states: Massachusetts, Pennsylvania, Rhode Island, Connecticut, New Jersey, New York, with smaller numbers in Chicago and on the Pacific coast.

16. Marc Fried, *The World of the Urban Working Class* (Cambridge, 1973), 40.

17. H. S. Nelli, "The Padrone System," *Labor History*, 5 (1964): 153-167.

18. Covello, 358-359. The 1920 census shows a trend away from farming toward skilled occupations; but most Italian Americans took heavy labor (unskilled) jobs: e.g., seventy-seven percent of all blast furnace and steam R.R. jobs were held by Italians, as were twenty-two percent of all coal mine workers. See Bureau of the Census, Department of Commerce, "Immigration and Children, 1920," prepared by Niles Carpenter, Census Monograph VII, Washington, D.C., 1927, American Immigration Collection, 283-288. On the other hand, Italian women formed the largest percentage of semi-skilled clothing and cotton factory operatives, over eighty percent in some cities: ibid., 289. Each census through 1940 showed heavy percentages of Italians in unskilled, heavy labor jobs, out of proportion to other nationalities. See U.S., Congress, House, *Report of the Industrial Commission*, vol. 15, "Immigration" 57th Congress, 1st Sess., 1901, 300-303; and Philip Taylor, *The Distant Magnet* (London, 1971), 197, 201. Some Italians did run truck farms in New Jersey, vineyards in California, cotton and fruit farms in Louisiana and Texas: Allen M. Jones, *American Immigration* (Chicago, 1960), 212; Edwin Fenton, *Immigrants and Unions, A Case Study: Italians and American Labor, 1870-1920* (New York, 1975), 584-585.

19. Fried, 160-161.

20. Ibid., 11, 94.

21. Class solidarity seems to have been retarded by the homogenization of ethnic solidarity. See J. C. Leggett, *Class, Race and Labor: Working Class Consciousness in Detroit* (New York, 1968), 30-32. This issue becomes a question of the politics of ethnic status versus the politics of class. Leggett says the achievement of class consciousness would probably foster competition and conflict between different class levels within the workers' community, including between workers and the emerging lower-middle class.

22. Fenton, 247-248; Leggett, 46-47, who feels unions did not flourish among Italian Americans because immigrants were too unskilled. See also Gerd Korman, *Industrialization, Immigrants and Americanizers: The View from Milwaukee, 1866-1921* (Madison, 1967), 53.

23. Edwin Fenton, "Italians in the Labor Movement," *Pennsylvania History*, 27 (April, 1959): 134; and Fenton, *Immigrants*, 201-202. Unions had little bargaining power outside the large metropolitan centers, especially with unskilled workers.

24. DeConde, 175. During the 1920s, trade union membership was declining. National Bureau of Economic Research, "Trade Union Membership, 1897-1962," prepared by Leo Troy, 92 (New York, 1965), 1, 4. Fenton, *Immigrants*, 376, said many unions refused to grant autonomy or equal representation to Italian immigrants.

25. Silvano Tomasi and Madeline Engel, *The Italian Experience in the United States* (New York, 1970), 112. Tomasi gives six reasons for this: lack of training, low standard of living, thrift, need to find work, desire for immediate gain, and the tractability of Italians. Fenton, *Immigrants*, 142, says it was a lack of information among Italians, the attitude of their leaders who were socialists and anarchists and scorned regular union channels, the dislike of regular union members for Italian immigrants, and again, lack of skills among Italians.

26. Sally Miller, *The Radical Immigrant* (New York, 1974), 118.

27. J. Dickenson, "Aspects of Italian Immigration to Philadelphia," *Pennsylvania Magazine of History and Biography*, 90 (1966): 459. In Philadelphia, most Italians were not responsive to union pressure partly due to language, and partly because they were economically disunited. Resistance to trade unionism was found to be an individual, rather than a group, phenomenon. See also Federal Writers Project, *Italians of New York* (New York, 1938), 64-67. In 1910 only ten percent of southern Italians in New York were organized, while 14.2 percent native-born workers were unionized. Southern Italians, who formed the bulk of the Italian population in the United States, were eighteen percent less organized than native-born Americans. U.S., Congress, Senate, *Reports of the Immigration Commission*, vol. 7, 61st Congress, 3rd Sess., 1910, 417-419; 530-531. Fenton, *Immigrants*, 158, says that part of their failure lay at the door of the 1920s depression, the manufacturer's drive for open shop, the emergence of the Communist Party, and the diversion of mutual aid societies to Fascism.

28. Joseph Lopreato, *Italian Americans* (New York, 1970), 96.

29. Fenton, *Immigrants*, 565.

30. Many groups refused to let Italian Americans take part in their union activities, e.g., the Masons of New York in the 1890s, as well as in the textile and shoe industries. See *Reports of the Immigration Commission*, vol. 3, 61st Congress, 2nd Sess., 1911; Fenton, *Immigrants*, 561.

31. Fenton, *Immigrants*, 158. During World War II, socialists managed to win support of the huge Sons of Italy, the Foresters of America, and other Italian mutual aid societies.

32. Fenton, *Immigrants*, 568. Italian socialists, syndicalists, and anarchists looked for identification of their interests in the United States and could not find it in the AFL: they then turned to the socialist-oriented Central Labor Federation of New York, the Socialist Trade Union Alliance, the Socialist Party, and IWW.

33. Fenton, *Immigrants*, 565.

34. In a poll conducted by *Fortune* magazine in November, 1939, Italians were considered by over 22 percent of Americans to have made the "worst" citizens, or the least participatory of the immigrant nationalities. This reflected their political powerlessness, deriving from their lack of control over working environments. See also Fried, 157.

35. Ibid., 195-196.

36. Nicholas Chiaramonte, "The Nature of Fascism," *The Living Age* (August, 1936), 516-517. He had joined the *Fascisti* in Italy in 1920-1922, but relented and eventually worked against Mussolini.

37. Writers Project. Until 1931 tailors, barbers, etc. were among the five occupations listed after "laborer" in the Italian American working class. After 1931, this was followed by mechanics, clerks, and salesmen.
38. Leggett, 36-38.
39. Chiaramonte, 518-519.
40. Reinhold Niebuhr, "Pawns for Fascism—Our Lower Middle Class," *American Scholar*, 6 (Spring, 1937): 146.
41. Nathan Glazer and D. Moynihan, *Beyond the Melting Pot* (Cambridge, 1963), 216. They said Italian Americans of New York were developing rapidly in the 1930s toward middle-class status. The "old proletariate city life" had already begun to disappear, and was being replaced by the new middle-class system, mores and all.
42. Denis Mack Smith, *Mussolini's Roman Empire* (New York, 1976), 180.
43. Chiaramonte, 520-521.
44. Ledeen, 114; Hughes, 97. We must not forget the positive effect the Concordat of 1929 with the Vatican had on the Italian American, who for fifty years had suffered from the separation of Church and Italian state. The settlement seemed to put their conflicts and principles to rest.
45. Angelo Del Boca and Mario Giovana, *Fascism Today*, trans. R. H. Boothroyd (New York, 1937), 31.
46. D. M. Smith, *Roman Empire*, 86.
47. "Our Black Shirts and the Reds," *Literary Digest*, 77 (April 7, 1923); 16. The lower-middle class, along with veterans, immigrants, the unemployed, etc. all supported Il Duce. There were branches in several states.
48. "Mussolini's Hand Across the Seas," *Literary Digest*, 87 (Dec. 26, 1925): 10; in an interview on August 7, 1978, with a former Italian American Fascist member (who wishes to remain anonymous), this writer had the concept of "dual citizenship" illustrated. When Giovanni Botta, then Minister of Education under Mussolini, made a tour of fasci of the New York area, during the summer of 1936, he spoke in Pleasant Park Bay, Bronx, and said: "Blackshirts! Remember the fatherland you left. If you are a good citizen of the U.S. you are also a good Italian; if you are a good Italian, you are a good citizen of the U.S. It is a position compatible to both." The witness had been a member of the Mario Morgantini Club of New York City.
49. Ledeen, 99.
50. Marcus Duffield, "Mussolini's American Empire," *Harpers*, 150 (November, 1929): 661-672.
51. "The War of Nerves: Hitler's Helper," *Fortune*, 22 (November, 1940): 108, 110.
52. Ibid.
53. The *dopolavoro* clubs were organized along lines similar to those in Italy.
54. Gaetano Salvemini, *Italian Fascist Activities in the United States*, ed. and intro. Philip V. Cannistraro (New York, 1977), 3-88. This book in itself is probably the most complete compendium of Fascist organizations and activities in the United States at the time.

55. *New York Times*, April 25, 1936, 19; May 19, 1936, 1; May 25, 1936, 4; May 27, 1936, 22; and May 31, 1936, 9. There even were some volunteers from the United States to fight on Italy's side in the war; Salvemini, 203; see also Martin Dies, *The Trojan Horse* (New York, 1977), 332, 336. *Fortune*, 22 (November, 1940), 85-86, estimated $200,000 had been given to Italy by Italian Americans between 1922 and 1937, in addition to bond issues by the United States investment banks, totaling $300 million between 1925-1931.

56. Charles Ferguson, "Embattled Haberdashery: The Fascist Shirts," *50 Million Brothers: A Panorama of American Lodges and Clubs* (New York, 1937), 3.

57. George E. Pozzetta, "Italians of New York City" (Ph.D. diss., University of North Carolina at Chapel Hill, 1971), 385; an August, 1978 interview with the anonymous "blackshirt": dues were fixed at $1.00/month, and the club was duly chartered by New York State. Salvemini, 215-242.

58. The anonymous witness said the local records of the Fasci "vanished" from the club rooms by December 11, 1941.

59. A. Parry, "Goodbye to the Immigrant Press," *American Mercury*, 28 (January, 1933): 57. Quoting *La Follia* of New York, Parry said the second generation did not read the immigrant press, and by 1932, 25 percent of the Italian papers in the United States were forced to add English-language sections to keep readership.

60. Duffiend, in *Harpers*, 665.

61. "The Italian-American Press on the Mussolini Regime," *Literary Digest*, 88 (January 30, 1926): 14-16. The *Digest* survey discovered fifteen pro-Fascist to six anti-Fascist Italian newspapers in the United States (with only five maintaining neutrality or non-committed positions.)

62. Salvemini, *passim*.

63. Neibuhr, 145-151; Chiaramonte, 518-519.

64. John P. Diggins, "Flirtation with Fascism: American Pragmatic Liberals and Mussolini's Italy," *American Historical Review*, 71 (January, 1966): 487-488; DeConde, 190-191; D. M. Smith, *Italy*, 399.

65. H. L. Varney, "The Truth About American Fascism," *American Mercury*, 41 (August, 1937): 388-389. A partial list included The Khaki Shirts. The Order of '76, The Silver Shirts, The Crusaders, The National Watchmen, The Ben Franklin Society, etc.; see also Frank Hanighen, "Foreign Political Movements in the United States," *Foreign Affairs*, 16 (October, 1937): 18.

66. John Gunther, *Inside U.S.A.* (New York, 1947), 382.

67. Cassels, 710.

68. Giuseppi Bottai, "The Corporate State and the NRA," *Foreign Affairs*, 13 (July, 1935): 612-624; Varney, 388-397.

69. M. B. Schnapper, "Mussolini's American Agents," *Nation*, 147 (October 15, 1938): *passim*; and ibid. (August 27, 1938): 198.

70. Edward Corsi, "Our Italian Fellow-Americans," *American Mercury*, 55 (August, 1942): 203.

71. Ibid., 200.

72. "A Contribution to American Victory and Italy's Freedom," *First Annual Report of the Italian American Labor Council* (pamphlet).

73. Niebuhr, 147.

The Italian American Working Class and the Vietnam War

Fred Milano

A Unique Form of Readaptation: The War Veteran

The "restructuring" of the individual's outlook and behavior was a common theme in many of the older sociological studies that focused upon newly arrived immigrant groups and their problems of adjustment within specific community settings. The central concern in these earlier community classics was the problem of initial adjustment. The Chicago school of sociology, flourishing from the 1920s to the 1940s, nurtured an interest in such problems through its extensive support of field research studies of "social disorganization" and "reorganization" in urban areas. Yet, the individual frequently was viewed as though locked into a given setting. Acculturation was the prime altering experience, and the expectation (of researchers) was one of continuity: first-generation members were seen as remaining firmly implanted in a single community for the duration of their lives. As for their offspring, it has been said that

> the Chicago school's contribution to our knowledge of urban processes is surer on "inter-generation" mobility processes: children moving "out" and "up" from Little Sicilies, than on "intra-generational" processes: leaving home to live in a rooming house or flat, and later moving to suburbia after marriage.[1]

Later generations of ethnics, however, were confronted by another qualitatively different form of change-inducing agent: participation in the military. The disorganizing effects of military service, and of possible exposure to war, were compounded by the difficulties of reconnecting one's previous life. Whereas the parent generation had preoccupied itself with integration into the American community, for the generations of ethnic veterans that followed, the struggle was one of re-integration into the normal functioning of the community. Though much of the research for community studies was conducted in the aftermath of either World War I or II, surprisingly few references regarding the veteran within the community were found. The sole exceptions were William F.

Whyte's *Street Corner Society* (1943) and W. Lloyd Warner's *Democracy in Jonesville* (1949). The former, a study of second-generation Italian Americans in Boston's North End, examined two male youth groups in the district, but did so in the years immediately prior to World War II. Thus, while Whyte observed that the "college boys" were more politically active than the "corner boys," neither group was exposed to the politicizing (and perhaps equalizing) effects of direct military participation. Returning to the same neighborhood in 1953, Whyte discussed the lone "street corner" boy who had entered the Marine Corps and served in both World War II and Korea. The author's discussion, however, was in the form of a description, tracing the individual's life since his departure from "Cornerville"; no account was given of his reaction to his military experience. But, more significant, because of the individual's decision to remain in the organization as a career soldier, Whyte was not presented with the opportunity to observe this person's re-entry into the community.

Warner's "Jonesville" study, by contrast, committed an entire chapter to the impact of World War II on a "typical" American community (Morris, Illinois), in particular, to the interaction between the civilian and veteran elements in its population. The ex-serviceman was portrayed as "above all a displaced person, a migrant, and an immigrant. He returned to his old community as a traveler . . . who has accustomed himself to a radically different way of life."[2] To some extent, however, this transformation may have entailed more than merely an alteration in "style of life."

> The experience of the citizens of Jonesville who stayed home or who were members of the military and returned had a profound effect on the community. No one felt himself to be quite the same, for life during wartime was different. That the effect of World Wars I and II was more than what happened to each individual who experienced them is displayed in the organization of veterans, but this permanent effect on the group is even more deeply felt in the secular and sacred ideology of the community.[3]

The veteran of Vietnam, in comparison to the ex-soldier of World War II or Korea, has perhaps undergone an even more thorough and severe politicizing experience. Based upon a 1973 survey of 3,522 youths between the ages of sixteen and twenty-five, Yankelovich noted that those among them who were veterans reflected "a relatively greater estrangement from American society than their peers."[4] It is these veterans—with this alienation—who must be considered against the backdrop of the milieu to which they inevitably and permanently returned. Although individuals may be changed by their military experience, such change is thereafter fed back into the community in which they live.

The Ethnic Community vs. Military Environment

According to Martindale, the community is a complete and total social system. But at the same time, change serves as the fundamental process underlying the relationship between community structure and extra-community involvement.[5] In considering the interaction between the military and civilian experiences then, emphasis must be given to the degree of transformation which may, or may not, occur within the citizen-soldier as he moves between these two worlds. Admittedly, there are a number of forces outside the confines of the ethnic community that can confront the individual member. However, in terms of a stratification or hierarchy of human experiences, the military is likely to have a greater impact on the individual consciousness than do others. Moreover, for the ethnic youth who has not been separated from his community for any appreciable length of time, the military may provide the initial—and perhaps most significant—"fresh contact." It is within this context that the following thesis is examined: other factors being equal, military service is expected to have a major politicizing effect on the behavior and attitudes of members of the Italian American community. The term "politicizing," as used here, refers to that process by which an individual undergoes a pronounced restructuring of his outlook as a result of a certain dramatic circumstance occurring within his life. In a sense, the socio-political maturation of the Italian American is accelerated (i.e., relative to his non-military contemporaries) by his exposure to the sharp discontinuity between the ethnic and military environments.

Considered alone, that is, isolated from the ethnic or any other such factor, the military in itself could be regarded as exerting a formidable politicizing influence. For instance, the essentially democratic and egalitarian ideology which the citizen-soldier brings with him is contradicted by an alien caste system of inequalities. In Stouffer's words,

> The Army was a new world for most civilian soldiers . . . [because] of its many contrasts with civilian institutions: (1) its authoritarian or-

ganization, demanding rigid obedience (2) its highly stratified social
system, in which hierarchies of deference were formally and minutely
established by official regulations, subject to penalties for infraction,
on and off duty (3) its emphasis on traditional ways of doing things
and its discouragement of initiative.[6]

Vidich and Stein, on the basis of observations drawn from their
own brief military careers, also refer to this marked discontinuity.

> The routine repetitiveness of training, the frequent appearance of
> senseless authority, the investiture of authority in regular noncoms
> who were frequently less educated than the recruit, the reduction of
> all training and participation to a common denominator—all of which
> were supported by established and unquestioned authority—gave
> pause to the civilian-minded recruit who brought with him a quite
> different set of attitudes.[7]

The personal tensions triggered by this pattern, and its seeming
imperviousness to change, may give way to a resigned tolerance as
the individual is gradually assimilated into the military organization. Yet such tolerance is not tantamount to acceptance. Furthermore, the precisely stratified structure of the military may have the
effect—unintended, though ironic—of forcing the working-class serviceman to recognize his relative class position, both within as well
as outside the armed forces. The aspect of "class," perhaps not
previously encountered in his ethnic community, is now thrust
dramatically upon him. A similar result is sometimes achieved by
middle-and upper-class youth with their greater ease of access to a
higher education. But, for others, the military may serve the equivalent function.

The politicization of the ethnic soldier may be further pronounced in that it conflicts with the values of the Italian American
community. It could perhaps be argued, on the one hand, that the
Italian American is easily assimilated by the armed forces because
of certain basic similarities between his ethnic and military environments. Both settings could conceivably be viewed as fostering
patterns of organization and behavior that place inordinate reliance
upon past convention or tradition. In each, for example, there are
expectations of loyalty toward the group and deference toward
superiors. Social institutions within the Italian community could
likewise be interpreted as being preparatory socializing agencies,
facilitating one's transition into the military—e.g., Catholicism,
with its teachings about obedience to authority. According to this
argument then, military values are simply superimposed on those

that the individual previously acquired as a civilian. What this ignores, however, is the prime de-socialization and homogenization function of the military, whereby the ethnic soldier is expected to subvert aspects of his former identity in the interests of the organization.

> It is abundantly clear that basic training aroused deep anxieties and resentment in the soldiers exposed to it, and that these anxieties and resentments were aroused by the assault made upon their previous life-patterns and self images . . . Americans from widely different class, ethnic, and religious backgrounds had to be stripped of old identities and coerced to accept new military roles, even though these violated many of their basic values and self-conceptions.[8]

There is, nevertheless, a series of sharp contrasts. Despite an apparent degree of overlap, the military is antithetical in many respects to the Italian American ethnic experience: the artificially created and maintained military unit as opposed to the naturally evolving community; the compulsory, contractual-type relationship as opposed to the strongly interpersonal and emotionally bound relationship; enforced segregation (according to positions of rank/ status) as opposed to physical proximity and open interaction; transient, short-lived associational ties as opposed to enduring, permanently envisioned social attachments. Such distinctions, moreover, are likely to be perceived only by those who are drawn out of the relative isolation of their civilian community and thrust into contact with the military.

Sample

The study was conducted in a small steel town (hereafter referred to as "Luketown") in the southeastern region of Pennsylvania. In 1970 Luketown had a population of 12,300. As is the case in many industrialized areas, the town contains a highly diverse ethnic population. One-fifth of the inhabitants are black. Among those of European background, the largest groups numerically (in descending order of size) are the Italians, Poles, Hungarians, Ukrainians, and Czechoslovakians. The data for this study were obtained by means of in-depth, tape-recorded interviews with 30 members (15 Vietnam veterans and 15 non-veterans) of the Italian American subcommunity and by the participant observation of the author. All 30 subjects were interviewed during the period from January through April, 1976.

The town itself contains a relatively homogeneous Italian American population. This commonality is reflected in the major social characteristics shared by the 30 respondents who were interviewed: sex (male), age group (23 to 33 years), ethnicity (Italian American), socio-economic background of parents (working class), religion (Roman Catholic—moreover, the town has only one Italian church), education (all had graduated from the town's solitary high school), and geographical place of residence (except for short absences such as the military service, all had lived their entire lives within this same town). The only outstanding factor which served to separate the two groups was their service or non-service in the armed forces.

An Ethnic Portrait

Beginning with the initial large-scale infusion of Italians into American society in the late nineteenth century, innumerable accounts have documented the unique character of the Italian American ethnic experience. Within the confines of the group or subcommunity, the ethnic individual is able to find total social and psychological sustenance. At the same time, there is a sharp awareness of the differences between the ethnic group's culture and the dominant culture. This realization has led one writer to remark:

> An ethnic group is not one because of the degree of measurable or observable difference from other groups; it is an ethnic group, on the contrary, because the people in it and the people out of it know that it is one; because both the *ins* and the *outs* talk, feel, and act as if they were a separate group.[10]

Despite attempts to resist encroachment by the surrounding society (i.e., to seek closure) and to retain its distinctiveness, an ethnic community is constantly exposed to forces which can modify or transform it. Foremost among these is perhaps the acculturation and assimilation of its youth, particularly those of the second and third generation.[11] Each new age group, through its "fresh contacts" with the on-going social world, confronts that world in a manner unlike that of the previous generations. But, even among contemporaries, there will be a differentiation of experiences. It is likely then that those who withdrew from their subcommunity and entered the armed forces during the Vietnam war acquired impressions and orientations that distinguished them from their non-military peers.

The concern of the present analysis is not with ethnicity per se. Rather, it is a purposely limited investigation of the interaction occurring between the military and ethnic experiences. The Italian American, regardless of his service or non-service background, generally maintains a strong allegiance toward his cultural heritage. But the veteran, having been severed from these bonds for a period of years, may over-compensate for his absence. In attempting to re-establish his former identity and position within the Italian community, he may pursue his ethnicity more vigorously and with more affection than his non-military companions. Thus, the returning Italian American serviceman may demonstrate a greater adherence to traditional ethnic values and practices than would the Italian American non-serviceman. To ascertain this, the two groups were compared on the following specific criteria: 1. ethnic self-identity; 2. ethnic preservation; 3. the "imagined" outsider's view of the Italian American; and 4. ethnic change.

Ethnic Self-Identity

The respondents were asked to classify themselves as Italian, Italian American, or American. Twice as many veterans (8) as non-veterans (4) identified themselves as "Italians." For those of "pure ancestry," this was a matter of considerable pride.

Army veteran: I guess I would be called an Italian American. But I like to think of the old way, that I'm Italian only.

Non-veteran: I am very proud of my heritage, of being a pure-blood.
For persons of mixed parentage, however, the decision was somewhat more complex.

Air Force veteran: It's funny, what with my mother being English and my father being Italian. I am aware that my mother is English. But I've always classified myself as being Italian. I've never, ever thought of myself as being English American, if you want to classify it like that . . . Because the Italian influence has always been there; it's always been number one.

Most of the interviewees, veterans as well as non-veterans, clearly and emphatically acknowledged their ethnic affiliation. Despite their status as native-born Americans, their primary orientation was decidedly Italian. In the case of one ex-serviceman, however, the ethnic dimension had been severely diminished. The generation that had raised him had sought to enhance his chances of survival in the dominant culture; in so doing, it had cut away an important element of his later self-identity.

> It's just something I've never really considered. That's one of the bad things of being from parents that are from the early 1920s generation. The thing of the 'melting pot' and the immigrants: 'We don't want to *look* like Italians; we don't want to *talk* like Italians; we want to be *Americans.*' And so they completely destroyed their ways. You know, *everything*: their ethnic background, their customs, and so forth. As quickly as possible they learned to speak English, and forgot about teaching their children Italian. So I guess you could say I'm an American because my parents lost my background for me. But it's also something that I'd like to see regained.

Ethnic Preservation

The desire of a group to protect and maintain its ethnicity—or the remnants of that ethnicity, as in the case of second-and-third-generation off-spring—manifests itself in a variety of forms. One of these is the way in which its members interpret the negative or prejudicial slurs that are directed against the group. Asked to comment on such labels as "wop," "dago," and "guinea," the veterans and non-veterans reacted similarly. Certainly these terms did not carry the same derisive connotation for them that they had for earlier generations of Italian Americans. For these men, such designations were seen as either unimportant ("they don't bother me") or tolerable within certain limits ("it depends on who says it and how it is meant"). Furthermore, although it is acceptable for members of the group to apply these labels jokingly in referring to one another, it is not equally acceptable if applied by outsiders.

> Navy veteran: They don't bother me because I am proud of my heritage. In fact, it generally causes problems to the guy that says it at work because there's usually about five or six of us Italians in the office. And a couple of times a guy will say something like "Boy, that guinea has got an easy job!" And when he turns around there are three guys standing there asking him if he has a problem.

> Army veteran: It depends on the content of the conversation. If it's used in a slanderous manner I'd probably take it to heart and get upset about it. But just in the kidding sense I don't mind.

Confronted by this label while in the service, one army veteran recounted how he had diverted it to his own purposes, using it to enhance his status among his military peers.

> I've always used things like that to my advantage. Like for instance, when I was stationed down South there was a little go-cart track right outside the base, and go-carts were just coming along then. I was kind of wild on those things. And they would call me "wop," being Italian and all that. So I labeled myself as "The Mad Wop" on the go-carts. And they thought that was great! So everybody called me that. But when they said it I know why they were saying it, because I planted the image. And I said, "I'll take it from there." And from that they just built on it. I did that constantly. When A. J. Foyt was popular, they used to call me "A. J. Wop."

Disguising one's ethnicity by alteration of the surname was unanimously rejected by both groups. On the basis of their self-reports, none of the thirty respondents had ever seriously considered changing their family name.

> Army veteran: No, I'd never change it, even though it's hard to pronounce. But I've never thought of changing mine. Like "Lou Ben." You know, you cut it down, leave everything off the end of it. But I like "Benevenuti." It's got a little class to it.

> Non-veteran: As a matter of fact, I changed it so that it was *more* Italian. It's B-w-c-c-i. My family pronounces it "Bucci" (Bee-yew-see). But some Italian friends in Lancaster told me that in Italy it would be pronounced "Bucci" (Boo-chee). So for three years now I have changed myself in the pronunciation and said "Bucci" (Boo-chee)—which *is* the correct pronunciation. So many people butcher their name. But I like it the right way, so I've kept it.

In only a single instance had an individual been tempted to "modify" his name.

In terms of marital patterns (for themselves) and marital expectations (for their children), a close similarity again existed between the serviceman and non-serviceman. Of the twelve married veterans, two had spouses of Italian descent. Moreover, no negative reactions were expressed by either group concerning intermarriage with other European ethnics. Some contrasts were nevertheless evident.

> Non-veteran: I have no qualms about that whatsoever. I really can't see why one religion should stay within its own boundaries. I would have no qualms about marrying a non-Italian or even a non-Catholic.

Navy veteran: I don't think there's anything wrong with that. But I know our parents frowned upon that. And I *know* our grandparents frowned upon it! "Is she Italian?" That's the first thing they said.

The resemblances between the two groups, however, are perhaps eclipsed by their differences. In areas other than those already cited, the attitudes and behavior of the servicemen appeared to vary significantly with those of the non-servicemen. Asked to indicate, for example, the type of neighborhood in which they would prefer to live, six of the veterans—as opposed to two of the non-veterans—chose the "Italian." Conversely, ten of the non-veterans—as against four of the veterans—preferred to reside in a "mixed" neighborhood. The remaining eight respondents reported "no preference."

Among all of the interviewees, only three (two veterans and one non-veteran) could claim fluency in speaking Italian. But this inability was not viewed in the same manner by members of the two groups; in general, a greater sense of ethnic loss was expressed by the ex-servicemen.

Army veteran: Call it the third generation blues! Yeah, I guess I really would like to speak it. Like I said, I play golf with my father—he speaks Italian—and a lot of the guys that we play golf with are of Italian descent. And they get to talking back and forth in Italian, and I nudge my Dad and say "Hey, what's he saying?" I wish I would have learned Italian when I was younger, but I just never did.

Navy veteran: I used to be able to understand it when my grandmother lived with us. She used to talk it all the time. I couldn't speak it but I *could* understand it. I always knew what she was saying. But I just never learned how to speak it.

Projecting into the future, a majority of the veterans preferred "Italian" as a second language for their children. By comparison, a majority of the non-veterans also considered it advantageous for their children to acquire a second language, but placed no like priority upon "Italian."

The strength of a person's ethnic allegiance is partly reflected by the desire, or lack of desire, to return to the country of their ancestry. Of the thirteen servicemen who had never traveled to Italy, ten expected to visit there within their lifetime; of the fourteen non-servicemen who had never been to Italy, seven intended to do so.

The military experience often clashed uncomfortably with elements that civilians brought with them from their previous life.

Yet, on occasion, the military unexpectedly served as a vehicle for rekindling an individual's ethnic sentiments.

Navy veteran: When I was over in Vietnam, these people from Italy —we have relations over there—they wrote me letters. And I can't even read Italian! I can't even talk Italian! I'd look at the letter, and there were pictures in there. And I didn't know who it was, who *any* of them were, nothing. They thought that was great, because this Italian boy was in America and he was going to war in Vietnam. So they wrote me letters, and I appreciated it. I think I still got them.

Navy veteran: I was cussing at the service every day I was in it. But one thing I really liked was the idea of traveling. I got a chance to go over to Europe like I always wanted to, and visit the European countries. And of course while I was over there I took a couple of weeks vacation and I went to Italy to see my relations.

The Outsider's "Image" of the Italian American

From the vantage point of the individual, how is their ethnic group judged by other factions in the community? For those who have maintained continual, day-to-day contact with non-Italians, a greater accommodation is likely to have developed. The "permanent residents," whose gradual adjustment to the town has been unbroken, may perceive local matters somewhat differently than the "returning residents." Whereas the Italian non-veteran downplays or minimizes intergroup frictions within the town, the Italian veteran becomes sensitized to incidents of discrimination.

Non-veteran: I think most people in the town have ignored the fact that there is a difference between Italian and American. I think they consider them all the same now. It's mainly because this area is made up of different nationalities, not what they would call the WASP's. I don't think there's much bad feeling around here. We have a lot of Jewish people, Italian people, Germans, and so forth. In fact, I think the WASP's are the minority to tell you the truth.

Veteran: I felt there was discrimination against us when we moved into this neighborhood. It's a fact! The reference made would indicate that it was ethnic-oriented. However, I think with those kind of individuals, had I been Jewish or whatever, there still would have been an ethnic slur. I am distinguished from the other Italian neighbor in that I'm the "guinea on the hill", whereas he's referred to as the "guinea in the valley".

Veteran: I've felt it a little bit where I'm working now, because the post office is run by the Irish. I think in general the whole post office system is, from the Postmaster General to most of the supervisors. I think I've felt a little uneasy about it.

Veteran: There's definitely been discrimination. It was job-related. Well, it happened and I couldn't understand why. And then later I found out that the reason it happened was that most of the bosses that I worked for when I went to the telephone company were Masons. And two of the people that were hired at the same time I was were Masons. And they got the best jobs and I was put on the digging crew.

Ethnic Change

Twice as many servicemen (six) as non-servicemen (three) felt that their interest in Italian ways of life had increased in the intervening years since their departure from high school. This heightened interest, moreover, manifested itself in a number of forms.

Army veteran: Even when I was small, I always listened to the old people talk. I liked to listen to them talk. In so many ways they're right. A lot of people used to laugh at this stuff a long time ago, but if you really sit down, their ways of life are right.

Navy veteran: When I was in high school I really didn't think about it. But since I've gotten out of high school, one of my best friends is an Italian guy. And we can see things eye to eye. I mean when he says something I understand. And when I say something to him, *he* understands. I have a lot of good friends that aren't Italian, and there's just a lot of things I don't have in common with them, customs and so forth.

In several cases, the death or incapacity of a central figure within the family was instrumental in disrupting, or even altering, the individual's attachment to his ethnicity.

Army veteran: When you're living with your parents, it's there all the time. But now I'm married and have my own family, and I live with a woman who knows nothing about Italian food or Italian customs or anything like that. I guess I've fallen away from it since my grandparents passed away. It used to be standard procedure two days a week to have spaghetti, and have my grandmother cook it every Sunday morning before we went to church. I kind of miss that.

Non-veteran: Things aren't the same anymore because of my grand-parents being deceased now, and my father too. My grandmother, she spoke very little English. But when I'd go down with my father to see her, I'd become really involved.

Army veteran: When we were kids, we always met at my grandmoth-er's house. But those days are over. My wife is Slovak; my mother is Polish. Grandmom is an invalid now so we don't meet at her house anymore.

Inasmuch as Catholicism has traditionally been an integral part of the Italian experience, the two groups were evaluated in terms of their religiosity. An almost identical proportion in either group—nine veterans and ten non-veterans—had retained their member-ship in the local Italian Catholic Church. (The remaining eleven respondents reported having no specific church or religious affilia-tion, although all had been raised in the Roman Catholic faith.) However, on the basis of church attendance, the participation of the non-servicemen (median attendance: eighteen per year) ex-ceeded that of the servicemen (median attendance: twelve per year).

Despite certain similarities, the two groups were strongly differ-entiated by the religious developments in their personal lives. Nine of the servicemen, as opposed to only four non-servicemen, stated that their religious attitudes had changed dramatically since leav-ing high school.

Non-veteran: I'm not as regimented as I was. I form my own opinions on certain things in the Church, such as confession and birth control and things of that nature. I don't attend church every week like I did when I was in high school. I guess one of the biggest stumbling blocks is confession, in that I don't feel as though you need to go to a priest to absolve your sins.

Veteran: When I was a kid, I used to go to church every Sunday. Sometimes two or three times a week. So as I grew up, it became a mandatory thing. But the way I am now, I don't feel that it was necessary to go every Sunday to church.

Veteran: Right now I have no religion. I was baptized and brought up in the Catholic religion. But religion now makes no sense to me. That's why I've lost interest in it as I've gotten older.

Veteran: My feelings about religion have *definitely* changed! I was married once before, and it turned out that this girl married me under false pretenses. And I couldn't get an annulment. The priest didn't take the time to look into my case; he just let it go . . . And I thought, "Well, they don't really care". I mean, if I had *money* they would care. Like my father, he was ill for fourteen years. And I don't think the priest came to see him twice in that whole time. He would go to Mass even though he was in terrific pain, because he had cancer . . . And I know that when somebody with money is sick, somebody who gives a lot of money to the church, they get special attention. So that just made me bitter. Not against the Catholic religion but against the people who *run* the Catholic religion. It's too impersonal anymore—unless you have money.

In some instances, the transformation of the individual's religious self could be traced to events occurring during their military service.

Navy veteran: Things started happening to me after I left. It was getting out of the little cultural shell of Luketown. It's all a part of growing up I guess. You get away from home and you see what the world is like . . . I got to meet people from here, from there. You're going to grow just from experiences that you've encountered. A Catholic from the South is a lot different from the Catholic in the North.

Navy veteran: I became disillusioned with the Catholic Church. I don't want another religion but I'm disillusioned with that one. When Angelo's baby was baptized, I took leave and came home from Vietnam. I stood for the baby . . . And when I came home on leave for it, I went up to ask the priest for a letter from the other church . . . And he [the priest] wanted to know why my envelopes weren't in the Sunday collection! And that kind of hit me. He didn't ask me where I was, why, or anything like that. Just, "Why don't I see your envelopes in the Sunday collection?"

Summary

On the basis of certain criteria (self-classification as Italian rather than Italian American, preference for residing in an Italian neighborhood, desire to visit Italy, political support of Italian Americans, etc.) the veterans did differ from their civilian counterparts. But due to the limited scope of this study, it would be hazardous to generalize the findings to other Italian American communities. Nevertheless, in the present case, the individuals' separation from their ethnic group and their subsequent encounter with the military seems to have led to a resurgence or "re-birth" of their ethnic identity. Even more than this the veteran's previous views toward ethnicity had undergone a restructuring or reshaping. Whereas the non-serviceman had maintained a "local" orientation, confining his interpretation of ethnicity to the immediate neighborhood or community, the veteran was characterized by a more "cosmopolitan" outlook that regarded ethnicity in a comparative and more encompassing way.

There is always the possibility that the serviceman, having been transformed by his experiences, acts as a carrier in introducing change to his community. But the individual's departure—and his return years later—involves a two-way accommodation. Upon returning, he is given a sympathetic welcome and slowly reabsorbed into the normal functioning of the community. In the process, he gradually relinquishes certain of the "foreign" traits acquired in the military. To some extent then, his "outside" experiences are neutralized. The effects of the military would be considerably greater were it not for the way in which the ethnic community retains the diffuse control over its members.

Notes

1. Colin Bell and Howard Newby, *Community Studies* (New York, 1972), 98.
2. W. Lloyd Warner, *Democracy in Jonesville* (New York, 1949), 276.
3. Ibid, 285-286.
4. Daniel Yankelovich, *The New Morality: A Profile of American Youth in the 70's* (New York, 1974), 143.
5. Don Martindale, *American Society* (Princeton, 1960); *American Social Structure* (New York, 1960); *Social Life and Cultural Change* (Princeton, 1962); *Community, Character, and Civilization* (New York, 1963); *Institutions, Organizations, and Mass Society* (Boston, 1965).
6. Samuel Stouffer, et. al., *The American Soldier: Combat and Its Aftermath* (Princeton, 1949), I, 55.
7. Arthur Vidich and Maurice Stein, *Identity and Anxiety* (Glencoe, 1960), 496.
8. Ibid, 497-498.
9. Karl Mannheim, "The Problem of Generations", in P. Kecskemeti, ed., *Essays on the Sociology of Knowledge* (London, 1952).

10. Everett Hughes, *Where Peoples Meet* (New York, 1952), 156.
11. The "first generation" is composed of foreign-born individuals who migrated to the United States. "Second generation" refers to those persons born in this country, one or both of whose parents were immigrants. The "third generation" consists of native-born children whose parents are likewise native-born; however, one or both of the grandparents must have been foreign-born.

Contributors

Betty Boyd Caroli is Professor of History at Kingsborough College of the City University of New York. She has published *Italian Repatriation from the United States, 1900-1914* and has just completed a photographic study of Italian Americans.

Colomba M. Furio recently completed her Ph.D. at New York University, School of Education, Health, Nursing, and the Arts Professions. She is particularly interested in the study of culture, cultural pluralism, and ethnicity.

Robert F. Harney is Professor of History at the University of Toronto. He is academic director of the Multicultural History Society of Ontario, and president of the Canadian Italian Historical Association. He has written extensively on Italian immigration and is co-author of *Immigrants: A Portrait of the Urban Experience, 1890-1930.*

Vincent M. Lombardi teaches at Sachem High School in Long Island, New York, and is adjunct Professor of History at Adelphi University. He is currently completing a study of seventeenth-century Italian history.

Fred Milano is an Assistant Professor of Sociology at Appalachian State University, North Carolina. He received his Ph.D. in Sociology from Pennsylvania State University in 1977.

Philip F. Notarianni is a doctoral candidate in history at the University of Utah. He is currently on the staff of the Utah State Historical Society as a preservation historian. His special interest has been Italian immigration into the states of the Intermountain West.

George E. Pozzetta is Associate Professor of History at the University of Florida, Gainesville. He has authored numerous studies of Italian immigration and has co-edited *America and the New Ethnicity.*

Jean R. Scarpaci is Associate Professor of History at Towson State University. She has published articles dealing with Italians in the South and the Italian American woman. She is currently working on a study of the Italian community of Baltimore.

Rudolph J. Vecoli is Professor of History and director of the Immigration History Research Center at the University of Minnesota. He is author of *The People of New Jersey*, and is currently working on a study of the Italian American Left.